ONE FREEMAN'S WAR

ONE FREEMAN'S WAR

WAR

IN THE SECOND AMERICAN REVOLUTION

3RD EDITION

Mark Emery

ISBN: 0692360980
ISBN 13: 9780692360989

Dedicated to all those who have suffered and struggle to maintain their heritage and identity as 'Free Men'.

This book started from notes, handwritten in pencil on blank paper, while sitting in a jail cell. Special thanks to 'Trudy' for her help and devotion to typing them out into a legible format which we could start working with!

And we know that all things work together for good to them that love God, to them who are the called according to his purpose.

- Romans 8:28

FREEMAN: "A person in the possession and enjoyment of all the civil and political rights accorded to the people under a free government..."
- Black's Law Dictionary (6th edition)

FREEMAN. One who is in the enjoyment of the right to do whatever he pleases, not forbidden by law. One in the possession of the civil rights enjoyed by the people generally.
- Bouvier's Law Dictionary 1856 Edition,
1 Bouv. Inst. n. 164. See 6 Watts, 556:

FREEDMEN. The name formerly given by the Romans to those persons who had been released from a state of servitude. Vide Liberti Libertini.
- Bouvier's Law Dictionary 1856 Edition

"It is proper to take alarm at the first experiment of our liberties. They hold this prudent jealousy to be the first duty of citizens, and one of the noblest characteristics of the late revolution. The freemen of America did not wait till usurped power had strengthened itself by exercise, and entangled the question in precedents. They saw all the consequences in the principle, and they avoided the consequences by denying the principle."
- James Madison

'...if you can get your freedom, get it. The person who was a slave when God called him is now the Lord's freeman. In the same way, the person who was a freeman when God called him is now Christ's slave. Christ paid a price for you; don't be slaves of men.'
- 1 Corinthians 7:22, 23

PREFACE

MORE PEOPLE ARE STARTING TO stand up for the principles of freedom, 'true' justice and liberty. America rose to be the greatest national success story in the history of the world because its people were 'good' and free.

When this book was originally drafted in the mid '90's the freedom movement was also referred to by various other names and labels. At that time, these folks were labeled 'fringe extremists', 'armed and dangerous', 'militia wackos' and were routinely marginalized, castigated and vilified. They still are today. Only today, it has been discovered that 'Bible believing', 'Evangelist', 'Constitutionalists' are considered 'the enemy' in federal agency training manuals.

The movement for liberty has taken root under many names and banners. The 'Tea Party' is most talked about today. We now see the same passions manifesting in more and more people across the spectrum who have since taken up the banner of freedom (Don't Tread on Me!) to try and preserve those morals and principles which made the USA great throughout its history. Yet still, few if any of these mainstream groups understand the real issues which this book represents and has to teach.

The examples of how tyranny is creeping into our lives at a steady pace are too numerous to count. It is frightful.

It is in this context where the story takes on greater significance than just a story of one individual. It now becomes in itself a microcosm and an embodiment of the dynamic events and trends which are shaping the political and moral landscape of the sleeping giant, 'We the People' who make up 'the republic of the united States of America'.

This struggle is largely one which very few understand to this day. There is a legal and moral distinction between the 'Republic' and the 'U.S. Corporate Democracy'. The Republic is an entity of organic law created to serve its creators, 'the people' by protecting their rights, heritage and 'opportunity' to achieve prosperity and to manage the common interests between the states which created it.

This is in distinct contrast to the corporate 'Democracy' of the federal 'UNITED STATES' which is a very limited corporate body politic by definition. These are two distinct juristic (legal) entities which have been confused and obfuscated in most peoples' understanding today. One has very little, if anything, to do with the other.

The elite money powers behind the social reformers have seized upon the opportunity created by generations of apathy and ignorance. They keep us all busy fighting amongst ourselves over relatively trivial 'red' and 'blue' political and social issues while the real damage is being done elsewhere.

Over the years they have manipulated the economy, the politics and our social structure by dumbing us down with state education and controlled media and using various influences to destroy the family unit which is 'the central unit of government'! If we cannot govern our families, how can a free people expect to govern themselves? This is a fundamental issue.

The result has been that this core governing and teaching unit (the family), has decayed to the point where we now have more than one generation which has grown up in a vacuum without proper values or guidance. This makes them that much easier to manipulate without roots well planted in traditional values and history which gives us roots with a national identity. So we all now struggle just to survive. We are indifferent to the forces that dismantle our country and many of us only seek instant gratification in our daily lives, while the fabric of a decent, prosperous and strong society is unraveling before us.

Under such conditions, helplessness and despair are on the increase. With those conditions also comes dependency. Instead of looking to God, family and community to fill the void, people increasingly depend on government for the reasons just stated above. God is no longer welcome in our public society, (unless you are Muslim!). He is being stuffed in the closet. And if you've noticed, the public square progressives are now openly chastising and marginalizing those of the Christian faith. Just read the headlines of any 'true' journalistic operation.

In recent headlines we've seen numerous instances where students cannot mention God or Jesus in a commencement graduation speech. Victorious athletes gesture praise to God with a simple finger pointed to heaven, and are disqualified and denied their obvious victory because they 'broke the new rules'. The stories go on and on. The signals are clear. The 'Legal Society' and mainstream America has turned from God and will reap the results. Read 'The Harbinger', a NY Times bestseller.

So where we ask for 'help' from government, government grows in power and influence in our lives. When we receive 'gifts' from government (benefits or protections), there are always strings (adhesion contracts) attached. These strings have the effect of shifting of power from the free independent sovereign people who were granted an inheritance from God under organic, immutable law, to our new 'protector' which is the government operating on the whims of 'legislative code' and are in fact the corporate bylaws for U.S. Inc.

We the People have now sold our inheritance of 'freedom' and 'just law' for a bowl of porridge just like Esau did in the book of Genesis. If we don't correct ourselves we will continue on a path for destruction. Thus, we have our situation today where God is pushed out of the equation (Jews and Christians only) and constitutional protections no longer have any meaning or impact in our lives, which this book will explain in ways you've never imagined.

You will come to understand that to be legally correct, U.S. Inc. could not legally force a free and independent people to give up their rights short of blatant force, which would never work with any legitimacy. They had to 'induce' you into 'voluntarily' giving up those rights in exchange for benefits and privileges. Thus, the porridge!

Benefits and privileges can be suspended and revoked. God given rights cannot! So long as you 'want' those benefits and privileges, you can be manipulated and controlled by those who issue them!

As you read this story, you'll see how the character, Rex Freeman renounced all of his government benefits and privileges. He didn't need them! Thus, he was free from that control! If he just left it at that, he probably would have been fine. However, he started teaching the masses in a big way and that's where the excitement begins in our story.

You have, and always had, the free right to travel on the highways without regulation unless you are involved in 'commerce', until you apply for the drivers license.

You always had the right to get married without the state, until you apply for the 'marriage license' seeking 'benefits'.

You always had the right to clean the gutters on the house and do home repairs free from interference, until you applied for a 'permit'.

You always had the right to have and rear your children without interference, until you applied for the 'BIRTH CERTIFICATE'.

You NEVER own your car so long as all you have is the CERTIFICATE OF TITLE!

I hope I have piqued your curiosity. These are fascinating subjects once you get into them and they MUST be understood for freedom to exist.

Let's look at the <u>hierarchy of order</u> of each side of the law, to help you understand how we have converted our God given rights, into state granted privileges via applications and contracts for 'benefits'. In the chart on the following page, we start with the highest authority first and descend to the lowest authority in ranking order.

The Organic Law (of Nature and Nature's God/'de jure')	The Corporate Legislative Code (U.S. Inc./commerce)
#1. God Reigns supreme over all and he created man in his own image granting him dominion over the earth and free will.	**#1. Federal Government** Created by the states, now dominates the states.
#2. Man Answers only to God. In the USA, the people (man) created the state governments to regulate their affairs and serve them.	**#2. Federal Agencies** IRS, EPA, OSHA, SSA, DHS, ICE, NSA, et al now <u>dictate</u> directly to the people and essentially rule over them.
#3, State Governments The state governments answer only to their creators, the people.	**#3. State Government** Is now subject and completely subservient to that which it created, by virtue of the power to tax and spend and wanton disregard for constitutional limitations.
#4, Federal Government Federal government was created by the states, to serve the states as a means to harmonise commercial relations and intercourse between the people of the several states. The federal government answers to its creator, the several states.	**#4. Man** Now finds himself in the unenviable position of being 'the low man on the totem pole'. The 'creator' of government is now subject to his own creation. . Upon the earth, 'Man' is the sovereign under God!
#5. Federal Agencies Agencies are then created to help administer the business of the Federal government. They answer to the federal government which is subject to the will of the states.	<u>Note:</u> One side is completely inverse to the other. Plus, there is one critical element in the hierarchy of Organic law, which does not appear in the Legislative Code. Can you find it?

This author reaches out and claims the label of 'Patriot' and 'Freeman' with pride and fervour in the fight to preserve the honor and dignity of the truth about our history, our heritage, our freedom and what's right. This is why I wrote this book.

This book will open your eyes to various issues you likely have never considered before. Upon reading it to its conclusion, you may never be the same again. I can only hope for such a result. Someone once said, "Once removed, ignorance is impossible to regain!" This book is a grave threat to many peoples' blissful ignorance!

The war for the minds of Americans has been waging for generations now. So far, this war has been a war of words and ideas. We can only hope and pray that it continues on that level. I fear the alternative.

Will it remain purely ideological as a war of ideas and fought only in the minds of men and the ballot box? Or will the conflict 'get hot' as more 'Ferguson Missouri events' are staged and stoked? More and more states are supporting secession from the Feds as we have seen in just the last few years. "ONE FREEMAN'S WAR..." may provide some additional insights for you to draw your own conclusions.

Note: This is a novel using a fictional character, but is based on actual experiences and issues which are razor sharp. Be careful! The names of 'some' people and places have been changed to avoid poking the sleeping bear with another sharp stick. Any resemblance of the fictitious names which are used, to real people, is strictly coincidental and unintended. Some of the stories in this book do use the actual names of people who have either since deceased, or who would benefit, so that you, the reader can do further research and explore the exciting world of freedom on your own! This book is written to entertain and inform on general issues. By no means should it be construed as legal advice. Do **Not** attempt any commercial or legal process without professional assistance!

TABLE OF CONTENTS

IV. STRATEGIC SUMMIT CONFERENCES

V. BATTLE CRY - THE ENEMY ENGAGED

INTRODUCTION

THIS BOOK TELLS THE TRUE story of an average hard working truth seeker who could not sit quietly and allow the fraud and abuse of power he was witnessing to continue without saying or doing something about it. So the book is based on actual experiences and substantive events. Some of the names of people and places have been changed to avoid further conflict. So for this reason, we'll call this a 'novel'. Nonetheless, it will likely change the paradigms of your belief systems and what you have held to be 'true' throughout your life.

The story is an account of how one man, in concert with many others across America, exposes fraud of historic proportions on several fronts! Not only does he help expose it, which in itself is quite significant, but the remedy is implemented. This is when the fireworks begin.

You will see how one man, Rex Freeman, sought after the truths that some would rather keep under wraps. He gains a lot of attention from the wrong places in doing so. People in positions of power and influence become very uncomfortable, which is his objective!

This book is an adventure story which highlights what can be done with a little knowledge and a smidgeon of courage. Once he starts on his quest of upsetting the local power structure, Rex begins to realize that his own local battles in fighting abuse of power are really indicative of a much broader, systematic problem rooted in the American legal and political system.

His unquenchable thirst for knowledge and how he applies it in his life sharing it with others in a very public way makes him a threat to the 'status quo'. He becomes a target for persecution and his 'War' is on!

In pursuit of righteousness and guided by the light of his faith with the strength of his convictions, he challenges the government powers head on with the truth and the law. In the process, he exposes their hand of iniquity for all to see. You can imagine the result.

This story is an educational lesson which all Americans must learn and understand. You see, this is not only Rex's war. It is a war currently being waged against ALL Americans and freedom lovers worldwide.

You will see many of the 'real issues' which have been hidden from you, with crystal clear clarity. You will see them from the eyes of 'Rex Freeman' whose exploits are quite entertaining as the story is told. Read. Enjoy. Learn!

For more information on the author and his work we recommend his website: www.onefreemanswar.com

PART I

THE MAKING OF A PATRIOT

CHAPTER 1
THE POTTER'S CLAY TAKES SHAPE

AS MANY AMERICANS PURSUE THEIR daily lives and pleasures they stand oblivious or indifferent to the fact that their nation is awash in a sea of corruption and perverse ideals which are diametrically opposed to those principals which have made this country the greatest political experiment in human history. The people are being buffeted by un-American and un-Godly doctrines like a powerless and rudderless ship adrift in high seas, which is destroying the society as we have known it.

This occurs, to a large extent, as a result of our lack of understanding as to who we are as a nation ('people' not politics) and where we came from. People are much easier to control when they don't know who they are or where they came from. This is the natural result of not having roots firmly planted in history and tradition which gives a sense of identity. We can reference today's students' and their current lack of comprehension of true history and geography. It is simply not being taught effectively anymore in public schools (search 'Common Core'). Our own lack of knowledge of the colourful and compelling history and civics lessons serves to sever us from our roots and inextricably changes our character as a society. Without this solid attachment to our roots we cannot stand tall and firm in the face of the corrupting winds of deceit and manipulation. Instead we turn in circles like a weather vane and fall over and collapse, being susceptible to the manipulations of half-truths or flat out lies when it really counts.

For this reason, and in order to gain a fuller perspective of what this book has to offer in later chapters, I ask you dear reader, to indulge me with a brief foray into Rex Freeman's background and history. While the details themselves may not be important or notable to some, they do help to more fully understand the development and mindset of this individual and what is to occur in later chapters. Thus it serves as a point of reference for the reader to have a base of understanding upon which we will build a case for freedom which should be important to us all.

Here we go...

Rex's family had roots in the near west suburbs of Chicago; Oak Park and River Forest, Illinois. His father Ned was an only child, an ex-Marine and 'all cities' Chicago football player from a working class neighbourhood in Oak Park. He was your basic 'kick butt' 'take charge' city kid who graduated from Fenwick, a private Catholic high school. Ned's dad died before Rex was born so Rex never knew him. Ned's Mom (Grandma F.) lived modestly as a widow on a railroad retirement pension.

Rex's mother Carole came from the upper middle class neighbourhood of River Forest. River Forest was a gorgeous place where the trees formed what appeared to be gothic arches over the streets to give a tunnel effect. The homes were stately mansions in many cases. River Forest was famous for being the home of the late Paul Harvey, long time radio personality on one side of the coin, and the likes of mobsters Sam Giancana who was killed in his home before he had a chance to testify on alleged mob connections to the J.F.K. murder before a Senate committee. Also known in the neighbourhood were Tony 'The Tuna' Acardo and a host of other 10 o'clock news favorites! It was a very nice neighbourhood (if you just kept your head down).

Carole's father Ted was a pharmacist and ran a successful business which he started with his brother on North Avenue and Lombard St. in

Chicago in 1912. Since then he was 'the rock' of the neighbourhood. Things were changing all around him over the years, but he was always there for his customers, his neighbours and his friends. There was no doubt that over the years he had some very 'colourful' associates and a curious private life that, to this day, his family still isn't sure that they have the whole story on. His business thrived during the prohibition days, which was the heyday of the mob and Al Capone. The pharmacy was a 'classic' with the old fashioned cherrywood cabinets and glass cases, marble countertops and old style soda fountain fixtures. It was always a thrill for the kids to visit him and sit down for an ice cream soda in his 'parlour'.

Grandpa had influence and he knew everybody worth knowing in his neighbourhood. As they grew up, Carole and her sister never paid a traffic ticket on their 'home turf'. Grandpa always had a way of 'fixing things'. He was always full of good humour, silly jokes and didn't have a mean bone in his body. This was amazing for a man who, over the years, was routinely held up and robbed at gunpoint or threatened at the end of a baseball bat as the neighbourhood started 'changing'. He was a happy survivor!

Today, much of the furniture, fixtures and equipment of his pharmacy (Rex's childhood) are preserved and displayed in the Chicago Museum of Science and Industry representing a 'turn of the century Walgreens pharmacy store' (circa 1900) in the 'Main Street to Yesteryear' exhibit. Mementos of Rex's childhood are preserved for the world to see as a look into his past. It's an honour and a very nice testament to his roots which brings back fond memories whenever he sees his grandpa's old 'store'.

Rex's mom Carole went to Trinity High School, a private Catholic school for girls in River Forest. She then continued on to receive her degree in music at Rosary College, a liberal arts school again run by nuns and the church.

Ned's high school football team (Fenwick H.S.) won the 'All City' football championship in Chicago during his time there. This was a pretty big deal. Ned later got his degree in electrical engineering after attending several colleges on football scholarships. He then sharpened his confidence and bravado in the U.S. Marines which provided him all the tools necessary to be a real s.o.b. whenever he needed to be. In fact, Ned always had his favorite book in his office. It was entitled: "W.N.G.F.A.S.O.B.S." The title is an abbreviation of: 'WHY NICE GUYS FAIL AND SONS OF BITCHES SUCCEED" Although it was not his nature to be (usually), he was very independent and often found himself at odds with the world for one reason or another as he stood firm on his principles at the expense of convenience or favour.

Ned and Carole got married in a traditional Catholic ceremony in River Forest. Rex was born in the late 50's and within a couple of years Ned and Carole wanted to get the family out of the city to find 'the good life" in a wholesome small town or rural area to raise their kids.

As a result of Ned's entrepreneurial spirit and through several business endeavours over the years, they left the Chicago home turf and the kids had the pleasure of being raised in several small towns and rural communities in Wisconsin and Minnesota. As youngsters growing up in small town America, it was always a thrill for them to go make the annual summer visit to the 'big city' to see the grandparents in Chicago. Once, they actually left the car at home and went in a real 'jet plane'! This was almost unimaginable at the time (mid to late 60's). It was a real bragging point at school!

The grandparents in River Forest had a large, old home with innumerable secret hiding places, a spooky attic and basement. Best of all, they had a wonderful private swimming pool which was the center of most activity as you might imagine. As kids from farm country, they didn't know anybody else who had a swimming pool. The kids thought that a private pool was only for 'rich' people. The kids would often have to be dragged out of the pool when it was time.

Rex attended private parochial school in grades one through six which helped instill in him a deep respect for authority (namely God and his *enforcers*, the nuns!) as well as basic values that would carry on through life. Corporal punishment was administered freely when required and, being a normal mischievous boy, he got more than his fair share of it.

Memories of the nuns at school cracking his knuckles with a ruler or dragging him down to the principal's office by his ear (that really hurts when you do it right!) are still clear as a bell. To this day he has big ears!

Back home, whenever necessary, Ned would even use the belt in spanking his rear which was seriously dreadful. There were times when he and his sisters were equally culpable of disobedience and they would have to quietly wait their respective turn for the spanking while they listened to the uncontrollable squeals and shrieks of the one ahead of them in line. They learned quickly that in life, actions generated consequences, good and bad. Contrary to contemporary psychology and 'group think', the only lasting effects from these disciplinary episodes are those which taught him quickly not to make the same mistake twice! Imagine that!

As a result, this young kid had a profound respect for his elders and authority. When they spoke, he jumped up, listened and followed orders. He made sure he listened, showed respect and had his shirt tucked in while he did it. Today, this is unheard of. But that's the subject for another series of books.

If he had to do it all over again, he wouldn't change a thing. Now as an adult, he can see where the strong disciplinarian (but loving) upbringing he had bears fruit every day and provides serious advantages over those unfortunate products of the soft guidance' 'hands off", 'don't hurt their feelings' child rearing crowd. The facts in Rex's life are clear: strong discipline bears strong character. There is no substitute. For this reason alone our military personnel are among the best citizens we have! Although even that is starting to suffer with the contamination of basic time tested principles.

As is often the case, it wouldn't be surprising if the spankings were harder on dad than they were on the kids. He never said anything about it, but aside from being the necessary disciplinarian, he was a huge fan and supporter of each of the kids in all that they did in and out of school. He was the scoutmaster in boy scouts, football coach or team scout contributing in any way he could to success and development and in whatever way necessary.

He was equally involved in Rex's sisters' gymnastics, competitive ice skating, marching band and other activities. He showed his love in providing support and enthusiasm when things were good, and discipline when needed on the other side of the coin. Even when he was giving welts on the backside, they always knew he loved them. This was never in question, athough it was not even contemplated at the time!

On the other hand, mom was always there to comfort and guide them with a helping hand. Growing up with each other and countless pets and outdoor animals, mom showed how to have a big heart and to care for ourselves, each other and others as well. She once brought in a homeless man off the street in a snowstorm to share an Easter dinner with him. Rex thought she was a bit crazy at the time, but this was mom. They learned compassion from her.

Over the years, they raised countless dogs, cats, birds, bunnies, turtles, sheep and even a couple of horses. They learned responsibility and care for other creatures.

So after spending several years in places like Oshkosh Wisconsin' and Northfield Minnesota, the family landed in La Crescent the "Apple Capitol of Minnesota". It was a small town with a population of only 2,000, nestled in the foothills of the Mississippi Valley in southeast Minnesota. Just across the Mississippi River was LaCrosse, Wisconsin. It is a college town where Ned was now getting involved in a machining and manufacturing business with a friend of his.

HIGH SCHOOL

It was in this picturesque setting that Rex, and by now his 3 younger sisters, went through the public high school... LaCrescent High. What a slice of Americana! This was a place where people worked hard to earn an honest living. They lived in decent homes, people raised their families, went to church and spent the winter's snowmobiling, ice fishing and skiing and the summers were spent on the beautiful and mighty Mississippi River, boating, fishing, skiing, and camping, among other things! This is where life has its rewards. You put in a good work week and spent the weekend in the splendour in 'God's Country'. Their lives were simple, of modest means and glorious.

Rex's high school experience was equally glorious and he didn't want it to end, contrary to the sentiments of most students that can't wait to 'get out' and 'get it over with'. Fortunately, he was one of few high school kids who realized this at the time. He knew he had it good and cherished every moment. He knew that once he left the cocoon of high school where they were well taken care of and very comfortable, where they were stars (at least in their own minds) in their own small fishbowl and pretty much had the run of the place. It was clear to him that his world would change dramatically once he ventured out into the world of work and adulthood.

Rex and his friends were rebels, like many at that age. They liked to push the envelope. They did things which got them into trouble as much as anybody. They pulled many a prank, ditched school, had beer parties and did all the stupid school kid stuff. Most of them survived. Some didn't. Drinking and driving in the treacherous roads through the hills took its toll and a number of kids from Rex's school killed themselves having too much fun. He was always able to maintain control, or maybe he was just lucky. In Rex's senior year, they got away with a lot. He and his friends were also the leaders of most of the school groups and activities and were given a broad berth.

Rex's and his friends dominated all the sports activities plus debate, music, theater, school politics and almost everything. Rex himself was editor of the school paper. They didn't like the editorial restrictions placed on them, so the kids set up their own competition and published an *underground paper* with 'no holds barred'. They attacked school policies in the editorials and mocked some teachers with satirical articles using thinly veiled references. An adult version of a 'connect the dots' puzzle got its share of snickers and chuckles. In essence it was kind of a cross between the off-center humor of MAD Magazine and Playboy, with the biting editorials of a political rag, if you can imagine that. Circulation immediately surpassed the official 'school paper' they were also managing simultaneously. At least they controlled their own competition! Too bad they didn't do it long enough to go commercial! They could have made some money.

Rex was captain and MVP of the football team as middle linebacker and power running back, setting a school record for most tackles in a season and he made the All-Conference and All-Region football teams among other honors received. As the power running back in Rex's senior year he had reduced playing time on offense due to an ankle injury and the fact that his greatest value was on defense where they needed him the most.

Playing full time on defense, they didn't want to wear him down too much so he played spot roles as running back. Rex's buddies would be the workhorses to carry the ball during the offensive drives and get the team downfield. As they got close to the goal line, they'd bring Rex in as running back, to score the touchdowns. He loved to run over people and was known as a real 'hitter'. Rex's buddies did most of the work and he came in for the scoring glory. It's a strategy that worked. Who can argue?

In the Concert Choir, they competed in a regional contest in Kansas City which saw 80 schools from the entire mid-west region vying for honors. This was a big deal. The choir director had to do some heavy politicking to get permission for them to make the long trip from Minnesota to Kansas City, raise the funds and all that goes with such a venture.

The musical piece they attempted in the competition was extremely complex and difficult with dissonant chords that didn't resonate in a natural way. This element was combined with complex timing patterns and syncopation that required machinelike precision to pull off. When performed properly, the music created was absolutely surreal and something out of this world. When NOT done correctly, it was a horrible mess from hell which was extremely difficult, if not impossible, to recover from gracefully, if at all. This was 'do or die' music! The director, Don Annis, was not in his element teaching these lowly high school bums. This guy was a super talented, highly driven 'pro' who deserved a choir much better than this one to direct. He pushed the choir and had the guts to attempt this piece which honestly, they really had no business even attempting. At least that would be the 'common wisdom'.

They got the approvals, raised the funds and made the trip to Kansas City. The day of reckoning had finally come. They took the stage in the big theater with a number of other schools watching and they quietly positioned themselves on the risers in front of the director. Honestly, at first it felt a bit like walking up to the gallows. This thing could go either way.

Then, Rex could feel determination start to well up inside of him. He was completely focused on the task ahead with anticipation and eagerness, just as he does before a football game when he's suited up, psyched and just can't wait to get onto the field and hit somebody! They had spent months preparing for this moment, often agonizingly so with many failures and frustrations in trying to do a piece that often seemed to be beyond them.

Mr. Annis in his black long tail tux followed the choir to the risers and took his position in front. His posture and movements were strident, confident and deliberate. The air was thick with anxiety and anticipation. He smiled to try and put the choir at ease (longshot!) and then acknowledged the judges and the audience. He turned around to face the choir again and stepped up on his podium. He deftly raised his white gloved hand and held it with a pregnant pause, capturing attention with silence and his steely eyes. For a moment, time stood still…you could hear a pin drop. Everyone in the choir all stood with breath ready. They were entirely focused as they looked into his confident, serious and determined eyes. They got their starting note, derived the opening chord from that….and with one motion of the directors hand, instantly, 54 people were 'one unit'. …they started the piece and were off!

They started off magnificently. Mr. Annis didn't miss a cue, he was spot on, anticipating and executing every entrance, every pause, every syncopated rhythm and counter balanced dissonant chord, directing multiple sections of the choir simultaneously. It was masterful. Music, sounds and organized rhythms were magically bouncing back and forth from the bass section to the altos, from the baritones to the sopranos and cycling in ways that seemed to take a life of its own. Their confidence began to swell and they were in a complete zone of their own. It was absolutely beautiful. The music combined with the energy and confidence of the choir created an electric atmosphere. A performance like this deserved Carnegie Hall.

The piece went on. It felt like a marathon and they were in the groove and at their best. As they neared the end of the song, the syncopation and dissonant chords hit a crescendo and then began to smooth out. Everything started coming together in a regular smooth rhythm and the highly charged, chaotic, organized energy started softening and finally landed back on earth in perfect, subtle but eerie harmony leaving the spectator aghast and wondering what they had just experienced!

The atmosphere was electric. The feeling was nothing short of pure exhilaration and absolute relief that they actually made it all the way through the piece with such strength and confidence and didn't 'botch' it. The choir rose to the occasion and pulled off the performance of a lifetime, just like Mr. Annis *expected* they would. The concert choir from little old LaCrescent, Minnesota took first place in the top tier of 80 schools from 12 states. They were thrilled and absolutely amazed.

This group of average, goofball kids from a small town (some of whom really didn't usually sing that well, honestly) responded to the exceptionally high expectations and rigorous demands of a 'professional' director, Mr. Annis. They accomplished the goal with a gutsy performance and had the gall to try something difficult which dared failure. The director was thrilled like everyone, but not so amazed. Given that the kids could somehow rise to the very high level demanded of them by Mr. Annis, he knew that they would be far and ahead of anybody else on their heels in the competition. That's the power of strong leadership with demanding discipline and high expectations!

This is a perfect example of leading and demanding that kids reach beyond their comfort zone to achieve something that would not normally be expected of them for fear of failure. Sure, they were poised for the perfect humiliating disaster. It was entirely possible, and perhaps even probable. Yet with the faith they had in their director who led by his own example, he dared the kids to achieve something exceptional. In fact, he 'willed it' against the odds. They were given the opportunity to fail and the expectation to reach into a new 'zone' and succeed. They responded to the challenge, earned their reward and learned something that would contribute to their lives henceforth.

Had they not done so well, they would have learned the value of having the courage to reach for high goals and give it a try. Even in failure, there is much to learn from and grow. Today, it seems many kids don't have that opportunity to fail or succeed. It could 'hurt their feelings'. Fortunately, they didn't go that route! Thanks Mr. Don!

Let's face it, being in the choir is not considered such a 'macho' activity and was not so popular among the guys. Rex was a staunch member of the choir from the beginning and being 'Mr. Jock' from the football and track teams and school leader in other ways, he broke the mold and led the way for other guys to follow his lead where a number of his buddies and a few others joined because it was now 'OK' and it was also an 'easy credit'.

Rex was later voted *most valuable male singer* by his peers in the choir. He loved to sing and, like everything he did, he took it seriously and poured himself into it with everything he had. Rex's dad taught him that, *"if you're going to do it, do it right!" He* was also involved in a Barbershop Quartet, Madrigal singers, he played guitar and sang at church, played in a couple 'garage rock bands' and more.

In a similar vein, Rex's gang of friends dominated the spring musicals and put on several productions. In the production '1776' which they did Rex's freshman year, he played Mr. Charles Dickinson, the annoying British sympathizer and constitutional convention delegate from Pennsylvania. Rex's costume was a 'black velvet' colonial style outfit which was perfect for the role of the 'spoiler'. He loved the role of the spoiler! This character's persona stuck with him ever since, as you'll soon see.

In his sophomore year they did the Broadway play "The Fantastics" where he did get one of the lead roles and had fun with it.

Senior year, they put on 'Man of La Mancha' where he played the pious 'Padre' the priest (no typecasting here – it was the bass voice they needed for the character's songs in the performance). 'Cervantes' or Don Quixote was the lead role in the musical which was written for a tenor, so he was immediately crossed off the list of candidates for that.

They learned that putting on a theater production was a huge 'team effort' and required a substantial amount of discipline and sacrifice by each member of the production from cast, set design, crew, musicians, director, costumes, makeup, cleanup and everyone else involved.

Rex's high school experience was rich in experience, but the point is this: He excelled. He achieved. He pushed the limits and also got into his share of trouble. Being the non-conformists that Rex and his buddies were, they got away with a lot but were also accomplished leaders at the same time and they had a ball with all of it.

He was too busy having fun and being a 'smart alec' to be an excellent student. But he did maintain a solid 'B' average in the midst of all the mayhem and got what he could out of school knowing full well that he would be going away to college to pursue a degree in International Business/ Marketing & Finance which was decided in his Junior year in high school.

Rex's first French language class was in the fourth grade. But his interest in international cultures was really sparked by his high school French teacher, Miss Papic, starting in the ninth grade. She later took them on a trip to France, his junior year in 1975. This was quite an eye opener! This was before email and internet and back then, going to a different country was like going to the moon!

It was a different world with stark cultural contrasts and once you went, communications back home were scant and expensive and not very reliable as the telephone connections were mostly by transatlantic cables. Remember that in the mid 70's this was before satellite communications were so prevalent and going to another continent was a place far, far, far away! You felt quite detached from your home environment. Today, with email and text chat on your personal phone, you may as well be next door than half way around the world. It's all the same! We have lost some of the romance, mystery and intrigue of travelling overseas.

Rex's participation in this wonderful trip was made possible by the love of his parents and their vision for his future and future success. They had to scrimp and scratch to find the money to send him, but they did. Little did they know at the time the direction this trip would steer Rex toward his future.

Rex's parents were not terribly political. They just wanted to be left alone to live their lives and to pursue the American dream. Ned was building his own business selling specialized machine parts to railroads in the US and abroad. It was a very small, one man business (secretary notwithstanding) and Rex often played a big role in what was going on there, which is where he cut his teeth in learning the business world.

Ned set Rex up with own business at the age of 15 selling certain proprietary parts to the Milwaukee Road railroad. He had the raw parts cast in a local aluminum foundry. He'd then have them machined in a local machine shop and assemble them before packing them up and shipping them out. Rex learned to issue invoices and collect the payments. It was interesting for a 15 year old kid.

The only political discussion he remembers his folks having was one around Halloween when kids came by looking for donations to U.N.I.C.E.F. the international U.N. children's fund. Ned was adamantly against giving any money whatsoever to an organization which operated under the auspices of the U.N. which is made up of predominantly communist or Marxist leaning countries. U.N.I.C.E.F also operates in 'communist countries' and thus his view was that they supported the 'communist governments' involved. He was very clear on that. Communism and Marxism were 'taboo' ideologies to be fought at every turn. Remember that this was still during the 'cold war' and that mind-set was prevalent.

Ned was a Marine after all, and served his country with a tour of duty during the Korean conflict which he was very proud of. As Boy Scout leader he was very serious in teaching how to properly fold and handle the flag with the utmost of respect. The flag was sacred. The family had a flag pole in front of the house, so raising the flag and bringing it down every night was a ceremonial ritual which was Rex's responsibility.

Rex's high school career was a full one. He had no special privileges other than what he might have earned from his hard work and personal ambition. He had no money other than what he could earn during the summer and from giving a few guitar lessons in his 'spare' time. He made some bad decisions along the way and suffered the consequences. Quite a bit had been learned that prepared him to excel in the big world he was about to enter.

COLLEGE

The main goal he had upon high school graduation was to 'get out of town'. Rex wanted to go to college to get out of the confines of his small town and to expand his horizons and see the world. He thought to himself, 'the good Lord put him on this earth for a sound reason and I'm going to find out what it is!" During the high school days, he had life 'whipped' in that small corner of the world. He was a big fish in a small pond. Rex was now ready for a bigger pond. So it was on to the next challenge and with the help of some scholarships, grants and student loans, he pieced it all together and was off to college.

Rex was loading up his car and getting ready to leave home for the first time in early August 1976. He got about 50 yards down the street and got a flat tire. He didn't get very far! His mom always remembered this as the iconic moment representing the challenges that always seemed to appear in Rex's life at the most inopportune times. He would often no sooner get started on something when obstacles would invariably appear. Maybe this has something to do with his temperament in not getting terribly upset when things do go wrong, as they usually do. He's used to it, so don't worry! Deal with it!

One critical factor in his choice of colleges was that he was invited to join the football team at St. Norbert College. The excruciating conditioning drills started in the heat of early August. The days were hot and humid when he arrived and he had the entire campus in DePere, Wisconsin (Green Bay suburb) almost all to himself as he came in early to report for football with his new teammates.

St. Norbert College was one of the few at the time that offered a full International Business and Language Area Studies program (IBLAS) which is the degree that he pursued from the beginning. That, plus his ability to play on the football team were Rex's main reasons for choosing St. Norbert College. The fact that St. Norbert was the training camp home for the Green Bay Packers at the time and that the two organizations had a close relationship with a variety of mutual benefits and exchanges may have had 'some' influence. He was a serious, die hard Packer fan. So that didn't hurt.

Being on the St. Norbert college football team meant that every year they had at least one 'sideline pass' to a Packer game on the hallowed 'Lambeau Field'. The St. Norbert football team would also use the Packers practice facility when they had to prepare for a game on artificial turf. The Packers had a 60 yard patch of turf indoors at the time. There were a few private parties Rex and his buddies had as students where a couple of the Packer players came over. This was a thrill. In fact, Larry Krause was an alumnus of St. Norbert who actually played well as a regular for the Packers during Rex's high school days and he remembers following his career. Krause was a smallish guy (by NFL standards) from a small school in a small town who had 'done good'. Maybe Rex could follow his path!?

Rex continued his singing and tried out for the Oratorio Concert Choir at St. Norbert. He got invited, no problem. If that weren't enough along with football, Rex met some musicians in the choir and formed a rock band in which he sang and played guitar. In his sophomore year, he joined a fraternity on top of it all. The best description of life in Phi Sig would be to compare it very closely with the movie "Animal House" starring John Belushi. The parallels are striking and some parts of the movie seemed more like home videos of Rex's own experience in Phi Sig at St. Norbert.

It was a typical college/football jock/fraternity experience: Girls, drinking, glaring examples of immaturity and general 24 hour lunacy were the rule. Shortly before Rex's freshman year ('76), St. Norbert was written up in Playboy as the most strident 'party school' in the country behind only USC who they didn't include on the list because Playboy considered them 'professionals'!? Surely the Jesuit priests at St. Norbert loved that writeup! One can only wonder if it ever came up at any alumni fundraising or board meetings!

There was no shortage of strange characters either. Despite this, he was able to stay out of jail and the emergency room! (Don't ask how!)

Ned had a heart attack Rex's junior year and Rex had to take one semester off to run his dad's business and help the family while his dad recovered. He somehow still made the Dean's List his senior year and amazingly reached the finish line with momentum having graduated with honors. With no other delay, in four and a half years, with a semester of exchange study living in southern France, which was an experience in itself, he had a college diploma and was now prepared to single handedly conquer the world! (Sure!)

Throughout Rex's childhood, his parents were loving, supportive and were involved in everything he did. Rex's father Ned rarely missed one of Rex's football 'practices' let alone a 'game'. He made every game, home and away, from grade school through college. St. Norbert was a 4 hour drive from home in La Crescent!

In high school, if Rex didn't do well in practice when he finally got home to rest and relax, Ned would take him out in the back yard and they'd have their own practice session where Ned would ride him hard. Lovely! Just what he wanted, right? After Rex's coach ran his ass to the ground, he got to finally go home to collapse and rest and then he'd have his dad continue riding him in the backyard to point out his weaknesses! Jeeez, Come on!

Ned put a lot of pressure on Rex to be the best he could be. Rex resented it at times (a lot), but his discipline and quest for near perfection made him into one of the best football players in the area: He was voted 'Most Valuable Defensive Player of the Year' ('75), 'Team MVP', 'All Conference' and even made the selection to 'Regional All Star'.

Rex was not the greatest athlete by any means but was deadly serious and disciplined about his football and he worked harder than anyone. This only to shows that he was taught how to excel and win with laser focus, not only in football, but in life. The formula for success does not include doing things 'half assed' or being lazy. Again, his motto: *'If you're going to do it, you may as well do it right'*. Anyone who is accomplished in any discipline can attest to the validity of this principle.

When Ned came down hard on Rex, as he often did, mom was always there to clean up the mess by consoling him and lifting Rex's spirits. Come to think of it, whether it was intentional or not, mom and dad had perfected the 'good guy/bad guy' routine!

Ned gave the same attention and support to Rex's sister Connie who excelled as a leader and champion in competitive gymnastics and figure skating, another sister Marcia was in marching band and travelled the country doing exhibitions and Collette had her own dance and music activities and related parenting challenges in life.

It's hard to say how good parents find the time for all of these things, but they do! But let's acknowledge that this was back in the mid 70's and life was a bit simpler back then!

So despite the normal family feuds, fights and disconnects, Rex's upbringing was about as good as one could ask for. His childhood years didn't lack anything. They had a close family life. Plus, after years of incessant teasing, taunting and harassment, Rex may have even toughened up his sisters along the way!

Rex was disciplined in an authoritarian household with maximum love and support to excel and achieve within the boundaries clearly defined by a respect for law (what dad says!) and morality. They were religious, rarely ever missing church on Sunday and all special religious days. As a rebellious kid, Rex put up with it as he had no choice in the matter. They prayed at home, prayed before meals and always had meals together because meal time was 'family time'. It was sacred not to be dishonored.

They were taught that there were many good things in life, all of which had to be earned. Life in these united States of America could be great. Rex's parents saw to it that even though they had modest means, the kids had all the tools they needed to make it so. They were rewarded when they lived up to high expectations and they got their butts kicked when they screwed up. So what? They are now achievers in a world awash in mediocrity.

With Ned's non-conformist, entrepreneurial attitude, they often had financial difficulties. But they never looked anywhere outside themselves in times of need. They found a way to make their own way and achieve their own dreams.

Ned had accomplished his dream; he finally got into a position after many years of hard work to put a brand new 30 foot Sea Ray cabin cruiser boat into a slip in the local marina. This was his love (the rest of the family didn't mind it too much either). Rex had his own classic runabout: a old wooden Thompson Lapstrake ski boat with an 80 horse Merc outboard motor to run up and down the Mississippi river in. Life was good. This was a beautiful boat and extremely fun to do some 'river running'.

It was this type of good, fruitful, productive living with loving families that so many before us have shed their blood and sacrificed their lives to preserve. Our right to seek a peaceful, productive life, protected by righteousness and a government which recognizes its constitutional limitations to interfere in our pursuit of such things, is what our forefathers established for us. Yet today we sleep and let this America slip away.

You don't see this kind of family unity and self-reliance as a 'common standard' today. And people wonder why society is unraveling at the seams? The central organ of good government is…'the family unit' which functions with order, discipline and solid values. With this as the basis, a 'Free Society' can function well. Without it, well, look around! Look at all of the abominations being tolerated, taught and even promoted in our public schools! As the family unit is being systematically destroyed with the 'Politically Correct' 'anti-Christian' mindset is it any wonder that the country and the world are in such a mess?

Growing up he always felt very 'normal' and an 'average guy' even after having spent 4 years in in college, where he was a smaller fish in a much bigger pond. There were much smarter kids than him in class and there were much faster and stronger guys than him on the football team. But few were more determined and prepared to succeed than he was.

Rex's childhood NFL dreams were dashed by reality. Nobody ever came knocking with a big contract. So now he had his work cut out for him. It was time to get busy.

CHAPTER 2

THE ALLURE OF FAR
AWAY LANDS

THE PRIMARY PURPOSE FOR GOING to college, in Rex's mind, was to expand his horizons and it didn't take long. With diploma in hand, a degree in International Business, living experience overseas (France twice) and experience in helping run his father's business which shipped to Canada, New Zealand and Australia, he began his job search feeling confident he would find something in the international business arena.

INTERNATIONAL EXECUTIVE

Rex's job search was typical and involved a lot of work making many contacts. There were countless mailings of his resume, letters, interviews, and ultimately, several bouts of exasperation along the way. It was a winding path where he felt like giving up more than once. Finally, he was actually given an offer by Federal Signal. By the time the offer came, he really had his sights set on another company, EKCO Housewares, whom he had been talking to about a really exciting job, but they weren't ready to make a decision. Federal Signal makes the emergency lights and light bars you see on police and emergency vehicles, among other signal and safety devices. This job offer was domestic sales. It wasn't international.

Rex was waiting on 'EKCO' which is a multinational manufacturer of housewares. You know the name and probably have some of their cutlery or kitchen gadgets in your home. EKCO was looking for some-one who had an MBA in international business (he didn't qualify), who had 5 years work experience (he didn't have it) and a list of other requirements to be their 'Area Market Manager for Europe and Africa'. This was Rex's dream job and was perfect for his training and goals! Both companies were in the Chicago area. Federal Signal was in Blue Island, a way south suburb and EKCO was in Franklin Park, which is a near west suburb near O'Hare airport.

Just like when the choir won the contest in Kansas City singing a song they really had no business attempting, Rex lobbied EKCO hard for this job even though he didn't 'qualify', as per their stated requirements. He had the *gall* to go after it anyway. He set his sights on this job and went at it hard. He might not get it, but he was not daunted from trying anyway. By now, he had learned long ago that 'limits' are there only to be 'tested'. Only bold action could break through!

He sold them on the fact that from working with his dad's company in the international railroad markets he had direct 'hands on' international marketing experience and then living overseas on two different occasions (once for only a week in high school jaunt and six months in a university program) combined with his language skills in French from grade school on, he most certainly had a rare command of the French language which was a prerequisite.

He sold them on the fact that his personal business experience was at least on a par, if not better than, any fresh MBA grad. His language skills were certainly better than some 'classroom trained' French student and that, as a lowly BBA grad, Rex's *price tag* was a bargain for them to get all this experience in comparison to their alternatives with MBA grads with the same experience. In fact, finding an MBA grad with this level of experience would be difficult AND expensive.

The problem was that the folks at EKCO were really dragging their feet on making their decision. He finally couldn't put Federal Signal off any longer, as they were really pressuring to start a group training program and they wanted him in the training. Finally, Ekco was still indecisive and he took the bird in the hand with Federal Signal. It was a good job, just not stellar and it wasn't 'international' which is what he was really groomed for. It was a very long job search and he felt he had to do something, so he took it almost out of desperation. He needed to start somewhere.

After joining Federal Signal he attended one week of special training in a south suburban hotel which they paid all the expenses for.

Then, Ekco finally came back. They finally offered the dream job he was waiting for after much deliberation on their part. It worked! Amazingly, they bought! BINGO! He set it up and then closed the deal to land his first professional job out of school (well, the first one that lasted more than a week anyway)! It was a dream job which he figured would take many years to work into. Rex busted the parameters with bold action!

Great! Now how does he handle this mess with Federal Signal?

He gave Federal Signal the bad news. He was leaving. They also dragged their feet before making offer on a Friday, and forced a decision by Monday so they could start their training the next week. That wasn't so great and after forcing Rex's hand so quickly, he didn't feel too bad about it.

He was only 22 years old and had maneuvered himself into the position of the 'Export Market Manager' for Europe & Africa with the International Division of EKCO Housewares International. Wow! He had hit the jackpot!

Before long he was traveling the world on a company expense account, living like a VIP and as his dad would say, 'high on the hog' at an early age.

The primary objective that EKCO had was to develop the markets in North and West Africa. West Africa included the countries of Senegal, Liberia, Ivory Coast, Cameroon and Nigeria. Nigeria was the cornerstone of the Marketing plan being an OPEC oil producing nation with a large population and lots of money and economic development. Then, up in northern Africa is the Arab world of Morocco, Algeria, Tunisia, Libya and the island of Malta in the Mediterranean.

Rex's boss was a Pakistani named Ali and while he was very serious and businesslike... He was also quite a funny character once you got him loosened up a little. They got along well. He took Rex under his wing and like Rex's father; he demanded a lot in no uncertain terms and he gave every opportunity to successfully meet his expectations.

They had a fond respect for each other and developed a good working relationship.

If you understand the history of Africa you know that only recently (in the second half of the 1900's) have the African nations emerged independent from the colonization by the European powers, namely France, Britain and Portugal.

Thus, all of North Africa and about half of West Africa have a strong French cultural influence including the language. So Rex's French was about to be put to the test. Rex's first project was to translate the entire EKCO housewares product catalog into French. Can you imagine what it's like to come up with the French equivalent of such things as; 'cherry pitter', 'egg slicer', 'butcher knife', 'skewer', 'potato peeler' and 'double boiler'? What a nightmare! Well, somehow he did it (or came close).

That first project being complete, Ali virtually handed him a one way ticket to Africa and said, "Rex, it's time for you to go. Don't come back until you sell something!"'

He'll never forget his first trip. After hours spent over the ocean on Air Afrique (which no longer exists), he looked out the window of the airplane as they were making final approach to land in Dakar Senegal. As he looked out and saw nothing but little scrub trees, a few bushes and dry desert. He asked himself, "Rex you've really done it now, what the hell are you doing here?" It was a little too late for second guessing. He was touching down on the West Africa bushland.

It was always fun to see the reaction of new acquaintances when they would ask what he did for a living. Rex's short response was "I sell pots and pans in Africa". You could see them pause for a moment, quietly envisioning him with a wicker basket of pots and pans going from hut to hut out in the bush villages. He was just your classic, tribal, door to door, pots and pans salesman you know!

Of course Rex's 'wicker basket' was, in reality, a twenty or forty foot sea container, similar in size to a semi-trailer, which was shipped to large distributors or retail chain stores.

For some reason people still have a hard time breaking out of the mentality of the old Tarzan movies and envisioning modern cities and big business in Africa.

Some of the executives he dealt with were placed in the home offices of large organizations based in Europe, primarily London & Paris which occasionally gave him the excuse to go make a visit. Hey, if you can get some French cheese, croissants and wine out of the deal, let's go!

Consequently, about half the time he was dealing with the French or British anyway. The smaller importers were typically either Lebanese, exiled from the strife in their homeland, East Indians or native black Africans to a lesser degree.

Of course all had their own customs, which he quickly learned with great admiration and enjoyment. Fortunately for him, during his visits they all treated him like a king. They offered him fantastic meals, chauffeured transportation, bodyguards where needed, you name it. He learned to love the Turkish coffee that the Lebanese served! Coffee drinkers haven't experienced coffee until they try Turkish style coffee. It's boiled in a special pot together with fine coffee grounds, almost powder, with sugar poured into an ornate, porcelain, slightly oversized shot glass served with a twist of lemon.

It's very, very strong! These people are absolutely amazed at how Americans can drink such huge cups of diluted coffee! Of course it's not the same thing. This stuff will grow hair on your fingernails! The grounds settle on the bottom of the glass and its custom to turn the glass over and let the wet grounds settle on the saucer. When it dries, the cracks that appear can be 'read' by fortune tellers much like your palm and gifted 'seers' can give you 'guidance' from what they see in your coffee!

Rex's first trip was proceeding along nicely as he was quickly getting the lay of the land in Monrovia Liberia, Abidjan Ivory Coast and then finally Lagos, Nigeria. He was immersed in a different world as anyone who has been in a third world country would attest. Things are done quite a bit differently there. He had to learn the "Dash" system in Nigeria. Very little got accomplished with government workers, customs and port officials, unless you knew the 'Dash' system.

Rex's containers simply would not move through the port unless or until he found the right guy to "dash" a little cash to over here and then "dash" a little cash to that guy over there and then magically, things began moving!

Selling is quite a bit more complicated in poor countries with exchange controls. The client may have plenty of money in the native currency. Then he had to get it converted into U.S. dollars to pay for the goods. Many third world countries have a very limited supply of foreign exchange and they ration it based upon national priorities. So after he'd sell a client he'd have to go to the government finance officials and sell them on issuing a permit to apply for the foreign exchange so the order could be paid for. Once this is approved (meaning you've 'dashed' the right official) Rex had to translate this arrangement into an irrevocable, international letter of credit with the local client's bank and have its acceptance confirmed by a U.S. bank.

Occasionally he would have to enlist the assistance of the U.S. embassy or consulate in the area for one purpose or another. Through Rex's experiences he was acquiring technical skills and influential political contacts very rapidly.

The closest thing that you can compare to living and doing business in West Africa is that it's like being on the frontier in the old Wild West. It's virtually a 'free for all' and may the best man win. Regimes change with the weather; political instability means you see armed military check points at various spots on the road. You never know what to expect. There have been several occasions where he's encountered dead bodies just pushed off to the side and nobody seems to bother themselves about it. You had to be alert. This was a wild frontier where 'anything goes'.

In Lagos, Nigeria, the building that housed the center for the entire national communications system was destroyed by a 'mysterious' fire just prior to election. Word on the street was that it was burned by outgoing officials for fear that the opposition in the new government would trace records of wired money transfers into politicians' private accounts in Europe. It's a crazy, crazy, mindset. But it does breed excitement and opportunity!

This freewheeling atmosphere and latitude allowed him to hook up with a wild Irishman named Shaun Kelly who was an entrepreneur to the end.

They finagled some large transactions together that you'd have to see to believe with cross trade and payments (exchanging goods instead of cash, doing transactions with those goods, making a profit on that and then generating the cash for the original intended transaction). It was a circus of characters and everyone came out a winner with the 'dash' system working in full glory on all sides to make things happen. They never taught him this stuff in school.

Ned was extremely excited by Rex's new career. On Rex's first trip to West Africa Ned had a world map up on the wall in his office back home and was tracking Rex's daily progress with stick pins on the map as he followed Rex's itinerary. With his map he was living vicariously through Rex's trip, day by day as it progressed. They were both excited and looking forward to getting together when he got back to re-live the adventure.

Well, that never happened. About three quarters of the way into Rex's first trip, after a history of heart trouble, Ned had a fatal heart attack and died at home. Rex was with his biggest client in Lagos Nigeria when he was called into the office of his counterpart there and received the news. The trip was cut short and he went back early for the funeral. As hard as Ned worked all his life to see his only son succeed, he never got to share the excitement of Rex's greatest success to date. What a shame.

Rex did well with EKCO for about three years. He traveled all over Europe and Africa and accumulated enough experiences, stories and adventures to last a lifetime. Then, Nigeria started to slip back into political and economic strife. Their foreign currency became more restricted and with it so did the prospects for business. Rex's market responsibilities were consolidated back under Ali's control and Rex's adventure with EKCO came to a close. So now he was back in the job market with one hell of a resume for a twenty-four year old kid. He had experienced some of the best of what the world has to offer and now had a hunger for more.

CHAPTER 3

CONTACT WITH
'THE COMPANY'

IT WASN'T MORE THAN A few weeks of putting out resumes, making phone calls, and networking with existing contacts that he started to get frustrated with the job search process, again. It's never easy, especially for such an exclusive type of job.

There just didn't seem to be any opportunities out there that would give him the same responsibility and experience like he had with EKCO. He was spoiled. But just when he started to get exasperated, Rex received an interesting phone call.

The caller mentioned his name quickly. It was unknown to Rex. The caller said he was a friend of a friend and he heard Rex was looking for an opportunity.

After a friendly and lengthy conversation about Rex's qualifications, experience, his contacts, language capabilities, goals and related topics, he ended the discussion abruptly by telling Rex, "Well, it sounds like you might qualify for a job opening I'm aware of. I'll have someone contact you by phone in the near future to discuss it further. They'll be in touch, goodbye." And that was it! 'click'!

Several weeks had gone by and he hadn't heard anything. In the meantime Rex was interviewing with Four Winds International, an International specialty shipping and moving company. They were interested enough to fly him out to New York to meet their brass up in beautiful Westchester County, just north of New York City. The interviews went well, they hit it off fine and shortly thereafter, he was hired. Rex proceeded through minimal training and began calling on large corporations in the Chicago area to solicit their international shipping business. It was really a step down for him, but he was still in 'international business' to keep the thread on Rex's resume intact.

PHASE 1

It wasn't until he was well into his new job with Four Winds that one Saturday morning Rex got the phone call that he had been promised some time back and now had nearly forgotten about. It was not the same man who he had talked with the first time. He identified himself as John Espinosa. Again, the conversation was cordial yet very direct and to the point. They rehashed over much of the information that was discussed with the first caller, quite extensively. Perhaps the caller was checking for B.S. or changes in 'the story'.

Finally, after repeated attempts on Rex's part to ask some questions, he broke through and started getting some information out of Espinosa.

But it didn't last long. Espinosa took control of the conversation again. "Mr. Freeman, he said, "the job we need to fill requires someone who has many of the skills and experience you have demonstrated. However, very few people we talk to ever end up coming to work with us, for many reasons. This job is not for everybody. We work with a branch of the government." Now he really had Rex's curiosity piqued.

"Mr. Freeman," he said again, "our interviewing process will probably take over six months, if we complete it at all. There will be several stages whereby we will evaluate you and you, us. If, at any one of these stages, either one of us wishes to terminate the process, it will be done. You will not meet anybody face to face until the final stage, if we make it that far." Espinosa continued, "the branch of government we work for is the Central Intelligence Agency. Have you heard of it?"

He continued, "From this point forward you are not to share this conversation or any information we discuss with anybody, even your family. In the future, if you find it necessary at any point to say anything about your affiliation you might just mention that it relates to gathering statistical market data for the government. Just keep it general. Understood?"

He went on, "You won't be told many specifics until the later part of the process. The first stage involves getting you familiar with what life is like working in this environment. We have a list of books that we want you to read. You can get these in just about any library. It is very important, if you want to proceed, to complete these tasks, as required, in the time frame given. We'll be back in touch with you in about six weeks. Any questions?"

Rex answered, "Yes, how do he get a hold of you or someone else, if needed?"

"You won't need to," he replied. "Just complete the tasks and we'll get back in touch with you when appropriate." He wound up the conversation by telling him, "Thanks for your time and interest, you'd better get busy. We'll talk to you further down the road. Goodbye."

This was all a bit overwhelming. He knew the C.I.A. ('company') was secretive but he had barely even begun the selection process and he was already keeping 'secrets'! Well if Rex's escapades in Africa whet Rex's appetite for adventure, he was now certainly back on the right track.

He quickly got down to the library and pulled three of the books from the list he had. William Casey's book was huge. It didn't take him long to figure out this would be no lark! He started reading as much as he could.

Whenever he could find the time, he was doing his homework reading what was a massive amount of material, trying to accomplish the task before the next call, whenever that would be. Rex's girlfriend at the time was a bit put off that all of a sudden he didn't seem to have all that much time for her. She dealt with it.

Rex began to learn about the key role that the 'company' played in Vietnam. It was not as much just gathering intelligence but the 'company men' were a direct force in the 'pacification' of the local Vietnamese, trying to win over their hearts and sympathies to the U.S. war effort in their country. The company had a huge propaganda effort in addition to direct financial and community support to those people. Rex was quite amazed at the scope of C.I.A. involvement in the war.

He read about the agents' work and personal lives in places like Botswana, Angola, Bolivia and other God forsaken ends of the earth. It was certainly not always a pretty picture. Those who equate this work with James Bond running in the fast lane with beautiful women in exotic venues would be highly disappointed.

If, by and large, C.I.A. agents were as these books depicted, he had a high esteem for the many personal sacrifices, and selfless acts done on behalf of their country, often without even a pat on the back from their superiors. Rex was told early on that "the greatest reward in this job that you should expect would be the knowledge that you did a good job for your country and little more."

That was kind of hard to swallow for a football jock and musician who was used to the limelight, glory and personal recognition for his accomplishments. Nevertheless he continued reading and studying.

Phase II

The next call came in about seven weeks from the last call. It was another lengthy interview lasting about three hours on the phone. He was tested on the content of what he had read to confirm that he had completed his assignment. He could tell that the important thing they were interested in was Rex's personal reaction and opinion about the stories told in those books. Espinosa was trying to determine if Rex's character and goals in life matched up at all with the reality of being a C.I.A. operative. Evidently he was satisfied as he asked Rex then, if he wished to proceed to the next level. This was the third step they had just completed.

The first was generating enough interest to be contacted in the first place.

The second was the lengthy initial phone interview. And this 'book report' discussion was the third phase which was now complete.

Rex affirmed his desire to move on to the fourth level and was told, "They'll be sending you some paperwork. Try to fill it out and send it back within three weeks." Rex thought to himself 'what's a little paperwork?' No problem! Once again Espinosa said, "We'll be in touch, goodbye.'"

The package soon arrived in the mail and upon opening it, Rex quickly realized that it would be all that he could do just to get 'this little bit of paperwork' completed in the three weeks requested. It was focused on Rex's biographical profile, family history, educational history, drug history and a lot of other kinds of history that he didn't even know he had!

Well guess what? The information was somewhere and he had to find it and reduce it to writing. The race was on! He was forced to do a lot of research on himself and in the process learned more about himself than he ever knew existed. He finally completed the project, although not a minute before the three weeks was up. He needed every bit of that time to put it all together. He shipped it off in the pre-addressed envelope to some nondescript address.

PHASE III

Several more weeks passed by and 'the call' came in. The profiles were reviewed and again, he passed this phase. The question came, "Would you like to continue?" Rex confirmed. They'd repeat the next process with another set of papers. This time it was a battery of psychological profiles and related testing.

Do you think you dulled your No. 2 pencil filling in dots of the S.A.T. and A.C.T. college entrance exams? Rex never saw so many circles and was never so glad to get any such testing over with as this.

So many questions were designed to trip you up and contradict your earlier answers to the same questions worded differently. There was no question but that if you weren't 100% on the ball, you'd go down in flames on this one. It was a maze of intertwined connections designed to frustrate. It was a mental agility test like none other.

They repeated the process. Several weeks after sending the tests in, he got the call. To his amazement, Rex passed again. Did he want to continue? Well, at this point he wasn't real sure. This was getting to be quite a pain, not to mention a crimp in Rex's social life and he thought if it's this difficult getting in, what's it going to be like once they want him to get serious?

Espinoza then told him, "You've now gone farther than 90% of our candidates. Your next step will be to meet with one of our people."

Finally! A meeting with a real person. Hallelujah! He was beginning to wonder if that would ever happen and was sure sick of the tests, profiles, reading and studying. He didn't know it at the time but this face to face interview was the 'next to last' step.

By this time he was almost into his second year with Four Winds International. This job wasn't nearly as fulfilling as was the one at EKCO, but he was comfortable. Rex thought to himself, 'to heck with it, I've come this far, let's keep going!

PHASE IV

So within a couple of weeks the 'company' flew a man out to Chicago. He called Rex when he got into town: "Mr. Freeman, this is Jim Hewlett. I'm with 'the company' staying out at the O'Hare Marriott. Can we get together tomorrow afternoon?'" Rex answered, "Sure... How does 1:30 sound?" He said that would be fine.

"'Great I'll stop by then and I'll look forward to seeing you.'" Rex's interest was starting to build again. Since he had made it this far along in the daunting process, his confidence was high and he intended on doing as much of the grilling as he could. After all, they had put him through a wringer and he felt like he deserved some answers, information and at least a few details about the job and proposed assignments!

He woke up the next morning in his quiet, suburban apartment and realized that 'this' was the day. This is the day to find out exactly what 'the company' had in mind for him. It had to be good or they wouldn't have gone to all this trouble, right? He was upbeat, positive and fired up.

It was Saturday so Rex's job wasn't going to get in the way. He had all afternoon. By now he should have anticipated that he'd *need* ALL afternoon! The morning rolled by and off he went to O'Hare to meet the wizard!

As he pulled up to the Marriott in his black Firebird Trans-Am he felt like he was moving into the world of high stakes poker in a James Bond movie. He thought to himself, "What the hell? Let's use the valet to park the car."

Rex gave the keys to the valet and moved through the lobby to the house phones, right on time, to ring the room. "Hello, Jim? This is Rex. Are you coming down or am I coming up?' He said, "'Come on up to room 617." 'I'll be right there!"

At that point in time, he felt as though he might be passing through a door in his life from which he may never come back through quite the same.

Rex knocked, entered and was invited to sit on a comfy sofa in a large spacious suite. He found Jim to be very pleasant and easy going. They began their discussion looking eye to eye over a coffee table and they quickly established rapport. They reviewed the procedures and exercises he had gone through and Jim explained much about them that was not previously explained to Rex. He said he was impressed with Rex's efficiency and the results.

Rex was anxious to talk about other things so, at the first opportunity, he interjected, "Jim, we've spent six months on process and procedure. Let's talk about the job. I've gone through hell the last six months trying to qualify for a job I'm not even familiar with. I'd like to know why I'm doing this, does that make sense? I'd like to get some specifics. At this point, and from your perspective, in what direction am I headed here?

He understood and appreciated Rex's forthrightness. They began to get down to brass tacks. Jim proceeded to explain the difference between 'private cover' and 'diplomatic cover' of field agents. If he were assigned to a post under 'diplomatic cover', he would be an attaché working directly out of a U.S. embassy overseas.

The advantage to that was that should he be caught in espionage activities or violating any laws, he had diplomatic immunity and would only be expelled from that country. The downside was that diplomats were obvious targets for counter-surveillance and thus were much more restricted and susceptible to exposure or worse.

Under 'private cover', he would actually be working and putting in a forty hour work week with a multi-national company just like he had done in the past. The difference was that he would also be then doing his government work along with, or over and above, his routine business activities. This would allow him much more flexibility and a deeper cover to get involved in extensive 'projects" and he would be that much more effective.

The down side to 'private cover' was twofold;

1) he would have to give back his private corporate salary and only receive government scale for working two jobs; and,
2) if he were exposed overseas in his covert activity, the U.S. government would wash their hands of him and leave him to fend for himself with no immunity, help or support. Hmm. 'Mighty nice of them' he thought.

Where did he fit in? Jim told him, "Rex, with your experience, work history and contacts I think you'd understand why we'd want to set you up under *'private cover'*.

He stressed the necessity of total and complete confidentiality as to the details of the work. Even a spouse could not have any intimate knowledge of the projects he would be involved in. There would be no glory or recognition, other than from perhaps a partner or fellow associate who was involved. The entire compensation structure was government work pay scale. He might have earned a 'hardship allowance' depending on what godawful place they sent him to suffer. How wonderful!

The biggest benefits he had to look forward to, was the satisfaction of serving his country and retirement with a nice government pension in his mid-forties.

"Now, after today, "' Jim said, "I will ask you to think about our discussion for a few days and we'll do the same. We'll contact you and if it's mutually agreeable, the last step in this process is to come out and spend a week to ten days in Langley (C.I.A. headquarters in Virginia).

PHASE V

Hewlett went on to explain that this was to be no comfy 'nickel tour' of spy central. It would be an intense and grueling week of emotional level testing to see how you react to confusion, stress, pressure, disorientation, etc. They would be taking numerous polygraph tests, and in general, when finished we would know exactly "what Rex Freeman is made of and what you can take emotionally."

The afternoon was productive, informative, intriguing and enjoyable. They parted with a mutual respect.

Rex didn't tell him right away, but his mind was made up. It was crystal clear. Rex had been on top of the world. He had seen and tasted the world as a proud American. He had lived by the fruit of his forefathers who left him the freedom to pursue whatever success and happiness he could achieve for himself. He was off to a fast start and striving for more.

Rex wanted to enjoy and capitalize on those freedoms and let his entrepreneurial spirit feed on them. He wasn't seeking the security of a government pension and he'd be damned if he was going to become an unknown martyr for politics in an arid wasteland somewhere, for nothing more than government scale! Thanks, but no thanks!

Further, one can only wonder though, that if the C.I.A. is used as a direct active force for political influence as they were in Vietnam and many other places, at what point do we cross the line where authority uses them to serve political and even corrupt ends?

Along this path, he had asked himself this very question and did a little more research of his own. Among other things, he found an interesting book: **C.I.A.: Cocaine in America?** by Kenneth C. Bucchi. Google it. This was a pretty resounding answer to that question. The book documents the C.I.A. involvement in highly criminal operations.

Many other whistleblowers have documented how the agency has gone off track serving political if not criminal ends. Rex would never last in such a politically charged, adverse environment and be able to keep his mouth shut. Being as principled as he is, he would never make it as a 'conformist' to just sit down, shut up and follow orders. It's not in Rex's character.

It's sad to think of the recruits who are brought into service thinking they will be helping their country when, in fact, the C.I.A. and related U.S. government agencies are probably the largest importer of illegal drugs in the country and one of the largest exporters of illegal weapons not to mention the myriad of other illicit or immoral enterprises the company has been known to engage in or set up as fronts for crooked politicians. How many of our well intentioned patriots are led into this cesspool of moral depravity from which there may be no living escape? How long can we as a people keep turning a blind eye to it all?

For Rex, it was an interesting ride. But when the final hoop was presented and the invitation to Langley finally came, he thanked Hewlett and politely declined. He had been where very few people have ever been, right at the gate of 'the company'.

Rex had other things in mind for his life. He wasn't cut from the cloth needed to make this suit. This learning experience gave him a deep appreciation and respect for all of the agents working out there, at least the honest ones. You are selfless Patriots and we take our hats off to you.

That was the end of Rex's relationship with the C.I.A.... at least for awhile.

PART II

BOOT CAMP

CHAPTER 4

HIDDEN SECRETS REVEALED

REX'S LIFE PROCEEDED ALONG QUITE nicely. It wasn't long before it was clear that his independent thinking nature was not a good fit for him to be playing corporate or organizational politics. He had forsaken the career climb up the corporate ladder after only two years with Four Winds. Instead, he followed the path of adventure and independence and dove into the arena of self-employment. He decided to enter the world of mergers and acquisitions as an independent consultant with a national network of business brokers. He became known in that community as an aggressive professional and a very competent 'business broker' in the Chicagoland area which hosted a franchised network of 12 independent offices at the time. The network of consultants throughout the area voted him 'Rookie Agent of the Year' which was a very nice honor. It was along this path of independence that he started to learn some life changing 'truths'.

TRANSITION

After several years of having great fun as a deal maker in the big city, he was ready for a change. Rex was near a burnout stage in his career with the huge pendulum swings back and forth on the financial side. He could put months of effort into a deal, only to have some cocky attorney come in from left field at the last minute and tell his client not to follow through because it was the only 'safe" thing to do. The straw that broke the camel's back hit October 17, 1987. It was known as 'Black Monday'. Rex had been working on his biggest deal yet. This one was the *coup de grace* and would put him on easy street for some time if he could pull it off. The business being sold was a large high end sporting goods store. Rex's client, the owner, was getting involved in ski ventures out west with a famous Austrian skier and Olympic gold medalist. He was anxious to get out of his retail business and into his new venture. Rex had finally struck a contract with a qualified buyer and the closing was set for two weeks. Then, before the closing, Black Monday hit and wiped out the buyer's ability to follow through on the deal. That was it! Rex needed something more stable and not so high flying. He wanted to enjoy life more with less stress. He was on the outs with his girlfriend and Chicago was cold, dark and gloomy for him both literally and figuratively. He was ready for a change. Rex hooked up with a health insurance marketing organization catering to small business. He got familiar with the operation while in Chicago and moved out to one of their new western offices in Denver where two of his sisters were already living at the time. He welcomed the opportunity. The money was good, fast, and fairly regular. It was a good fit.

In his first year, he topped the sales charts and was doing great in the health insurance and financial planning business. He was enjoying life. Denver was a great place to be young and single. He traveled every week in his job and got to meet great people all over Colorado state. He was serving the small business and rural farm and ranch markets. It was good wholesome living. He lived in an upper end penthouse apartment in Denver with a view of the Denver Skyline and the entire front range from Long's Peak seventy miles to the north and Pike's Peak seventy miles to the south. He was doing well and life was good!

As often comes with prosperity, so does the I.R.S.! Rex worked really hard doing well in the insurance business and earned a $6,000.00 bonus check. This was really nice! The problem was that the I.R.S. wanted most of it. Well, Rex worked damned hard for that bonus and didn't quite see it from their viewpoint. To make a long story short they didn't get what they wanted and started getting nasty with him.

This just wasn't right. Some things you just feel in your gut are not right and he just knew there had to be a way to legally beat those I.R.S. bastards. He was going to find it 'come hell or high water'! (Rex's dad's favorite expression). It was this impetus that started him on the path of studying the law in an effort to know and protect his God given rights to private property and the fruits of his labor.

LIBERTY FOUNDATION

The quest for the silver bullet was on. After several months of inquiries and networking with friends and associates Rex discovered what he thought was the 'holy grail'! He had found 'The Liberty Foundation' formerly known as the 'Pilot Connection' formed by Phil & Marlene Marsh to educate Americans on the tax law and how it really is written as opposed to what most of us think we understand. Not only was he in his glory in starting to understand the fraud and blatant deception and thievery of the I.R.S. but, then based in California, Phil and Marlene were soon to be moving out to Rex's home town in Colorado in the Denver area! The timing couldn't have been better for him.

Phil & Marlene had established a nationwide network of managers to help people legally withdraw from the voluntary income tax structure. They had paralegals on staff, a sizeable administrative organization and numerous 'victory' letters from the I.R.S. showing how the I.R.S. had backed off from many 'legally protected' clients. Rex soaked up their introductory, informational meetings and read Phil Marsh's book, 'THE COMPLEAT PATRIOT'. After several crash courses in government, the constitution and Title 26 of the U.S. Code (Internal Revenue Code) he was ready to jump. There was only one problem. He didn't have the $2,500.00 necessary to start the legal and administrative process. He had to wait.

In the meantime, Phil & Marlene had moved their organization out to Parker Colorado, in a very nice two level wood frame office building which they occupied entirely. First time visitors could always find it easily if unsure of the exact location. They always flew a very large U.S. flag on a tall pole outside in front, upside down. This is the sign of a nation in distress and he now understood that between the I.R.S. and the Federal Reserve, this country certainly is in great distress.

In June of 1993 the Marsh's held an annual convention at the Denver Tech Center Hilton Hotel. It turned out to be quite an event with a variety of credentialed professionals from across the nation as guest speakers. Not only was it exciting to be able to meet so many nice and informed people and continue the learning curve, but Rex entered a raffle and he won the most exciting door prize of his life, a $2,500.00 credit toward 'the' Untaxing Program! What a thrill! Think of it, not only did he win a prize worth $2,500.00 but think of the monetary value in future years from money potentially NOT sent to the I.R.S. and the alternative economic opportunity which that could create, if it worked as advertised. What a difference that could make in peoples' lives!

Not only does the I.R.S. unlawfully seize incomes, bank accounts, businesses, assets and livelihoods, but people have no idea how many divorces, broken families, and even suicides have been directly related to the blood thirsty, satanic system and the heartless vultures who work it. We all know the score, so let's not try and sugar coat it! It would be one thing if it were a proper and correct legal system which is implemented fairly and enforced according to due process, but it's not. The entire system is based on pure fraud and abuse of power preying on people's ignorance. In addition to legal fraud and deception, the arrogance and abuse of power wielded by their minions is far beyond the pale that any citizen should have to endure. They see that now with the revelations coming from the congressional hearings exposing the political targeting, stonewalling with complete arrogance. It is this evil that cannot stand in the face of truth.

The Liberty Foundation's 'Untaxing Program', which was now in Rex's hands, exposed this reality in the written law. The truth, once uncovered, was absolutely unavoidable. Rex went home with his binder, legal research, sample paperwork and instructions and immediately got to work in the books.

In the meantime, the Liberty Foundation was achieving phenomenal growth and success nationwide. It wasn't known until much later, but our illustrious leaders in government couldn't stand the light of the truth and started to conspire on ways to bring down Phil & Marlene and their entire organization. It started with an attempted smear campaign by the media. The network news show 20/20 did a televised interview of Phil & Marlene with ABC correspondent Lynn Scherr. All indications were that the truth was about to hit mainstream media! This was false hope. The interview was used to take quotes and partial statements out of context and twist them to discredit the couple and the organization. The attempted smear backfired. While attempting to make Phil & Marlene look like wacko kooks, an I.R.S. representative admitted in an aired segment included in the presentation that "it could be done if you knew what you were doing." The "it" of course was removing yourself from 'voluntary' income taxes. You can't buy advertising like that!

Subsequently, and under cover, the I.R.S. began its most exhaustive and expensive investigation in history. Plants inside the organization were established. Surveillance commenced, asset searches and personal research was underway to dig up dirt on numerous Liberty Foundation people nationwide. Thousands upon thousands of man hours were expended.

All of this was to put away two humble Christian people who lawfully sought the truth as it was written in the law. There was no hyperbole or opinions involved, just the law. They shared it with as many as they could, using their rights to free speech, which they exercised under the protection of their 1st amendment to the constitution.

After months of work by the U.S. Justice Department, the day finally came. RAID! The Liberty Foundation building in Parker, Colorado was surrounded by jack booted thugs during business hours. They burst through the front door with force and automatic weapons. What proceeded from there was a comical situation of Keystone Cops.

Phil & Marlene's staff was primarily comprised of paralegals who knew the law and their personal rights and how to protect them very well. They were not people who were going to be buffaloed and intimidated into blind submission to false authority, and they weren't. Once the attackers and government minions were inside the building, the tables quickly turned. The working staff on site made fools of the unprepared 'Rambos', which is often easy to do if you know anything about your rights and the law. The uninvited gestapo units in black suits were quickly put on the defensive.

The entire episode was recorded on audio tape and is not only a beautiful 'live fire' lesson on how to handle yourself in preserving your rights, but it was also quite hysterical in parts. To summarize and paraphrase some of the highlights; first of all, the timing of the raid was very poor as only a few individuals were in the building at the time and they did not include Phil or Marlene. So the primary targets were missed by a mile.

Once they entered the building brandishing military garb and exotic high powered weapons, they told people in the front room to get back against the wall. The typical classic response from the office workers was, "Why should we?" "Who are you?"' "Where are you from?" "Who do you work for? Identify yourself" "What gives you the right to threaten us this way?" These were some of the questions that were launched in the first couple of tense minutes. The victims in the building were not getting satisfactory answers from the armed thugs and quickly went for the jugular. "Where's your warrant?" "Let me see your warrant.' 'Now! Right now, where is it?" "You let me see that valid warrant right now or get off this property!" The chief invading officer replied "Shut up lady!" and she fired right back, "we don't have to shut up, don't tell us to shut up, you show us your warrant or we'll call the sheriff and have you arrested on Federal weapons and attempted kidnapping charges! Under Title 18 of the U.S. code sections 241 and 242 you are attempting to deprive our liberty under the 'color of law'. That's a federal crime mister!" Under title 42 of the U.S. Code you are violating our civil rights. Under state law, you are impersonating an officer, restricting our liberty and threatening us with a deadly weapon without giving us proper I.D. shall we continue?"

The thugs didn't expect this kind of reaction. After all, when you show up in military garb and big weapons, aren't people supposed to cower in fear and follow every order, blindly? Their resolve quickly began to bend under the resistance put up by these people who knew their rights and the law and they began to sweat a little. Two of the officers scrambled out to one of the vehicles to supposedly get 'the warrant'.

Well, unfortunately for the officers, a valid warrant was not readily available and the thugs didn't quite know how to handle the situation. When they came back from the car they had dug out some kind of paperwork and flashed it quickly in the face of Rex's paralegal friend Linda who was 'point man' (very petite woman of 100 pounds or so) for the defensive counter attack. "Wait! I didn't read that." She said. "Bring it back here and let me read that warrant!" she demanded.

Upon closer review, she screamed, "That's not a warrant for you to come in here and threaten us this way." "That paper is for *California*. We are in *Colorado*!" The date is a year old! You have nothing here! Where's the phone? Let me call the sheriff! I'm putting you gentlemen under arrest. Up against the wall! Give me your weapons!" she screamed.

The alleged warrant they used was outdated by a year and was for the old "Pilot Connection" offices in California which was completely irrelevant and of no legal effect for the present circumstances.

Nonetheless, they had the guns and they didn't leave without their computers and seizures of other personal property along the way. One woman had cash in her personal purse which was obviously not on any warrant list. She was on her way to pay bills to the tune of a couple thousand dollars. They grabbed her private purse and took the cash for themselves. Hey, why not? They had the guns and they were in control!

This is how many of our law enforcement people operate these days' folks. It's not funny! What it is, is sickening, because these people knowingly and routinely violate the laws that are there to protect us and they think they can get away with it. They are rarely challenged and thus get sloppy and don't follow the law because nobody requires them to! They operate mainly on bluff and bravado and the people generally let them get away with it. It's time for this to stop!

The priority in our courts these days is not justice, but convictions. Convictions accelerate careers, seizures fill the coffers, and prisoners feed the fastest growing industry in America: law enforcement.

When it was all said and done, with simultaneous raids on Liberty Foundation associates all across the country, under the force of arms and threat of physical violence, the Liberty Foundation computers, files and everything which were needed to continue the operation were confiscated. Phil & Marlene were arrested later and a beacon of truth was unlawfully unplugged by thugs.

Interestingly enough, the charges brought against Phil & Marlene had nothing to do with taxes! Absolutely no tax charges were filed! They were charged with 'deceptive trade practices' relating to their marketing of the program. What does that tell us about the message Phil & Marlene were spreading? They were right on the money! Government was smart enough not to bring a losing issue into court where it would be a part of the permanent record so they picked another angle to try and nail them.

After a year of unlawful incarceration awaiting trial without bail, Phil, who was already in his 70's, was acquitted of the most serious charges and Marlene was completely exonerated. The most elaborate I.R.S. sting in history failed miserably in the courtroom but it still accomplished its primary objective: it destroyed the organization and many peoples' lives with it. Using this as an 'example' and a public relations opportunity - 'Anti-Tax Couple Arrested!' - the result was that they scared away many of their followers who were numbered in the thousands all across the country.

Rex was fortunate though. He got a powerful start to his education. The first stop on the road to truth was complete for him with a resounding wakeup call and some real fighting in the trenches!

THE QUINTESSENTIAL COP

Through some of Rex's compatriots at the Liberty Foundation he was made aware of a presentation being given by a retired cop from Phoenix who was in town. He was speaking on how police were being prepared for the New World Order. The speaker was Officer Jack McLamb. It sounded interesting so Rex put it on his calendar.

As he walked into the hotel ballroom for the event he was surprised at the turnout. There had to be over two hundred fifty people in attendance. Officer McLamb was welcomed with great enthusiasm and a standing ovation. Evidently these people knew something more about him than Rex did.

As it turned out, Jack was a latecomer to the Police Academy in Phoenix enrolling when he was about thirty years old. He was more mature than the average young cadet. He proceeded on a fast track to national stardom in the field of law enforcement. Jack was nominated by his fellow officers on several occasions, the once in a lifetime award of "Police Officer of the Year" for his commitment to the force, his innovative and effective community programs, his character and his allegiance to his motto 'to serve and protect.' He became a media darling and public speaker in high demand all over the country while still an active police officer. He achieved the epitome of success in his selected career of law enforcement.

In telling his own story, he explained that one day, as he was speaking to a group of retirees out in Sun City, a little old man who had been sleeping through most of Jack's presentation asked McLamb if he knew what the Fourth Amendment to the constitution was. Jack was embarrassed as he didn't know. The little old man asked several more basic questions on the constitution to which Jack had no reply. His halo was now badly stained by this old guy who then asked this big 'Cop star', "How can you serve and protect the people if you don't know what the peoples' rights are that you are supposed to be protecting?"

This embarrassment led Jack to do some serious introspection. He started questioning his superiors why he hadn't been trained in those areas which seem so basic and fundamental. He was told to forget about it. It wasn't important. To make a long and very interesting story short, Jack made his superiors very uncomfortable with his regular challenges and questions about police procedure. Jack began to realize some of the fundamental flaws in his training. And as he inquired and tried to get answers, the rebuttals and lack of interest he got from his superiors made him realize that police procedure across the country had acquired an "Us vs. Them"" mentality that had total disregard for the rights and liberty of the people.

As quickly as he had become a star in his ignorance, Jack had more quickly become a politically incorrect black sheep on the force with his questions. His rising star quickly burned out and fell. He was soon edged off the force and was now in a different mode of law enforcement. Jack soon became a rising star again for the people and took up the crusade of educating other law enforcement and military people, along with the citizens, as to how the forces of the New World Order were shaping our enforcers into Gestapo like armies formed to the detriment of the people which is contrary to their intended purposes.

Jack was also known for going up to Ruby Ridge in Idaho with Bo Gritz to try and get Randy Weaver and the living remainder of his family out of the cabin alive when they were under siege by F.B.I. and B.A.T.F. If you recall the story, Randy Weaver's wife was shot in the head by an F.B.I. agent while she was holding her baby as the family was trying to mind their own business in their home after Weaver was 'set up' on weapons charges by the Feds.

Well, when the Liberty Foundation had their annual conference in Denver in June of 1993 they brought Jack up as a guest speaker.

After the convention was over, Rex was very fortunate to be able to spend several hours with Jack and a small group of folks just having some lively discussion in the Liberty Foundation offices (before the raid). His experiences with his unique insights and perspectives left an indelible impression on Rex. He is a very humble and sincere man with the love of

God in his heart. He is truly concerned about the people of America and the path we seem to be on. His commitment is selfless and honorable.

After the meeting he thought to himself, "Here is a true American hero. We need more men like him if we are going to save our country."

Everybody must read his book 'Operation Vampire Killer 2000'. Read it more than once and distribute copies far and wide. Google it. Many of those in Rex's circle of friends carried extra copies all the time and gave them, as a gift of thanks, to law enforcement personnel whenever they had the chance. Look it up and get it free online.

Talking with Jack and learning about his story, opened Rex's eyes to the bigger picture in the world, which started when he was studying the law on tax matters. One fraud led him to another fraud and Rex's eyes were being opened in a big way. The pieces were starting to fit for him.

Rex continued in his quest for truth and justice. Most of all, he wanted to find a way for honest people to protect themselves against this tyranny which he was learning about and seeing first hand.

CHAPTER 5

A Strand of Truth Into Fabric

As he began learning amazing truths in law, politics and government, Rex's mind was a sponge and open to try and absorb as much knowledge as he could. One discovery seemed to lead to another, and then another and he soon learned that he was not the only one 'waking' up in this world. There was an army of people who were determined to preserve their rights and liberties. He began following these 'threads' that he was finding in his study and research.

As he was accumulating knowledge, little as it was at the time and he was only beginning, people began to look to him for solutions. He started getting folks coming to him with all sorts of problems, looking for help and answers. He may have known only a 'little more' about the subject than they did, but that made him 'the expert' in comparison. This thrust him into learning more, much quicker than he had planned on.

This 'need' sprouted a seed in Rex's mind. He was tapping into a wealth of important knowledge that people obviously needed. As the knowledge came, so did the demand for it through people around him who needed help. Rex decided to form a grass roots organization which would organize this information and make it available. Hence, The 'American Law Club' was formed. Chapter 7 will explore more on this.

Rex continued his search for powerful resources for knowledge and here we list a few that he found along the way. You can google any of these for much more detailed and fascinating information. When you do, you will find that most of these people are now, or have been, thrown in jail for one excuse or another. Their only real crime was: that their knowledge challenged the current 'system' of power and control, as you will see.

BARRISTERS INN SCHOOL OF COMMON LAW

The Liberty Foundation was only a beginning for him. He weaned himself from tax studies and delved into a more general study of law and courtroom procedure with 'Barrister's Inn School of Common Law'. They offered an extensive forty hour video training course on the basics of *'pro se'* litigation and legal procedure showing people how to become a 'belligerent claimant (of rights') in person'. The idea is that if you don't actively claim your rights (as a belligerent), the court takes silent judicial notice and then those rights are presumed waived and thus trampled and ignored.

Bob Hallstrom and George Gordon of Barristers' Inn not only educated but also entertained students through a very thorough and fun program backed up by extensive research and sample paperwork which included detailed briefs, case law, definitions, etc. Through their own personal experiences and numerous war stories, this program planted the seeds which showed how much fun it could be to know the law and run circles around the so called "professionals' who want to bluff and intimidate ignorant people into submission and acquiescence while they themselves have little grasp of the essential 'lawful' concepts involved.

Whenever a 'less than knowledgeable' official would run up against an 'informed' and 'capable' citizen it was often fodder for amusement certainly, and usually trouble for one side or the other if not both.

HARTFORD VAN DYKE

From studies in Common Law Rex moved into Commercial Law. He spent about a year under the personal tutelage of Hartford VanDyke.

Hartford's great uncle, Gerald Mason Van Dyke was the Army intelligence officer who telegraphed the message about the impending Japanese attack on Pearl Harbor, three days in advance!

"They knew well in advance that the Japanese were going to attack. It was a lie that they didn't have direct radio communication with Washington DC." --Lt. Col. Clifford M. Andrew

The secretaries of the departments of Defense and Navy, Frank Knox and Forrestal were both making plans to move all ships out of the harbor in a defensive perimeter but, F.D.R. had Knox and Forrestal detained and quarantined which prevented the orders from being implemented. They allowed a necessary 'devastating attack' upon our nation in order to rally public support for entry into the war in the Pacific arena. Yes folks, our own President deliberately conspired to set up the massive death and agony of our own men and women at Pearl Harbor! Believe it, it's true. This is from the man who personally gave the warning three days in advance!

Ever since that time, Hartford and his dad and uncle before him, had been seeking ways to directly and effectively hold such traitors accountable for their actions when the corrupt political and judicial systems would not. He was a second generation 'Patriot' and is/has been the nation's preeminent expert on commercial processes and fundamental commercial law. His avenue of accountability, if you will, is the use of the commercial lien on the assets and/or bond and accounts of public officials and private parties. The effect is to freeze them out of continued misconduct and to recompense for damages. This process also takes away the financial incentive for corruption as the moment ill-gotten gains are had, they can be lost or frozen by the people who have been damaged or oppressed.

This commercial process is beautiful because it is completely 'non-judicial', meaning there is no need to go into the corrupt courts. It is done entirely in the realm of commerce using the Uniform Commercial Code and the 'court of public opinion' using public notices and the County Recorder. Rex greatly enjoyed learning from Hartford. It was a long distance phone relationship. Rex never met him personally but the truths he taught him went to the core and are timeless and immutable. He often felt when he was calling Hartford, like the pilgrim climbing the mountain to see the wise old sage seeking the secrets of the universe. And many secrets did he receive. Thank you Hartford. His teachings provided a true foundation for understanding the complete fraud of the I.R.S. commercial processes among many other things. Rex would later use this commercial lien process against a local judge and others. More on that later.

DEVVY KIDD & 'THE PROJECT ON WINNING ECONOMIC REFORM'

As Rex began to get a reputation in his local area he had the great pleasure of meeting another very prominent gladiator battling I.R.S. oppression at the time. Her name was Devvy Kidd.

In the summer of 1993, he was fortunate to have had several opportunities to meet with Devvy. Devvy is an attractive, one time Max Factor girl who ended up with extensive experience in administration for the Department of Defense and Air Force Space Command. She married a now retired Army Colonel and was not only the spearhead for P.O.W.E.R. (Project on Winning Economic Reform) in which over three million people nationwide participated, but she also made another run for Congress in her California District for the fall 1996 elections and later wrote a book on extensive vote fraud which is worthy of attention.

P.O.W.E.R. was a nationwide grass roots effort to abolish the economic oppression of the private corporation known as the Federal Reserve and its enforcers; the I.R.S. Devvy has a straight forward and common sense alternative to supplant these foes of America. It's called the constitution. What a great idea! Why haven't any of our politicians for the last 100 years thought of that? We'll talk more about the Fed and the money system in later chapters.

Rex went down to the 16th Street Mall in Denver one bright sunny afternoon In September of 1993 to help Devvy and many of her supporters picket the Federal Reserve Building in Denver. They had a ball and educated a lot of people. Of course Rex's bell curve of networking, contacts and influence continued sharply this beautiful day. He made some new friends and one very interesting contact which we'll discuss later as well. He also happened to run into his brother in law Fred who stopped to see what his wife's lunatic brother was up to now! Fred always did think Rex was crazy. It's a charge to this day he cannot deny.

Dr. Eugene Schroder & 'The American Agricultural Movement'

Dr. Gene Schroder is a rural veterinarian and lived in a remote rural area which Rex knew well from his travels in the insurance business. It was a tiny little rural hamlet in southeast Colorado near the Oklahoma panhandle known as Campo, Colorado. If you ever want to 'get away from it all' this is the place to go. Not that it has much to offer, but it is definitely 'away from it all'!

Dr. Schroder realized that family farmers were quickly being eliminated, due in part to the total control over agriculture exerted by the federal government. He questioned why he and other farmers had to ask government agencies what they could plant, how much they could plant, and what they would be paid for their products. Each year farmers went into debt a little deeper until finally many lost their farms.

Schroder and others founded the American Agriculture Movement in 1977 in an effort to save the family farm. After several years of struggle, farmers were broke, tired, and discouraged. The movement finally waned, but Gene Schroder continued to question and investigate.

He and other researchers uncovered how the use of 'emergency powers' was a way for government to set aside the constitution. The Agricultural Adjustment Act, a curse to farmers for so many years, was a key piece of legislation in these emergency powers; for it took the power to coin and regulate money away from congress (as provided in the Constitution) and gave it to the president.

The results of this extensive research are contained in Dr. Schroder's book *Constitution: Fact or Fiction*. We highly recommend it.

The last he checked, Dr. Schroder still lived in Campo with his wife Laurie, near his parents' farm. Two daughters have made him the proud grandfather of three. It is for his children's and grandchildren's heritage in America that he continues to fight armed with knowledge of the truth found in our history. His book is not only fascinating but provides 'the key' as to how the feds can supersede the states as they now do regularly.

JOHN KOTMAIR & THE 'SAVE A PATRIOT FOUNDATION'

Through these folks Rex learned about the S.A.P. (Save-a-Patriot) Foundation on the east coast. This group assisted people in defeating the I.R.S. using a power of attorney relationship. In other words S.A.P. did the work and papers, etc., for you to help minimize errors. While this was very convenient and effective, Rex didn't feel it did much for personal empowerment through knowledge. But being a marketing man he tested them out with his own personal membership and later felt confident that there was a niche in the market for their services. He especially liked their mutual assistance program where, if you as a member lost any property or ended up in jail because of your fight with the I.R.S., the S.A.P. Foundation would compensate you handsomely for the loss. He never found anyone that needed it but it was a nice selling point.

JOE HOLLAND & THE 'NORTH AMERICAN FREEDOM COUNCIL'

About that same time he was introduced to Joe Holland and the North American Freedom Council. Joe is a very colorful character and his N.A.F.C., based in Indiana, was a national membership organization dealing in personal freedom issues such as property protection, I.R.S. and Social Security liberation, allodial title, right to travel, removal and separation of yourself from the Babylonian 'system, and much more.

Much like Bob Halstrom and George Gorden of Barristers Inn, Joe, through his gruff and inimitable 'never say die' style, showed how much fun it was to put cocky overzealous, over reaching public servants back in their proper place. He looks and talks like a big ol' trucker, (probably because that's what he was) not too polished but he gets his point across without question and leaves no doubt about the seriousness of his intent. He'd be great to have as a friend and he'd be a formidable foe.

The list of services and education N.A.F.C. offered was extensive. They filled a gap in the portfolio of A.L.C. so he organized their information and put another arrow in Rex's quiver for those who might benefit from it.

CHAPTER 6

HIDDEN TREASURE FOUND

THROUGH REX'S NETWORK WHICH WAS quickly swelling up around him, he had been approached to assist in a project that was almost beyond comprehension in its scope. It was known as 'TreasuryGate'.

'TreasuryGate' is a scandal involving huge amounts of money in certificates of obligation drawn upon the Federal Reserve, Swiss, Japanese, and other prime banks. The existence of these certificates is denied by the big banks and government.

The U.S. certificates are essentially the property of the people of the U.S.A. They were not listed in the Federal Register and were being not only hidden but put in the names, and for the use of some of America's greatest adversaries. Some of these names included Muammar Qadaffi, Saddam Hussein, Manuel Noriega, Ferdinand Marcos, the Shah of Iran, Idi Amin, Adnan Kashogi, Fidel Castro, and others.

The amounts of 'hidden" money were large enough to pay off the national debt with enough left over to change the face of the American lifestyle for everybody. This was the goal of a man known as Tommy 'TreasuryGate' Buckley. The TreasuryGate story is extremely complicated and involves the highest levels of governmental and banking authority on an international scale.

Buckley tried to deal with these worldly powers and formed a support group called 'GreenLight'. As a member of GreenLight, a substantial amount of confidential and very sensitive documentation crossed Rex's desk.

This story by itself, due to its scope, its lengthy duration and complexity could fill volumes. You can find more on this on your own.

The following is a very cursory review of the background and beginnings of this story which became a big part of Rex's life for some time.

BEGINNING

Buckley had been a Texas oil and gas man. He had spent time as a gas pipeline buyer for a major pipeline company in Texas. It was owned by Parker Drilling Company which is a major New York Stock Exchange company.

He went Independent right In the middle of the oil boom and acquired a bunch of acreage in southwestern Pennsylvania. It was about 40,000 acres that he was going to drill for gas. It took him about six months to acquire the contract on that acreage and after acquiring it the oil bust hit. Oil went down to $9.95 a barrel and you couldn't give gas away. He couldn't find any domestic driIling money for that project so he went international for it. In the process of going international in search of capital he ran into an Indonesian government official and businessman by the name of Edison Damanik.

They didn't do any business for several years but in that time they got to know each other and become friends. At a point in time when Damanik trusted Buckley's group he asked them to do something for him, which they did.

They met in Los Angeles in October 1989. Damanik brought what they thought at the time were a bunch of international certificates of deposit.

They ended up being certificates of obligation. He wanted Buckley's group to have them verified and then follow instructions for cashing them.

Mr. Damanik was an Assistant Financial Monitor for Indonesia which is, in essence, an Assistant Finance Minister. He was also retired from the Special Forces and Armed Services and is a very close friend of then President Suharto. They fought together in the resistance in World War II.

Mr. Damanik had a job to do which was to come to the U.S. and force the U.S. government to acknowledge the certificates.

The Indonesian finance ministry had attracted the foreign certificates as follows:

For about 30 years during the cold war, Indonesia had been the head of the non-aligned countries which were 110 nations that didn't take either the communist or capitalist side. They were neutral. The CIA worked hard to bring Indonesia and its allies into allegiance with the Western powers. They did this in Iran in 1954. It's well documented that it was the CIA who put the Shah into power. And as a reward for playing the role, the Shah got one of the certificates that were now in Buckley's possession.

As an inducement to get Indonesia to move out of the 'non-aligned nations' camp into the U.S. sphere of influence, the CIA helped Indonesia attract the U.S. Federal Reserve certificates and the Japanese certificates, the Marcos, Noriega, Qadaffi certificates, etc.

But once Indonesia got a hold of all these certificates, they told the CIA to take a hike.

So now that Indonesia had all of these certificates of obligation, which were investment grade commercial instruments, they had to go into the financial markets to negotiate, hypothecate, or otherwise liquidate them at a discount, possibly up to 50%.

Indonesia now had all this money and it didn't want to align with the U.S. The CIA was extremely ticked off, as one might imagine. The question then arises, "Who knew what was going on?"

People at the top knew about it. The President, the head of each CIA team allegedly knew about it, Bush's cabinet including William Barr and James Baker allegedly knew about it and on down the line. This was all going to be brought out in a lawsuit in the Washington D.C. Court of Claims due to the continued stonewalling.

ATTEMPTED REDEMPTION

Eight certificates of obligation were presented to Tommy Buckley by Damanik. These were primarily from Swiss banks. A certificate of obligation is like a bond. It is an evidence of debt. As a form of commercial paper it is negotiable for cash in the financial markets by the bearer.

One group of the certificates was written in U.S. dollars and guaranteed by the Swiss government. The principal was around $800 billion. With accrued interest the total amount was about $1.8 trillion.

Buckley's group proceeded to approach a number of different banks taking in one or more certificates at a time for authentication. Buckley brought two certificates with him to a bank in Mexico City in December 1990. He got further with that bank than he had anywhere else. But as in other instances, he got all the way up to the top office of the bank and had received written confirmations that everything was fine and that they "would do it!" Then, mysteriously everybody stopped talking.

Damanik asked Buckley to put them in a trust account at Citibank while getting them verified. They deposited them and proceeded with the bank to send telexes out for verification. They were well on their way of getting all that done when all of a sudden everything stopped.

Now these guys were oil and gas people and were used to some big money but they didn't know what they had their hands on. They were having trouble trying to get them verified as the banks in Europe wouldn't talk anymore. They were dealing with Credit Suisse, Union Bank of Switzerland and Lloyds Bank in London primarily.

Once the banks realized that they had the 'real McCoy' they clammed up. Over the course of the next few months Buckley and his team did everything in the world that they could think of to get authentication.

APPROACHING THE FED

In late spring of 1991, Damanik flew from Djakarta, Indonesia into Austin Texas, and brought additional instruments. These were U.S. Federal Reserve bank certificates and a very large group of Japanese certificates.

As much trouble as they had with the Swiss certificates they thought it would be relatively simple with the U.S. Federal Reserve instruments. Their plan was to find out whether or not these documents were any good. That's all.

The U.S. instruments were even larger than the Swiss ones and these were the ones in the names of Saddam Hussein, Col. Muammar el - Qadaffi, Ferdinand Marcos and Manuel Noriega.

They sought out a gentleman in Scottsdale, Arizona, named Robert Johnson who was a friend and confidant of Ronald Reagan and George Bush. They knew now that what they had was volatile and they wanted to take precautions. That's why they approached Mr. Johnson. They were walking in with 166 trillion dollars (plus) in instruments. Because the Federal Reserve instruments had been stamped by the Federal Reserve they were the obvious source to validate their authenticity. This was a move that needed to be cleared diplomatically as well as from a business standpoint.

So Buckley and four associates met with Robert Johnson in Scottsdale.

They showed him the documents and he cleared the way for them to go into the Federal Reserve Bank in Dallas.

Buckley went in with two of his associates at 10:00 A.M. on July 8, 1991. The bankers were expecting them and as soon as they arrived they went downstairs to a private meeting room. They spent only about 25 minutes there. The two ladies they met were very cordial.

The bankers were shown the certificate in Saddam Hussein's name in the amount of $33 billion and were told that all Buckley wanted to do was to verify the certificate's authenticity.

The Federal Reserve employees made a photocopy of the certificate and said they were going to fax it to the head office of the Federal Reserve in New York.

Buckley was asked where he was staying. The woman said it would take a few hours for the main office to respond and they would call as soon as they received a response.

BUSHWHACKED

When Buckley's group was back at the hotel, one of the attorneys for the bank in Dallas called and said the certificate was good. However, he said since the U.S. was in conflict with Saddam at the time, all of his assets were frozen.

About mid-afternoon eight Secret Service Agents with guns drawn, burst into Buckley's hotel room. They demanded to know where their guns were. Buckley said they didn't have any and that he was there on business. There was a fourth man in the group at the hotel who was not present at the Federal Reserve Bank meeting earlier. One of the three who were present at the earlier meeting at the Fed was now not in the room. This surprised the agents. One of the 'three' was gone and a 'wildcard' was present.

Buckley was convinced that their objective when they came into the room was to make sure that they were all dead and then take the certificates.

But the fourth man in the room threw them a curve.

Tommy's suspicions were confirmed later in December when he was informed by telephone that the intent of the raid was to have the group assassinated and the certificates confiscated. Within about two weeks of this phone call he received three affidavits that stated not only were the financial instruments valid, but there actually was an order for the assassination. Mr. Damanik told Tommy in person that those who ordered it were John H. Sununu, the President's chief of staff and Brent Scowcroft.

The information from the affidavits came from an F.B.I. report.

Buckley's group was taken down to the federal building and they gave statements over a period of six hours, after which time they learned that they were under formal arrest. The group was put in jail at a maximum security prison for a week and denied bond. Tommy begged for the right to call an attorney for hours and hours but they denied him that right, even when he went to court the next morning.

No charges were ever brought forward. Of course there was no warrant either. They were put in prison on the basis of a complaint that they intentionally tried to defraud the United States government out of over $33 billion. That's what the Secret Service testified to on the stand at the hearing. Buckley and company were not allowed to speak at their own hearing.

They were finally released after a week, on their own recognizance even though they were alleged to have tried to perpetrate the greatest fraud in the history of the U.S. government.

Now, one would think that this would make for a worthy news story. Buckley contacted numerous media... and with the exception of Radio Free America, nobody would touch the story.

Buckley's Indonesian friend, Mr. Damanik, was also arrested in his Austin hotel room on the same day Buckley's group was arrested in Dallas. Buckley was truthful in outlining the whole story and his association with Mr. Damanik during his interrogation.

Damanik was held in jail for about 70 days and now nobody from the Indonesian government would touch him.

He finally got out on bail. Even though a trial date was set they knew all along it would never get that far. The charges would be dropped for the same reason they dropped the charges on Tommy. They didn't want this information exposed to the public.

THE ISSUE GOES TO WASHINGTON

While Damanik was in jail Tommy was able to get a lot of information from him. Damanik put in writing what he wanted Congress to do with the funds from the certificates. He wanted to retire the national debt. He wanted to fund the super collider project. He wanted to provide an adequate amount of money to reform public education in America and to provide better health care. He wanted to make loans and grants to small businesses and farmers and more.

They took their case to Washington. Damanik actually received a written invitation from Representative Charlie Rose (D-N.C.) to testify before the Agriculture Committee.

Sharon Pierce was a U.S. prosecutor in Dallas and was involved in Buckley's arrest and subsequent court appearance. She called Charlie Rose's office and said she would not allow Damanik to go to Washington unless she was present during the meetings. This upset Rose and his people and the congressman went to the counsel for the Speaker of the House.

Steven Ross, the Speaker's attorney said, "Well, we can handle this. we'll just declare this a technical congressional investigation. That way the prosecutor cannot subpoena anybody in Washington as to what was said."

Hence, jurisdiction was effectively nullified.

Edison Damanik finally got on the plane to come to Washington and while in the air, a clerk from federal judge Newton's office (Dallas) called Rose's office and said, "You don't want to meet Mr. Damanik. He's highly contagious with tuberculosis." This scared Rose's office to death.

Even though while in jail Damanik went through the normal health screening process and came out with a clean bill of health, they went through four days of meetings with doctors and boards of health in Washington and Austin putting together the paperwork to prove he was all right. The bottom line was that he never got to meet with Rose, only one of his assistants, Tom Strarninski. This upset Damanik because he had a written invitation to meet Rose and the Agriculture Committee.

Straminski pursued the matter though. He wanted an affidavit, a copy of a power of attorney, a copy of one of the original certificates and an offering agreement. He wanted to know what Damanik was offering for the benefit of the citizens of the United States of America in order for Congress to take this project under their wing and do something about it.

This was playing right into Damanik's and Buckley's hands because they knew now that an enticement would be necessary to negotiate these instruments. Being such a political hot potato, they weren't going to just walk in somewhere and cash them. The United States was the leader of the Western World, and as such was on the inside of all the financial circles. Indonesia, while a leader of the non-aligned nations, was not a financial insider to the world banking community. So in order to get it done they had to entice the United States to open doors for them.

Damanik was prepared, and did so in writing, to commit enough funds to retire the stated national debt of America. At that time it was about 4- 1/4 trillion dollars. He was prepared and committed under oath to fund the Super Collider which by the way was then a dead project after Congress killed it due to lack of funding. He was prepared and committed to hundreds of millions of dollars in low interest loans to small businesses and farmers throughout America. He was prepared to revitalize the educational and health care systems of the country which would work for everybody.

This was all put in writing and accepted by Congress. The reason they accepted it was that they knew the certificates are good. This was conveyed to Buckley in more than one conversation which he had on tape.

Buckley and Damanik went beyond what Rose's office requested. They provided one of the original Swiss certificates and endorsed it over to Congress for the benefit of the United States. The intent was to gradually introduce these funds into the economy over a period of time to prevent monetary imbalances and runaway inflation.

Rose's office gave Buckley's group a date when all this was going to be resolved. The first date was December 2, 1991. The second date was December 15. It didn't happen. The holidays come around and nothing happened and at that point Rose's office stopped talking.

Tommy made numerous attempts to maintain dialogue but to no avail. Finally in February 1992 he put them on NOTICE that if he didn't hear something, he was going to take his story public.

The stonewalling continued and Tommy set out to court the media. Nobody would touch him. Nobody except Tom Valentine and his Radio Free America show on shortwave. Through this media R.F.A. listeners were mustered to start a letter writing campaign and through this national networking the word was starting to get out despite the blackout from the controlled mainstream media.

At one point Texas Senator Phil Gramm came forward and said that he would negotiate the transaction but he personally wanted 70% for himself.

Now we've known politicians to be greedy and put themselves ahead of their constituents but that was absolutely ridiculous.

A 70% cut of (300 billion dollars of certificates ($560 billion) is not what you would call a reasonable commission especially when he was already being paid by the people to do the job anyway as U.S. Senator.

Buckley and Damanik obviously said no and got quite angry at his pompous posture.

Resolution?

After the Radio Free America broadcast and the subsequent letter-writing campaign which started to blossom, a CIA operative told one of Buckley's associates that if Buckley backed off from going public they would bring the money in from all over the world and make good on the certificates.

The primary funds to take care of the Fed certificates were going to be brought back into the United States in the form of gold and gold certificates from Europe to Mexico and then from Mexico to the Federal Reserve Bank in Dallas. That started in May of 1992 and is very well documented that it carried on through the summertime.

Prior to May of 92 Tommy received a visit from a Green light member Raymond W. Ray told Tommy that he was informed to tell Buckley to shut up and back off or unfortunate things could happen to him. Tommy didn't listen right away but was convinced within a week.

Ray had been informed about TreasuryGate and brought into the Green light fold. However there was no apparent connection with his business dealings with Doug 'X' of Dallas which involved the sale of used farm equipment to Mexico and the importation of Mexican cattle into the U.S. and other foreign markets, namely Japan. It didn't take too long though, before the connection did become apparent.

In Mexico's involvement with Indonesia and the U.S.A. Ray's name came up on his dealings with Doug 'X'. They found out that Mexico had helped the U.S.A. and Indonesia in moving hundreds of billions of dollars from the successful resolution of all the certificates from the U.S., Swiss and Japanese banks. The money moved from the U.S.A. to England, Switzerland and Germany. Fifty U.S. certificates were resolved, sixteen of which they had in their possession during the Dallas fiasco. Thirty-four more had been brought up from Indonesia by Mr. Damanik. President Salinas from Mexico was the key to not only moving the funds, but has provided a majority of information to Doug 'X', then on to Ray, then on to Buckley.

For all of May and most of June 1992, Ray was incommunicado with one exception. He, Buckley and several GreenLight members met in the middle of a cow pasture near one of their homes in Texas. During this meeting Ray advised the group of the following:

1. The deal (resolution of the certificates) is done and had been done months ago in Washington, D.C.

2. Telephones, homes and cars were bugged.
3. Tommy was not to go near the remaining certificates or risk imprisonment, or worse.
4. The U.S. government did not want us to get paid and would make our lives miserable if they were paid.
5. Mexico would see to it that they got paid through an offshore entity.
6. The date for complete resolution was July 1, 1992, at the latest.

At this meeting in the cow pasture, Ray reluctantly agreed to communicate with Buckley either by cell phone to pay phone, vice versa, or cell to cell. During the next few weeks they would talk almost every day.

Ray would inform Buckley that the U.S. had delayed the resolution until August 1, for political reasons. Buckley demanded a meeting with Ray to review information he had.

They met in a parking lot and during the meeting listened to a tape recording of a conversation between Ray and Doug 'X' from the presidential airplane of President Salinas of Mexico. Doug "X' mentioned in the tape that someone very important had been caught in a big lie.

We'll talk more about this lie in a little bit. In the meantime they learned that resolution would occur on the gold standard. Money was being transferred for charter flights for Doug as he retrieved the lost certificates from Europe and the Far East. Salinas was making the arrangements for much of the transportation and provided the financing.

In a meeting on 8-26-92 Tommy drove to Lubbock for a brief meeting with Ray where he found out that:

1. Doug "X' had just returned from overseas after obtaining two plane loads of gold which was put in a bonded customs warehouse.
2. The person who caused many of the problems to date had been discovered. He was also the source of information of the big lie

just referenced previously. This problem maker was Senator Phil Gramm and he was caught spreading his lie to President Bush and Salinas.

What he was promulgating was the concept that Buckley and GreenLight were attempting to destabilize and overthrow the U.S. government, putting them obviously in the light of being the bad guys. How this could be construed when Mr. Damanik had spelled out his intentions to Congress in writing whereby he was virtually giving the certificates back to the U.S. for the benefit of the American people is not only a stretch of the imagination, but is also indicative of Gramm's childish temper tantrum for his sour grapes over losing out on his 70% commission which he felt he deserved more than the American People.

They later learned that Gramm had been involved for two and a half years behind the scenes through other parties trying to get the whole commission for himself. This explained a lot.

While in Dallas, Gramm's insider contact was wired money and instructions to orchestrate a break-in of Doug's home looking for information that was deliberately kept from Gramm. He got into Doug's home but got nothing of value or importance. All this really did was blow Gramm's cover and expose his true intentions and modus operandi. His lie though did set the project back and took quite a bit of undoing by Tommy and GreenLight.

They were so close to resolution.

What was happening was that Bush handed the project to the CIA which was really running the show anyway. When they got close to the fall elections Tommy began to smell a rat. If they kept holding off on resolution Tommy wouldn't be able to get this as public as he wanted to. So on October 1st he went back on the Tom Valentine show to tell the world that the Congress and White House hadn't lived up to their promises.

Tommy was scheduled to go back on the Valentine show again on the 7th of October which he did. But just prior to going on the air he received a phone call from a dear friend of his who has a close association and contact with a sitting U.S. Supreme Court Justice. This friend informed Tommy that he had asked his justice friend to go down to the CIA in Langley, Virginia to find out what was going on. He did that and told Buckley's friend to tell Buckley to shut up and stand down. Everything was going to be taken care of by October 23. "if he keeps raising his head and making a fuss, people will be embarrassed and nothing will happen."

So Buckley waited in silence from October 7th to the 23rd and again nothing happened. The justice came back and said "I think that what they're telling him is that they will finish it by election time. Again, it didn't happen.

Then he gave us some personal advice. He said "Sue them."

That's exactly what They did. A civil lawsuit was brought against the F.R.B. of Dallas and Lloyd Bentsen in the U.S. District Court in the Northern District of Texas, case number 2-93-CV-030 filed February 16, 1993. The idea was not to break the government but to set a precedent. So the good old boys wanted to cover up their shenanigans instead of coming out the hero and 'bring this to the American people'. If it's hardball they want, it's hardball they'll get!'

Once again we see where the boys who control the money control the government and the best interests of the people play a distant second or third fiddle at best.

A LITTLE FREEDOM

There were the endless twists and turns in this saga. The intrigue, promised deals, infiltrators, betrayals and mysterious players did only one thing: screwed the American people... This is a battle which is yet to be settled. The sad thing is that our so called representative form of government refuses to even let the American people know about it, let alone have a voice in it.

Tommy forced the issue into the public purview. The government finally had enough playing on the defensive and they brought bogus indictments against Tommy for mail fraud based on the fact that Tommy was accepting voluntary donations from supporters via the mail to sustain his efforts and expenses.

It was too much. All Tommy wanted to do was use these previously issued and newly discovered certificates to eliminate the national debt, fund the supercollider to advance his country, and a host of other projects beneficial to the American people. The money powers would have none of it.

Tommy was convicted of the mail fraud charges and committed suicide while awaiting sentencing in June of 2011.

So much for government of, by and for the people. This experience added to Rex's understanding of the world and how things 'really are'. Rex's experience with GreenLight sharpened his hunger for justice and his quest for truth continued.

Tommy thank you for your commitment and unswerving devotion to the truth. Surely you are in good hands now!

CHAPTER 7

THE AMERICAN LAW CLUB

As Rex gained an education from the likes of Phil and Marlene Marsh, Jack McLamb and many others, he in turn began teaching others what he had learned, whenever he had the opportunity. He used the tools from a significant accumulation of research, information and related literature, books, video and audio tapes, the list of which grew rapidly.

The accumulation of so much information from so many different sources quickly became a quagmire, yet it was so valuable he felt people needed to have all of this readily accessible in some organized fashion.

A Hobby Blossoms

What started out as a sideline interest soon became a full time obsession as Rex's time spent involved in these matters of the law soon eclipsed the time he was spending in his financial planning business at the time.

It's funny how, as soon as one cracks a book and gains a sliver or two of knowledge in one area, some people immediately look up to that person as "the expert" problem solver in that area. That's what happened to Rex as mentioned previously. He was but a fledgling babe in matters of law but soon word got out that he had solutions to people's problems. With this new found public persona, Rex's activity snowballed.

He could see that he was going to need to get organized to deal with the onslaught, and so he did. The 'American Law Club' was born. He started out as an extension office for a friend, Jeff Michner, who had been quietly doing similar educational activities for some time across town in Denver.

Jeff got him started with a forty hour video training course from Barrister's Inn School of Common Law. This was an excellent primer in understanding the principles and maxims of law, judicial procedure and how to have fun with it all. Jeff also had produced his own series of training videos dealing with 'Initial Contact" with law officers and a variety of other issues. This was all a very good basis to start learning.

However, being a marketing man, Rex saw a much bigger picture in terms of what the market offered and demanded, relating to educating the citizenry of the good and bad of what was going on in this country and what they could do or not do about it. Rex's version of the American Law Club was to provide a continually growing informational resource center/library for people who;

1) ... had a hunger for the truth, and,
2) ... wanted to lawfully protect and defend their rights, property and family.

He networked with legal researchers, pro-se litigants, public speakers, local politicians and authors from across the country. Soon word got out and the people came.

They dealt with issues as diverse as; traffic tickets, bank fraud & the money issue, state control of 501(c)(3) tax-exempt churches and false arrest. They studied issues from the Internal Revenue Code and the Code of Federal Regulations to common law and the power of the sheriff and notary positions. The more the American Law Club (A.L.C.) grew, the more horror stories of abuse of power and injustice against the American people came to light. Of course, and unfortunately, the majority of people do not acquire an interest in the law and civic duty until they are beaten and bloodied by the strong arm of the authorities.

Until that happens, most of us lie sleeping. Despite that fact, he soon realized that 'the truth' is a threat to the status quo and those who benefit from it. Rex's resolve for the 'crusade' intensified.

The A.L.C. began having weekly meetings which were open to the public.

They could be more appropriately labeled 'training sessions' and/ or discussion groups depending on the topic and the agenda or guest speaker.

The meetings started out being held in Rex's offices for National Consumer Advocates which were nicely appointed and well equipped for small group presentations. They started with a small group of regulars which consistently grew and the usual numbers who would come once and go. Some people were concerned about Rex's open door policy and that it might lead to persecution when the inevitable government informant would show up.

That didn't bother him. After all, the whole purpose was to serve notice on public servants that they had better do the job they were elected or appointed to do, because they were being watched! Perhaps it would have bothered him if they were doing something illegal and subversive. But if all they were doing was discussing the law and how they could or should use it to protect their God given rights, liberties and freedoms, why worry about the fact that our illustrious American Bar Association, politicians, bureaucrats and law enforcers have buried themselves in a quagmire of fraud, deception and inconsistencies? It would seem to him that they should be the ones concerned that the citizenry was waking up.

So, on that basis he welcomed any public servants to attend and held out a standing invitation so that they could work together. After all, how can we expect good government if our public servants are ignorant of the truth and the people don't care?

Aren't they entitled to know the same truths that the people are learning about? He thought so and publicly welcomed any and all government guests, plants or spies regardless of their intentions. It was not uncommon for an occasional 'interesting character' who was previously unknown and who was not referred by anyone to show up from time to time. Rex thought it was great. If nothing else it would serve to put our public servants on 'Notice' that the sleeping giant was awakening and that they had better get their act together before they get caught with their hand in the cookie jar.

A COMMON TRAINING GROUND

For illustration purposes let's just take a quick look at one very simple scenario that we can all relate to and how we, as citizens, are tricked into doing things we would never do if we were fully informed. This common denominator that we all have probably dealt with is the proverbial and dreaded 'traffic ticket'. This of course was a common issue of the A.L.C.

We know it's a 'traffic ticket' when we get one because we are told that we were in 'traffic' when we committed the offense. Besides, right up on top of the ticket it has a box that is checked off by the issuing officer that says 'traffic" related offense, right?

Let's look at the legal meaning of the word 'traffic' as defined in Black's Law Dictionary, Fifth Edition which derives its definitions from actual court rulings and determinations:

> *"Traffic- Commerce-. Trade: sale or exchange of merchandise, bills, money, and the like. The passing of goods and commodities from one person to another for an equivalent in goods or money. The subjects of transportation on a route as persons or goods-. The passing to and fro of persons, animals, vehicles, or vessels, along a route of transportation, as along a street, highway, etc. See Commerce-"*

Well now, that's a very clear definition don't you think? Let's say you were in your automobile and on your way to pick up grandma and take her to church. So you weren't involved in 'commerce or trade' were you?

So then perhaps you fall under the part where it refers to "subjects of *transportation* on a route".

Let's see how Black's defines *transportation.*

"Transportation. The movement of goods or persons from one place to another, by a carrier."

Okay, so what's a 'carrier'?

"Carrier. Individual or organization engaged in transporting passengers or goods for hire. 'Carrier' means any person engaged in the transportation of passengers or property by land, as a common contract, or private carrier, or freight forwarder as those terms are used in the Interstate Commerce Act, and officers, agents and employees of such carriers. 18 U.S.C.A. Section 831"

"Well", you say, "I wasn't involved in transportation for hire, it was personal."

You'd better check the definition of 'route':

Route- Course or line of travel from one place to another. Cities or towns between which common carriers or airlines are permitted by I.C.C./ C.A.B.- etc. to carry goods or passengers.

Wait a minute! You say, "I'm not involved with the Interstate Commerce Commission or the Civil Aeronautics Board. I'm not a 'carrier involved in 'transportation'. I'm not involved in 'commerce' or 'trade' when I take grandmother to church or go to the grocery store. Now that I understand what 'traffic' is, I'm not involved in that. This ticket doesn't apply to me!"

You would be partially right in saying that. 'Partially' only because it didn't apply to you ... until you signed it, or accepted it. As soon as you accepted it and either paid the ticket or showed up in court you 'failed to object' to the premises of the ticket, therefore you agreed to them and thus you granted jurisdiction on the basis of those false presumptions which you have now acquiesced to. The court takes silent judicial notice

that you are agreeing (by failure to object) to the fact that you were engaged In Commerce, that the rules of 'traffic" do apply to you, etc.

A 'ticket' is a U.C.C. (Uniform Commercial Code) *presentment* which
you can accept or refuse 'for cause'.

When you sign it you accept all of the liability and legal presumptions therein contained, and there are many. One of those presumptions is that you were engaged in *commercial traffic*. After all, the officer
checked the 'traffic" box and you agreed (accepted the presumption)
by signing it.

There are different ways to handle this. One way is to go to court
and put the issuing officer on the stand as a witness for the defense.
Your questioning could go something like this; (D - denotes your defense, O - denotes the officer).

D: Officer Strongarm, you said earlier on the stand that you've
been on the police force for three years, is that correct?

O: Yes, Sir.

D: And in those three years would you say that you've learned your
job quite well?

O: Yes, Sir.

D: Officer Strongarm, are you P.O.S.T. certified? (Police Officers
Standards Testing program)

O: Yes, Sir.

D: So you of course would understand your job requirements which
would be to say that you would necessarily have to understand the laws
that you enforce every day, is that correct?

O: Yes, Sir.

D: Officer Strongarm, on the day that you issued the ticket in question, do you recall if there were any passengers or was I alone?

O: You were alone Sir.

D: Did you observe any quantity of packaged goods or commodities
in the car at that time?

O: No sir the vehicle was empty except for a briefcase and a blanket
in the back seat.

D: So then Officer Strongarm, would it be fair to say that, based upon your recollection of the facts, that you would have no reason to believe that I was engaged in commerce or the transportation of goods or passengers for hire? Would that be correct?

O: Yes, Sir.

D: (Handing him your copy of the ticket) Officer Strongarm, do you recognize this document?

O: Yes Sir, this is your copy of the citation he issued on that date.

D: Officer did you check the 'traffic' box on the top of this ticket?

O: Yes Sir, I did.

D: So this is a traffic ticket, correct?

O: Yes, Sir.

D: Officer Strongarm, what is 'traffic'?

O: (He'll come up with his own definition, something like – the movement of vehicles on the roadway.)

D: Is that the 'legal' definition or 'your' definition?

O: 'my' definition.

D: How close is 'your' definition to the 'legal' definition?

O: I don't really know.

D: (Handing him the statutory code definition or the Black's Law Dictionary) would you read the legal definition to us please?

O: (He does) (You might go into 'transportation' and 'carrier' as well.)

D: Now Officer Strongarm, just a minute ago you said I was not involved in commerce or the transportation of passengers and goods for hire, yet you also said, right here on the stand, that I was involved in traffic which, as we can see by legal definition, is the same thing.

Now Officer Strongarm, one of three situations exists here. Either;

1.   you were lying to me on the stand, which is perjury, or
2.   you are incompetent as an officer and a witness, or
3.   the issuance of this ticket is a mistake!

Which one is it?

Now, you've got him cornered. If he sticks to his guns on the ticket he commits perjury, a crime. If he admits to incompetence, his testimony is impeached and his job is in jeopardy. He'll admit it was a 'mistake'.

D: No further questions your honor (we hate using that term unless they can show that they have any) "I would move the court for dismissal."

Do you see why an understanding of the law can be so much fun? Do you also see how much money is extracted from the people based on fraud, tricks and/or ignorance of the law?

We're only talking about 'traffic' tickets here. Think about similar fraud in the areas of taxes, registrations, licenses, permits, etc., etc., etc. It's all there.

AMERICAN LAW CLUB GETS ATTENTION

The A.L.C. meetings grew substantially and attendance numbers began ranging from twenty five to one hundred. Of course by this time they had outgrown their little offices and were now meeting in the V.F.W. hall (Veterans of Foreign Wars) in downtown Denver which was two blocks down from the city police station.

They'd have tables set up with literature, research papers, books and tapes for home use. Some people would come in from the mountains. Others came from their farms and ranches as far as 60 miles away or more. After the main meeting, where they'd often have guest speakers as well as an open floor time for anyone who had anything to present, they'd go across the street to the upscale Racine's restaurant for food, drink and private meetings after the main event. It turned into quite a social and networking event and was educational as well for everyone.

Racine's was a popular hangout for Denver police officers, city hall officials, even legislators from Capitol Hill and other power brokers and business moguls. There were certainly some interesting comments and looks from people sitting nearby as they would overhear some of the lively conversations.

In one particular meeting at the V.F.W. there were two interesting characters who showed up who didn't seem very sociable at all. It seemed quite obvious what their general purpose was. When Rex did his usual welcome to any and all public servants at the beginning, he looked one right in the eye. He seemed a little bit nervous and his body language gave him away,

That particular night's presentation was a good one. They delved into several critical issues one of which was the requirement that each and every statute on the books requires a bond for any possible damage it may cause the public due to its enactment into law. Through their own diligent efforts, the A.L.C. discovered that not a single one of Colorado's statutes was bonded as required. Oops! This results in the statute being null and void if brought up properly in the courts. Think about the ramifications of that one for a minute!

These two mysterious characters left just as the group began wrapping up. They were standing out in the parking lot talking briefly between themselves. Unbeknownst to them, the spouse of one of the regular members was sitting in her car nearby having a cigarette when she overheard one of the men say, "These people are dangerous! Something needs to be done!"

He was right, although not in the sense that he meant it. The 'truth' is dangerous to those who would pervert it and something 'does' need to be done to the criminals who subvert it! The American Law Club was making its mark!

ALLODIAL TITLE

In the meantime, there was a sister organization across town, run by another passionate freedom lover and non-bar association legal student who was doing similar things. This group was called TEAM LAW. They specialized in Federal U.S. Code Title 42 civil rights lawsuits against government officials who felt it necessary to violate peoples' rights under *'color of law'*. Another area they had perfected was gaining 'allodial title' to private property, namely automobiles.

Let's provide you a little background on this issue. We can start with Black's definition of 'allodial':

> ***Allodial - Free: not beholden of any lord or superior: owned without obligation of vassalage or fealty: the opposite of feudal.***

Here's a great example: Most of us believe that once we pay off the bank loan, we own our car, right?

Wrong. You never own your car in ***allodial title*** so long as it is registered to the state and so long as you maintain a ***'certificate of title'***.

Consider this: You've seen the license plates which are marked 'For Official Use' and you instantly recognize that as a 'State owned' vehicle, correct? This is common knowledge. Now, check the hairline printing embedded in the background of your annual registration stickers in the corner of the plate on your 'private' car. You guessed it... 'For Official Use'. This is not only referring to your sticker. Your sticker is attached to your license plate which is attached to your car and the entire package is 'For Official Use'. Your car is owned as state property! How do you like that?

You're not yet convinced? Let's look and see how that happens: when your car comes off the manufacturer's assembly line, the original, true title of ownership is called a 'Manufacturer's Statement of Origin' or M.S.O. and this is the lawful 'title' which accompanies the car to the dealer. The dealer, upon sale, allows you to 'register the vehicle' with the state, if you request state registration and its commercial benefits. In this process he then sends the M.S.O. to the State D.M.V. which now holds the *'true title'*. You, because of your ignorance of the law, apply only for the *'certificate of title'* in the registration process. And even though everyone calls it the 'title' it is NOT!

Stay with us here. Have you ever had a group insurance plan with your employer? If so, you know that you only got a 'certificate of insurance' which is proof that an insurance policy exists, somewhere. Your employer holds the actual (true) policy contract. He's the principal and he's paying for it. Fine. But you don't get the actual policy, you only get the 'certificate of insurance'. The employer owns the master policy and he is in control of it. The same holds true with your car.

You don't get the true title because you don't own it, THE STATE does!

You only have *conditional use* of the car, provided that you take care of it the way the owner wants you to. What happens when you don't pay the owner his annual use tax (registration)? He'll take it away from you. What happens when you don't follow all the rules for insurance, emissions, speed regulations, licensing, etc., etc., etc.? He fines you and if you get too many fines, he takes 'his property' away from you. Does that sound like allodial ownership to you? Of course not. So you ask, 'what good is a 'certificate of title? Let's look at Black's Law Dictionary 5th edition:

> *"Certificate of Title- See Title Insurance"*

That's right. Your *'certificate of title'* is nothing more than a private insurance contract whereby you ask and pay the state to protect you from secret liens on your car. Because you are asking for a commercial benefit from government, you signed a contract in the application and now you have strict liability performance that is required from you in return. Do you see how this works? Now there is nothing inherently wrong with this, provided the people are aware that they have a choice. The fact that you were never told that this is optional is where the fraud lies. It's called 'coercion', 'unconscionable contracts' and 'lack of informed consent' among other things.

TEAM LAW had figured out how to lawfully remove property from this private contractual arrangement with THE STATE. Now with full allodial title, such property was not subject to the strict liability performance requirements and the police couldn't touch these people with bothersome nuisance items like 'traffic tickets' and all sorts of other rules and regulations intended and applicable only to 'state owned vehicles' or other contracts with the corporate municipality. About half of the cars in the parking lot for some of the law club meetings had *private allodial owner-ship* plates instead of the state issued version. They were 'private' vehicles, not 'state owned' vehicles engaged in the commerce of transportation!

On numerous occasions, many people with these plates were circled and followed by police cars. But once the cops realized what they were dealing with, that they had no jurisdiction, they would just go away.

On one occasion, a member named George had his whole family in the car out near Stapleton airport in Denver. It was a rare occasion but a cop, not knowing better, went so far as to pull him over. George understood very well the nature of voluntary contracts with the state, jurisdiction, etc. and previously got rid of his state drivers license so he had no standard corporate commercial (state) documents to give the cop when he asked for them. He did give the police officer the appro-priate paperwork for his allodial ownership and proper filings with the County Clerk & Recorder in order to be socially responsible for I.D. /etc. The cop read the paperwork and went back to his cruiser and called his dispatcher to see what the hell to do with this.

After waiting what seemed like an inordinate amount of time, George turned around to see the cop banging his hands on his dash-board in disgust and anger. He couldn't write a ticket and spun a quick u-turn and peeled out, leaving George and his family to continue on their way, without ever returning his documentation. It was OK, they were just copies which could be replaced.

Think about what this would cost THE STATE in lost revenue if everyone discovered how to claim their God given allodial property rights? This is the single most important reason for willful oppression: money and control!

Do you see now how some people (the powers that be) have a vested interest in fraud, deception and manipulation of the people? Would you believe that someone in THE STATE felt that this business of teach-ing about allodial property had to be stopped?

As soon as this procedure gained a toehold in the ever growing public meetings and started spreading, the attacks began. Allodial property on the streets started getting seized and impounded under *color of law*. They even sent camera crews and news anchors from the local network affiliate to A.L.C. meetings, doing ambush interviews in the parking lots, etc. with the only intention to smear and demonize the group and rally public opinion against 'these extremists' who thought that they were 'above the law'.

Surprisingly though, despite the slant towards demonization, the local T.V. station did present some of the truth behind the issues. So, contrary to their intent, the spots did educate the public viewers to some degree. Don't you love how some truth always seems to slip out despite their worst intentions?

As soon as the seizures of private allodial property began, so did the title 42 Federal civil rights lawsuits. The head to head conflict between government control and the truth had begun on one front.

ACTION AGAINST THE IRS

On another front, Rex and a number of those in A.L.C. also got involved in multi-party, multi-action lawsuit against the commissioner of the IRS. This suit was coordinated by Lindsey Springer, a Christian, non lawyer man who has devoted his recent life to this suit. It was very interesting, apart from its unique legal arguments to prove the fraud and misapplication of the Internal Revenue Code, for the reason that about eleven similar actions were filed in eleven different states (federal districts) around the country.

This accomplished a couple of things. First, when a federal judge made a favorable ruling in one of the related cases in one federal district, Springer's team could play this ruling against the other judges in the other jurisdictions, which is sort of like lighting the candle (IRS) at both ends and working toward the middle. If it was an adverse ruling on an issue, they would again work that to their advantage in the other cases where they would then be prepared and streamlined in a manner of speaking to correctly anticipate the opposition. Secondly, with the multiple suits, they occupied the defense attorneys in the U.S. Department of Justice, on a full time basis. They could spend 30 days or more responding to one motion in each of all eleven district courts.

The suit sought damages for unauthorized collection actions and asked for refunds of all income taxes paid on the basis that the plaintiffs were not engaged in a 'Trade or Business in the United States' (by legal definition) which is the basis to collect income taxes under subtitle A in the Internal Revenue Code.

Again, you have to look at definitions in the law books. Take a minute to understand this critical issue. It's fascinating and it's easy to follow!

Have a look at 'the law' direct from the Internal Revenue Code:

<u>26 USC 7701 (a)(9), (10), (26) & (31)</u>

<u>Sec. 7701. Definitions</u>

(A)When used in this title, where not otherwise distinctly expressed or manifestly incompatible with the intent thereof.

(9) **United States.** The term *"United States"* when used in a geographic sense includes **only** the states and the District of Columbia.

(10) **State.** The term *"state"*shall be construed to include the District of Columbia...

(26) **Trade or Business.** The term *"Trade or Business"* includes the performance of the functions of a public office.

(27) **Foreign Estate or Trust.** The terms *"foreign estate or trust"* mean an estate or trust...the income of which from sources without the United States which is not effectively connected with the conduct of a *trade or business* within the *United States*, is <u>not includable in gross income under subtitle A.</u>

Note: in law, when it says *'shall include'* it means intrinsically (if nothing else is defined as being 'included'), *'at the exclusion of everything else'*, or in other words, you can replace 'includes' with 'only'. So in this example definition 10 would be interpreted to mean:

> (10) **State.** The term *"state"* shall be construed to include only the District of Columbia...

Therefore, without the legalese:

> **(9)** **United States.** The term *"United States"* when used in a geographic sense includes **only** the District of Columbia.

Now, based on the legal definition taken directly from the U.S. Code Title 26 which is the Internal Revenue Code, in order for you to be legally determined to be engaged in a <u>*'trade or business in the United States'*</u> (taxable activity under subtitle A), you would have to be engaged in **<u>*'the functions of a public office in the District of Columbia'*</u>** to be subject.

It's pretty cut and dried don't you think?

According to the legal definitions, do Subtitle A 'Income Taxes' apply to you? Not unless you are an elected public servant working in ten square miles of Washington D.C. If victorious, all multi-party plaintiffs would have proven that the IRS tax laws didn't apply to them and would be getting permanent exemption from income taxes with full refunds of all taxes ever paid, plus damages. If only...!

To make a long and very interesting story very short, you have to know that the government would never let this issue be decided on its merits in a court room of public record. This would collapse the system and set all the slaves free!

Ultimately, the case was dismissed by the court on the basis that *'Springer had failed to exhaust his administrative remedies and the court had no jurisdiction.'* Chickenshit.

It's funny isn't it? That the court is happy to decide that it has 'no jurisdiction' when you are suing the government on an important, black and white, legal issue you are sure to win, but when they want to try to apply all kinds of laws and heap them upon your shoulders to get 'you' to comply with things that don't apply to you, they ignore your arguments of 'lack of jurisdiction'. This is the state of lawlessness in U.S. courts.

Later, to teach him a lesson, the government indicted Springer on the criminal charges for 'willful failure to file'. Of course it's not 'willful' if you have a pending issue before the court which needs determination in order to clarify your status and how the law applies to you, or not in this case.

Springer didn't want to argue that issue. He chose another approach. This is a very interesting case due to the fact that the government included in its list of charges against Lindsey, a variety of statutes 'and' their supporting regulations which he has 'allegedly' violated.

Knowing the law perfectly, Springer knows that the ONLY regulations that exist in the Internal Revenue Code (IRC) apply ONLY to Title 27 which ONLY applies to alcohol, tobacco and firearms. Of course Springer has nothing to do with ATF (again). The court granted him his request for a *'Bill of Particulars'* and in essence agreed with him in May of 2009, that the government is required to produce those *regulations* if they are alleging that Springer willfully violated them. They obviously need to be specific about what regulations he is allegedly guilty of violating, in order to prosecute. If those regulations only apply to ATF statutes, then they need to present to the court the evidence that he was engaged in ATF activity, which of course they can't do because he had no activity in that arena.

The regulations don't exist outside of alcohol, tobacco and fire-arms, and thus the 'statutes' the government is alleging Lindsey to have violated (Title 26 – IRC), have no teeth (implementing regulations) and cannot be prosecuted. This is another fraud which is absolutely clear in the law, but is being misapplied in the courts at the expense of the people.

If a statute has no implementing regulations it cannot be enforced and is in effect 'not law'! The only 'implementing regulations' behind the Internal Revenue statutes in Title 26 of the U.S. Code, which are being applied to you and your personal income, relate to ATF in title 27. Are you involved in producing, distributing or merchandising alcohol, tobacco or firearms?

Why don't they just change the law? Because they won't expose themselves. It's all a big fraud and if everyone became aware of it, with all the damages caused over the years as a result, can you imagine the backlash and virtually limitless liability?

You can find Lindsey Springer online and follow this if you like. It's interesting and very educational. Look for the posts on ram-v-irs.com

One thing was for sure. Rex and his American Law Club were mixing it up. They were getting peoples' attention and it was coming from all corners. Whatever your opinions on the matter, you have to acknowledge one thing, they were shaking the foundations of the 'status quo' and could not be ignored.

The 'People' were mobilizing!

For more on these subjects see the author's video workshops at www.vimeo.com/markemery

CHAPTER 8

THE CITIZEN'S RIGHTS FORUM

WITH THE A.L.C. ORGANIZED AND running like a fine tuned engine, it was now time to reach out to the masses. Rex began advertising on conservative radio starting with KNUS, a local Denver talk station.

It actually surprised him that he was getting a direct return on his advertising dollars. People liked what the A.L.C. was doing. He had expected to run in the red in the short term but build profitability through developing goodwill, referrals and word of mouth advertising for long-term benefits. It only took a couple of new A.L.C. members to pay for the advertising and he got a lot of interest and several new members right away.

Nearing the end of Rex's first ad contract, KNUS was planning a unique concept for a radio broadcast. They were organizing a special show with their prime time host Bob Heckler. This show was to be a public town hall meeting held once a week in a posh auditorium in the downtown Marriott.

A panel of guests would be assembled with the public invited to attend and participate in discussion and debate over the hot issues of the day. It was a great concept!

Rex was asked to help sponsor the event, which he did gladly. Of course by being a sponsor he attended the town hall meetings, promoted the A.L.C. and most important, was networking with all kinds of interesting people. There were times when the star studded guest panel was rivalled by the interesting personalities in the public seating. This radio business was fun!

KHNC

Later, he was made aware of a new station on the scene which he had previously never heard of because their signal did not reach into Denver. It is a small station situated in Johnstown, a tiny farm town in rural Colorado just south of Greeley about 60 miles north of Denver. The station was KHNC 1360 A.M. formerly known as the 'U.S.A. Patriot Network' and later the 'American Freedom Network' and now ' The America News Network'. The owner Don is a Messianic Jew in his beliefs and was open to all kinds of discussion from diverging viewpoints on his network.   Their shows focused on numerous conservative issues such as the New World Order, survival and self-sufficiency, P.O.W.s, home schooling, homeopathic and herbal health care, I.R.S., government abuse, the real stories behind the politics, etc.

KHNC was a bona fide alternative media source and they really let it all hang out. It seemed almost too good to be true. Of course he wanted to support them and reach out to their listeners. This was right up Rex's alley.

While their A.M. signal was only 500 watts it did cover most of the eastern plains of Colorado.   However, they also had affiliates across the country that picked up the broadcasts and many listeners nationwide would listen by pulling in the signal off of their satellite dishes. Furthermore, with sufficient sponsorship, shortwave broadcasts were possible by linking up with the Worldwide Christian Radio Network.

Rex gave the advertising a try. He had come in to the station a couple of times and cut his own spots. He was told that he had a good radio voice. As a matter of fact, ever since Rex's college days, new acquaintances would often ask him, "haven't we heard you on the radio before?" Of course he had no experience whatsoever with radio except for listening to it and paying for it with KNUS.

A Radio Show is born

It wasn't long before the owner Don, who is a wonderful and humble God loving man, asked him if he would like to do a show. At first he didn't know what to say. He was not at all technically inclined and wouldn't have a clue on how to run a board full of buttons, knobs, and levers.

He said not to worry about that, the engineer Dana would take care of the technical stuff. "We have a slot this Saturday at 10:00 A.M. Why don't you give it a try and we'll see what happens," Don said. Rex was a bit astounded and taken back by the proposition. He had never considered such a thing. Well, so what? Why not? So he accepted the offer and 'The Citizens' Rights Forum' radio show was born.

The first show, like anything new, was a little clumsy. He was so used to listening to KNUS in Denver he mistakenly give the wrong call letters a couple times just out of habit. Aside from feeling stupid about those goofs, the show went reasonably well. He didn't have any guests on and spent the hour discussing a person's rights during 'initial contact' with law enforcement. They even had a couple of callers. Glory be!

He quickly settled into the role of radio jock and looked forward to the shows every Saturday. He would usually drive up to Johnstown to do the show in the studio. But when he had tighter time constraints he would do the broadcast over the phone from his office at home or wherever he needed to be. The only drawback to not being in the studio was not getting the visual cues from Dana as to how much time he had before break. He had to force himself to watch the synchronized clock for break times. Being that much closer he occasionally goofed.

Rex's listenership grew steadily and he started bringing in some powerhouse guests. It wasn't long before he had an offer to sponsor his show to go up on shortwave. He was surprised at how many listeners pulled in the show off of satellite from all over the country. Now going up on the WWCR (Worldwide Christian Radio) on shortwave would be a powerful injection of new listeners.

This was fun and he started to feel like he might actually be able to make a small difference in the world. Rex's listeners would call in and often express how appreciative they were about how he was getting the truth out, which our mainstream media refuses to touch. He was told by many that Rex's show was the only source they had to learn the kinds of things they would get from the Citizens Rights Forum. One listener who came out on a trip from Washington state made a special effort to stop in just to meet him in person as he was on his way to Florida. Gosh, he felt special!

This is what he needed to see, not so much for his own ego, but to know that his efforts were making a difference in peoples' lives. He wasn't getting paid to do the show. To take the time to prepare for the show, arrange guests, drive up, spend a couple of hours at the studio and drive back was quite a commitment for a 'volunteer' who has many other things to do. Overall, he was happy with the way things were going.

He didn't want to be another forum for whiners and complainers. They were absolutely 'solution oriented' just like A.L.C. A problem issue was not raised unless he could offer an alternative solution that was viable for people to consider. This was a forum of ideas, solutions and positive information that people could use and apply in their lives. To get a flavor for the subject matter discussed, the following is a small sampler of some of the guests and related subject matter.

PETER KERSHAW AND 'HEAL OUR LAND MINISTRIES'

Peter is a researcher and author who has written on the issue of churches who incorporate and claim the IRC 501(c)(3) tax exempt status. Peter's research shows that churches have always been tax exempt and by becoming a corporation they become a creature (subject) of *the state* instead of God. Thus, they end up serving two masters which is obviously not correct. This is especially true when they apply for the 501(c)(3) status which stipulates that to preserve the tax exempt status, the church must not get involved in political issues.

Well, if the church is to fulfil its great commission from God it must get involved in all issues of the spirit. However, today that includes abortion, homosexuality, ethics in government and exposing the truth about political candidates, etc. Many 501(c)(3) tax exempt churches have been shut down and their assets seized for honoring their great commission in violation of the 'statutory requirements' of the tax exempt status. Serving two masters is a big problem. Peter provides a method and the legal support to get churches out from under the thumb of civil government and back in full commitment to God.

Peter's research is thorough and compelling and Rex had a very interesting discussion on air. Peter was actually Rex's very first guest in the early days of the show. When the show was over Peter was very pleased and complimentary on the way it was handled.

Rex had known of Peter from his books and Peter had visited the weekly Law Club meetings as a speaker once before. He lived in the area.

Rex later had one fun experience involving Peter. Peter had a civil issue in court that was pressing upon him and he asked Rex to help him. He asked if Rex would appear with him in the court hearing to provide some support. It was a contract dispute relating to foreclosure. Rex had no idea what to expect or what support he could provide, but Peter didn't have an attorney to represent him so Rex said 'fine'.

They appeared in a small courtroom in Denver as did his counter parties, a couple who did have an attorney representing them. At one point in the hearing the judge was stumped on a particular issue and asked both parties if they had any court references on previous rulings on this issue to support their position. Neither party had the requested support. So the judge called a recess to give everyone time to go downstairs to the law library and come back in 20 minutes with the references to show why the judge should rule in the prevailing party's favor.

They went down to the law library. In about 10 minutes Rex had 3 or 4 solid court rulings which were spot on and supported Peters position. He couldn't help but notice that the attorney for the other party was wandering around the library like a lost puppy looking for his owner.

The time was up and they were called back into the courtroom. The judge first asked the opposing attorney what he had. The attorney stuttered and stammered and finally admitted that he couldn't find anything and had nothing for the judge. Zilch.

The judge looked at Peter who presented the case law which Rex had found and it was strong. The judge ruled in Peter's favor and that was it. They were in and out and it was a done deal for Peter. Peter was thrilled!

Surely, the opposing couple wasn't too happy to have spent good money on this attorney to represent them when he obviously didn't even know his way around the law library. But that's typical, really.

But that's not the end of the story. A few months later, Rex and a bunch of the A.L.C. crew were in municipal court to provide support for one of the members who was there on a traffic issue and they had big plans for the hearing.

The judge came into the courtroom... 'All rise'. They didn't rise. The judge enters and you'll never guess who the judge was. Yep! It was this same attorney whose butt Rex kicked in that hearing with Peter! The judge looked at Rex and froze for a moment. You could sense a chill in the room. In anticipation of a challenge from our group, the judge gave a speech about respecting the 'office' of the judge and not necessarily the 'man'.

Sometimes being a smart aleck is terribly fun! The law club member was finally called and this person was prepared. He drove the 'judge' nuts with stipulations and challenges and for the time, got his issue deferred since the court was not 'able' to make a determination on the critical issues that were raised by this 'defendant'. Surprised ?

Dr. Tom Hutchison

Dr. Tom was a teacher on personal sovereignty issues. He focused on understanding five key legal issues; status, standing, agency, action and commencement of action as these relate to public servants, you and the courts.

Your legal status as a human being is important to understand along with who you really are and how you relate to others in the legal juristic world. Your status and the status of others determine who has proper standing to be heard in court. Agency helps us determine exactly who is working for whom and with what authority. Action and commencement of action determines how it all falls out or comes together, whatever the case may be. His teachings were powerful and fundamental providing all with a good base for further work.

PAM BEESLY

Pam is known for her work in researching and following social management delivery systems. Rex's discussions with Pam focused on the Goals 2000 program which was being sold to the public as an educational program for kids but is in fact was a cradle to grave social management program. Her revelations were shocking. She pointed out through her diligent and exhaustive research, how 'America' would be merged, ideologically, with the communist Soviet Union through the implementation of Goals 2000.

Pam was a guest on more than one occasion and interest in her research proved so great she soon had her own show on the network.

STATE SENATOR CHARLIE DUKE

Senator Duke was on with Rex a couple of times. The first time they were together Rex broadcast a nationwide conference call between Charlie, Representative Dick Rogers from California, and several other legislators from other parts of the country who were all involved in passing the 10th Amendment state sovereignty resolutions in their respective state legislatures. It was an effort by the states to re-assert state independence from the Feds in Washington D.C.

They did another remote broadcast at a 2nd Amendment rally live on the capitol steps in Denver where Charlie briefly appeared on the show after addressing the rally.

Charlie was also the focal point of what was probably Rex's best show ever, done at the common law grand jury event down in Cañon

City, Colorado. That broadcast is discussed in greater detail in chapter twelve.

Barry Smith

Barry was a legal researcher and pro-se litigant much like Rex, although he was far advanced in his knowledge compared to Rex, at least in Rex's early days. Barry has co-produced an excellent video on do-it-yourself legal research and was actively involved in teaching people the ins and outs of law and judicial procedure. He was also a 'Front Line Master' alumnus with the Right Way L.A.W. group in Ohio.

The particular focus in this broadcast was Title 42 civil rights lawsuits against public officials who overstep their bounds of authority to violate federally guaranteed rights under color of state law. In the one hour they had together they touched on some of the key points as to what constitutes a cause of action, how to overcome immunity defenses and other defensive attempts they use to try and get the case thrown out. This was an interesting discussion for pro-se litigants albeit somewhat technical. Barry and he spent a fair amount of time together and he taught Rex a few things. His mind was a walking encyclopedia.

General Ben Partin

Retired Brigadier General (U.S.A.F.) Ben Partin spent over twenty five years as a Pentagon munitions expert. General Partin's analysis of the bombing of the Alfred P. Murrah building in Oklahoma City was very revealing, precise and scientific. By inspecting the layout of the support columns in the building and looking at the pattern of damage done, he revealed some interesting facts which were contrary to the 'official' story.

First, the primary heavy, load bearing columns of the building went the length of the building in two rows in the interior area. The parallel rows of columns on the exterior were much lighter and more susceptible to damage from a blast. Interestingly enough, if the blast that did the real damage actually came from the truck in the street, as our illustrious leaders and media have told us it did, the lighter non-load bearing columns on the exterior, closest to the truck, would have incurred greater damage than the heavier interior load bearing columns which were further away from the blast, right? Of course. You don't need to be a scientist to understand this.

General Partin's Analysis: the section of the building that came down did so by virtue of the load bearing interior columns being 'sheared' off and giving way, while some of the lighter non-load bearing exterior columns, closest to the 'alleged' blast remained intact.

Conclusion:

A) Due to the 'bruisance' or blast pattern of the McVeigh fertilizer truck bomb in the street, the concrete in the columns should have been 'pulverized' into dust particles, not sheared off.

B) For the damage to occur in the manner that it did, and in that pattern could mean only one thing; the death and mayhem was caused not by a fertilizer bomb parked out front, but instead by heavy explosives actually attached to the interior support columns which would explain the 'shearing' effect. This hypothesis was supported by seismographic reports from the Oklahoma City Omniplex Museum which showed not one, but three explosions occurring according to seismologist Ray Brown of the Oklahoma Geological Survey.

Rex discussed this in detail with General Partin and he did a great job outlining his analysis and the apparently obvious conclusion. This show brought only two questions to mind:

1) Why hasn't this been a part of the 'official' report of what happened?
2) Why didn't the media investigate and report on these obviously crucial developments?

The General was very public about his findings but it was all ignored and completely swept under the rug. Think about it! In this case, there was another agenda which was better served by hiding the truth. This leads to many more questions and theories we won't get into here. Do your own research to find the truth.

RONN JACKSON

Ronn claims to have spent years working as a runner for one member of the Committee of 16. The Committee of 16 essentially is the shadow government behind all governments. They direct the Club of Rome, the Council on Foreign Relations and the Tri-Lateral Commission among others. While Ronn is a controversial figure, he spoke with much authority and information that few people would be expected to be able to gain access to. That, coupled with his many determined efforts to expose corruption and gain back our Republic, made Rex more of a believer than not.

Ronn was a regular guest and they talked about many intriguing issues. They made the biggest waves however when Ronn revealed that he had a sworn statement from a U.S. Justice Department employee indicating possible government complicity in, and foreknowledge of, the Oklahoma City bombing.

This affidavit, of which he had a sanitized copy, alleged a 'mock scenario' that was conducted by the U. S. Department of Justice in preparation for a terrorist attack on a domestic American target. The details of the 'mock' scenario were identical to the actual results of the Oklahoma City debacle down to the position and type of bomb 'allegedly' used. In fact the players in this game were substituted an actual photograph of the Alfred P. Murrah building in place of a photo they originally were given of another building. We now see these 'false flags' occurring routinely.

The signatures of the affidavit were witnessed by several people including a lawyer, a member of the House of Representatives and a retired military officer among others. All signatures were sanitized on copies made public, allegedly for the protection of the people involved, some of whom were whisked out of the country according to Ronn.

This story hit the airwaves like a full out nuclear blast. Pam Beesly heard about it and put the story out over the fax networks. Rex's phone started ringing and didn't stop for about six weeks straight. He got calls from a TIME correspondent, 20/20 called, Associated Press correspondents and editors and reporters from every newsletter, magazine, radio and T.V. show he'd ever heard of and many that he hadn't. He couldn't possibly even begin to return all the calls that he received. He did talk to Joe Del Monico of Dateline NBC. Joe wanted to send a camera crew to interview Rex about the revelations but he declined. "Since it was actually Ronn's news he should be the one to be interviewed," he told Joe.

At the time, Ronn was in prison on a tax issue as a matter of principle and was soon to be released. Rex talked to him about doing the interview and he was fine with it. So he got back to Joe at NBC and gave him the contact information. Arrangements were made to fly a crew out to see Ronn in Nevada. The interview went fine and Ronn was surprisingly impressed with the apparent sincere interest and objectivity that the crew had during the interview.

When the network aired the piece, they only used a small clip which was only a few seconds long. Nothing else from the entire lengthy interview was used or taken into consideration in the presentation. They took it completely out of context and used it only to try and discredit Ronn. So the interview was a complete waste of time. It's amazing how the news we get is so often skewed so as to present an 'alternative' to reality. But as usual, some truth did get through despite their worst intentions.

Even though he didn't participate in any way in the interview, NBC still used a taped segment of Rex's show wherein he signed on introducing himself, the show and Ronn as Rex's guest.

Ronn and Rex developed a nice working relationship and shared a lot of information both on and off the air. 'The' famous radio broadcast was April 29th, 1995. Ronn was due to be released in June. In return for

Rex's help and for providing him a forum, Ronn offered to fly him and two or three other select individuals overseas by private jet to interview these Justice Department officials. Rex was initially very excited by the offer but ultimately was unable to accept due to other complications in his life which will be explored later.

Rex never got to talk much with others from the station as nobody came in on Saturday mornings. It was like a mausoleum. Dana, Rex's board operator and he pretty much had the place to themselves. On one Saturday, however, before the show, 'Rock' was in. Rock was the wordsmith/editor of the American Freedom magazine which the station published.

Rock had just brought in a fancy piece of communications equipment. It was a scanner that was able to monitor hundreds of frequencies. He collared him before Rex's show wanting to show him his new toy and said, "Rex, do you want to see something interesting?" he said, "Sure, what are you up to?"' He took him in his office and gave him a brief explanation and demonstration of his new gizmo. He then said, "But look at this!" He showed him his frequency directory and referred to a series of channels used by the Federal government. He told him "You won't believe what the Feds talk about on that channel!" He continued, "Let's tune it in, I'll show you." He did and coming in loud and clear was the KHNC radio broadcast! Evidently, the Feds monitored all the broadcasts of KHNC every day. Good! Let the truth be known! The light is shining on all!

PART III

SKIRMISHES

CHAPTER 9

BREAKING THE CODE

THROUGH MUCH STUDY AND RESEARCH, Rex had come to learn that the single most important and devastating problem we face as a nation is the unjust weights and measures fraudulently imposed upon all Americans by the Federal Reserve Banking system and their fiat paper money and fractional reserve program in place today.

This entire story relates to Rex's personal quest for freedom. His study of the monetary system and how it works, held the keys to that freedom and was the underpinning to everything.

If you don't agree with this, then you likely just don't understand it completely and maybe this chapter will help.

On the worldly plane, aside from Satan himself, this is the enemy. The money powers force and coerce worship, allegiance and downright slavery through economic control and manipulation of government, media, industry, labor, churches and every facet of daily life. Volumes have been written about the Federal Reserve and we don't need to rehash it all. But this issue must be understood by all Americans. There is much information available for independent research. However, Devvy Kidd's booklet entitled **"Why a Bankrupt America?"** is highly recommended. It's only forty small pages, is easy to read and packs a punch.

Let's look at just a few cursory highlights that we should keep in mind as the basis for our understanding.

Let us examine in the words of several knowledgeable, credible individuals just how this system really works. These are taken from Devvy's booklet.

Chairman Louis T. McFadden of the House Banking and Currency Committee, addressed the House of Representatives on June 10, 1932:

"Some people think the Federal Reserve Banks are U.S. government institutions. They are not government institutions. They are private credit monopolies which prey upon the people of the U.S. for the benefit of themselves and their foreign and domestic swindlers, and rich and predatory money lenders."

- 75 Congressional Record 125950-12603

"It is mathematically impossible to pay off the national debt. In examining the origin of money under this central banking system", according to William H. Ferkler, Manager of Public Affairs at The Department of Treasury, Bureau of Engraving & Printing in Washington, D.C.:

"As we have advised, the Federal Reserve is currently paying the Bureau approximately $23 for each 1,000 notes printed. This does include the cost of printing, paper, ink, labor, etc. Therefore, 10,000 notes of any denomination, including the $100 note would cost the Federal Reserve $230. In addition, the Federal Reserve must secure a pledge of collateral equal to the face value of the notes." (from the U.S. government - i.e. taxpayer slaves!)

The Federal Reserve, by printing these notes into existence at a total cost of $230 to the Federal Reserve, this banking cartel - not the government of We the People - thereby obtains a pledge of collateral equal to their face value, namely $1 million if $100 notes. This pledge is made to the Reserve cartel by Congress, and the collateral which Congress pledges is the land, labor and assets of the American people. What a racket! They rent funny money from the private Fed that is so debt laden, They can never have a balanced budget or pay off this rent, even if They all lived to be one million years old!

Lewis T. McFadden, Chairman of the House Banking Commission and Member of Congress, speaking about the international financial conspirators during the very time they were taking over the monetary control of America said this:

"They have in this country one of the most corrupt institutions the world has ever known. We refer to the Federal Reserve Board and the Federal Reserve Banks, hereinafter called the Fed. They are not government institutions. They are private monopolies which prey upon the People of the United States for the benefit of themselves and their foreign and domestic swindlers; rich and predatory moneylenders."

- McFadden died mysteriously in 1936 after three previous attempts on his life.

George W. Malone, U.S. Senator from Nevada speaking before Congress in 1957 alluded to the families that secretly own the Federal Reserve Bank and control the finances of the United States:

"We believe that if the people of this nation fully understood what Congress has done to them over the past 49 years, they would move on Washington, they would not wait for an election... It adds up to a preconceived plan to destroy the economic and social independence of the United States."

Soon 100% of every federal income tax dollar you are coerced to pay will go just to service the interest on the national debt. It cannot be done!

"The actual deficits are almost twice as large as those admitted by the government. So why hasn't our economy collapsed? Because the American people still have confidence in 'the system.' The heart of the system depends on borrowing to fund the budget deficits each year." - Larry Burkett, The Coming Economic Earthquake, pg. 90

"Erskine Bowles, a co-chair of the president's bipartisan deficit-reduction commission known as "Simpson-Bowles," has called the nation's compound interest burden one of the biggest long-term challenges facing the United States. "We'll be spending over $1 trillion a year on interest by 2020. That's $1 trillion we can't spend to educate our kids or to replace our badly worn-out infrastructure," said Bowles at a recent forum hosted by IHS Global Insight. - U.S. News & World Report Nov. 19, 2012

To further illustrate how the Fed is robbing you, look up the U.S. Inflation Calculator. You´ll find there that if you purchased a $20 item in 1913, when the Fed was created, that same item would now (2014) cost you $477.07 reflecting a cumulative inflation rate of 2285.4%. This is a 'hidden tax' that nobody wants to talk about. Inflation steals your buying power and makes you poorer. Is it any wonder almost every family needs two incomes just to survive and the traditional family unit is being decimated?

The first problem we need to recognize is that many people are just unaware of the facts. They don't know that a problem exists because of the fact that they have forgotten who they are and where they came from. They are ignorant of history, economics, the constitution and the intent of the founding fathers. The roots of our heritage are being stolen from us with state sponsored and politically correct educational institutions and many just don't realize it or worse, just don't care.

If we spent any time whatsoever using the intelligence God gave us to study, learn and be responsible, we would know many things that are much more important than what's on T.V. tonight and who's playing ball this weekend.

One of the things we should all know at the junior high school level is that money was intended by our founding fathers to be 'spent' into circulation through public works without interest. If this were still the case there would be virtually NO national debt and virtually NO taxes compared to current levels.

Instead, each and every American in the nation carries a personal share of the national debt totaling nearly $60,000 at birth, most all of which goes toward interest. Those who are paying income taxes to the Fed work from January through most of June to pay for this burden and it never gets reduced! It only goes up!

You can look up your share of the national debt based on your age. Look up 'calculate my share of national debt'. Mine is $166,000 based on being born in the late 50's. And in view of all this, government is spending billions giving away cell phones and bicycle helmets to anybody who will take one (or more), including dead people!

How much better off would we be if people worked for themselves from January to June? How many mothers would be back in the home keeping our families together and society functioning properly? How many kids would get the attention and love they need and deserve to be good productive people instead of dropping out of school, getting pregnant, joining gangs, committing crime and costing society in so many ways? How much money could we save for our own financial security which in turn would stimulate the economy with a cheap money supply for business, investment and development? Think about the potential benefits!

Here is why and how the Fed is destroying America. According to William H. Ferkler, Manager of Public Affairs at 'The Department of the Treasury, Bureau of Engraving & Printing in Washington, D.C., he tells us (paraphrasing):

"The collateral talked about here is U.S. Government Bonds that cover the face amount of the notes PLUS INTEREST. What a great private business enterprise! The Fed manufactures a finished product that you need and can't get anywhere else for a cost of $230, does nothing to it and turns around and sells it retail for up to $1,000,000 PLUS INTEREST. Who are the suckers that would pay such a huge markup at retail from a foreigner (the Fed) when they could buy it wholesale by having their own government control and issue the money as is stipulated in the constitution?

The American people, that's who!"

The taxpayers are saddled to cover the bonds and notes issued as collateral. The problem is that the money to pay the interest is never created. Therefore, to pay the interest we have to borrow more. It's like using one credit card to pay off another. It only works for so long before you crash and burn.

There is never enough money to pay the principal <u>and</u> interest without borrowing more and going deeper into debt. Thus, every single dollar bill in circulation or on the books is backed by the debt (labor) of the people. Our labor, assets, bank accounts, property and future earning potential are 'the collateral'. You are owned! You are a slave!

This is why 'They the people' are considered by the international bankers to be 'natural resources' and 'chattel'. They own us through our public debt money. And if we paid the debt, there would be no money in circulation. If we all knew and recognized this we wouldn't waste any time talking about a balanced budget or eliminating the debt while the Fed is still in place. If we did, under the fraudulent Fed system none of us would have any money and we'd still have debt! It's all a hoax. The debt will automatically go away if we go back to a lawful money system and abolish the Fed and the IRS! That's what we should be talking about instead of national health care, bailouts, balanced budgets and other issues which are pure nonsense and distractions from the real issue of false weights and measures.

Ron Paul has it right! Audit the Fed. Uncover the fraud. Do something about it!

Rex's reaction to this revelation was natural: anger and contempt for the international bankers and ALL of the politicians who refuse to tell us the truth. It also laid a foundation of understanding for what was to come. It didn't end there.

The fraud and deception perpetrated on the American people resembles an onion. Once you get through one layer you're met with many more.

FREEDOM FROM THE VULTURE'S CLUTCHES

Because of the exposure of this monetary scam, some concerned American's had done further cutting into this onion and made some very interesting discoveries. They found ways of using the banker's rules in a 'beneficial' way. Rex learned more about this when a new friend whom he had met downtown picketing the Fed building with Devvy, introduced him to some people in Wisconsin who called themselves the Family Farm Preservation Group. They had broken the banker's code and monopoly on money and were helping people fight off the predatory bankers by accessing the *peoples' private banking system* or 'private credit money' as opposed to "public debt (Fed) money'.

Since public debt money is created by nothing more than the stroke of pen by a private corporation and the Sherman Anti-Trust Act was still in force (prohibiting monopolies), there must be opportunities for other private entities to utilize the banking laws as well.

Here are a few things that the 'Family Farm Preservation' group from Tigerton Wisconsin helped people understand:

The so called money we carry around and spend every day is called a 'Federal Reserve Note' or FRN. Well now, we know it's not *'Federal'*, it's 'private'. The Fed has nothing in *'reserve'*. And a *'note'* is nothing more than a promise to pay. Since our FRN's are not redeemable, the promise is fraudulent. It is never kept. All They exchange everyday are 'promises'. A promise to pay is a form of 'credit'. Thus, our medium of exchange is nothing more than non-redeemable credit using *'Notes'* or 'promises to pay' which <u>*never get paid*</u>! They only get exchanged for more promises!

Bouvier's Law Dictionary, 6th Edition, defines 'Money' as follows:

Gold, silver, and some other less precious metals, in the progress of civilization and commerce, have become the common standards of value; in order to avoid the delay and inconvenience of regulating their weight and quality whenever passed, the governments of the civilized world have caused them to be manufactured in certain portions, and marked with a Stamp which attests their value; this is called money. 1 Inst. 207; 1 Hale's Hist. 188; 1 Pardess. n.22; Dom. Lois civ. liv. prel. t.3, s.2, n. 6.

If a Note (FRN) is, by legal definition, NOT money, then what is our money? There must be something in the Federal law to tell us, right?

There is! Title 31 of the U.S. Code (Federal Statutes) Annotated Section 371 (5101 rev.) tells us:

The word "money" is substituted for "money of account" to eliminate unnecessary words. As far as can be determined, the phrase "money of account" has not been interpreted by any court or government agency.

Wait a minute! If the federal government has never determined what our 'money of account' is, then who has and what is it?

The Uniform Commercial Code (U.C.C.) tells us in 1-201(24) that; **"Money"** means a *medium of exchange* authorized or adopted by a domestic or foreign government and includes a monetary unit of account established by an intergovernmental organization or by agreement between two or more nations.

FRNs have written right on them that they are 'legal tender'. What's that?

Legal Tender' from Black's Law Dictionary:

Lawfully established national currency denominations. Legally required commercial exchange medium for money-debt payment. Differs widely from country to country. Creditors, lenders, and sellers retain the option to accept financial vehicles, such as checks and postal orders that are not legal tender, for payment of debt. Also known as lawful money.

Well, 'lawful money' according to your state constitution is defined very specifically as 'gold or silver'. So here is a conflict or a fraud, depending on how you look at it.

Black's Law Dictionary further elaborates in its definition of 'Money':

1. *The medium of exchange authorized or adopted by its government as part of its currency.*

So in this case, it's clear that the FRN (private credit) has been adopted as part of the currency and therefore **private notes** or private credit are the *'medium of exchange'* which can be included in the 'money' circulation.

Black's further defines money to include:

2. *Current money*
3. *Fiat money*

4.   *Hard money*
5.   *Lawful money*
6.   *Paper money*
7.   *Real money*

Confused? Compare any of these definitions with what your state constitution says is 'lawful money' and you'll go back full circle to gold and silver.

So *'money'* or *'money of account'* is much more than just *'legal tender'*

The courts must have encountered this issue and made some rulings to help us. So Rex started looking. Family Farm had already done the research.

Here is *some* of what they found:

First National Bank of Montgomery vs. Jerome Daly in Credit River Township, Minnesota was a foreclosure case in 1967.

In 1964, Mr. Daly approached the bank and obtained a 'loan' for $14,000 to buy a house in Scott County, Minnesota, signing a mortgage on the house to the bank. He paid on the loan for about 3 years then quit paying and the mortgage went into default. The house was then sold at a sheriff sale on June 26, 1967 and the bank instituted this action in court to get possession of the property.

The bank president, Mr. L.V. Morgan, took the witness stand and admitted that all of the money or 'credit' which was used as consideration for the note and mortgage 'WAS CREATED ON THE BANK'S BOOKS'. He explained that this was standard banking procedure which was exercised in combination with the Federal Reserve Bank of Minneapolis, which is of course another private bank. He went on to admit that he knew of no United States statutes or law that gave him or the bank the authority to do so. Mr. Morgan argued that Mr. Daly waived his right to complain about the 'consideration' for the contract because he used the 'credit entry' and paid on the loan for three years.

The issue for the jury to decide was whether the 'credit entry' (loan) issued by the bank to Mr. Daly was in fact and in law, a lawful consideration to support the contract (note & mortgage) and in fact if Mr. Daly had waived his right to complain.

It didn't take long for the jury to render a verdict in Mr. Daly's favor. They determined that the bank had given nothing of substance to Mr. Daly (no money) and therefore the bank had no right title or interest in the property and was entitled to get nothing back.

The Justice of the Peace presiding over the case, Martin V. Mahoney issued a memorandum which summarized the issues as follows;

"The issues in this case were simple. There was no material dispute of the facts for the jury to resolve.

Plaintiff (the bank) admitted that, in combination with the Federal Reserve Bank of Minneapolis, which for all practical purposes, because of their interlocking activity and practices, and both being banking Institutions incorporated under the laws of the United States, are in the Law to be treated as one and the same bank, did create the entire $14,000 in money or credit upon its own books by bookkeeping entry. That this was the consideration used to support the note dated May 8, 1964 and the mortgage of the same date. The money and credit first came into existence when they created it. Mr. Morgan admitted that no United States Law or Statute existed which gave him the right to do this.

'Lawful consideration must exist and be tendered to support the note' see Anheuser-Busch Brewing Co. v. Emma Mason, 44 Minn. 318, 46 N.W. 558 and Wingate v. Wingate, 11 Tex. 430, 437.

The Jury found that there was no lawful consideration and we agree. Only God can create something out of nothing. Even if Defendant could be charged with waiver or estopped as a matter of Law this is no defense to the Plaintiff. The Law leaves wrongdoers where it finds them. See actions 50, 51, and 52 of AmJur 2d 'transactions' on page 584 - 'no action will lie to recover on a claim based upon, or in any manner depending upon, a fraudulent, illegal, or immoral transaction or contract to which Plaintiff was a party.'

Plaintiff's act of creating credit is not authorized by the constitution or laws of the United States, is unconstitutional and void and is not lawful consideration in the eyes of the law to support any thing or upon which any lawful rights can be built.

Nothing in the Constitution of the United States limits the jurisdiction of this Court, which is one of original jurisdiction with right of trial by jury guaranteed. This is a common law action. Minnesota cannot limit or impair the power of this Court to render complete Justice between the parties.

Any provisions in the Constitution and laws of Minnesota which attempt to do so is repugnant to the Constitution of the United States and void. No question as to the Jurisdiction of this court was raised by either party at the trial. Both parties were given complete liberty to submit any and all facts to the Jury, at least in so far as they saw fit.

No complaint was made by Plaintiff that Plaintiff did not receive a fair trial. From the admissions made by Mr. Morgan and the path of duty was made direct and clear for the Jury.

Their verdict could not reasonably have been otherwise. Justice was rendered completely and without denial, promptly and without delay, freely and without purchase, conformable to the laws in this Court on December 7, 1968

December 9, 1968

BY THE COURT

MARTIN V. MAHONEY

Justice of the Peace

Credit River Township

Scott County, Minnesota

Note: It has never been doubted that a Note given on a consideration which is prohibited by law is void. It has been determined, independent of Acts of Congress, that sailing under the license of an enemy is illegal. The emission of Bills of Credit upon the private corporations (banks) for the purposes of private gain is not warranted by the constitution of the United States and is unlawful. See Craig v. Mo, 4 Peters Reports 912 This Court can tread only that path which is marked out by duty'

- M. V. M.

The justice went on to order the return of the house back to Mr. Daly after it had already been sold. There are numerous case law decisions which state that "Banks cannot loan credits. Just a couple for your research are; First National Bank v. Monroe, 69 S.E. 1123; Best v. State

Bank of Bruce, 197 Wis. 20, 221 N.W. 379; and Citizens Nat'l Bank v. Good Roads Gravel Co., 236 S.W. 153, and there are many others.

Justice Mahoney's patriotic efforts however, did not end there. On January 6, 1969, his court filed a "NOTICE OF REFUSAL TO ALLOW APPEAL WITH THE CLERK OF DISTRICT COURT" pertaining to the same case.

His refusal was based upon the fact that the attorneys filed the notice of appeal and paid the filing fees to the clerk of court with two so-called 'One Dollar' Federal Reserve Notes issued by the Federal Reserve Bank of San Francisco.

Justice Mahoney ruled, *"These Federal Reserve Notes are not lawful money within the contemplation of the Constitution of the United States and are null and void. Further, the Notes on their face are not redeemable in Gold or Silver coin nor is there a fund set aside anywhere for the redemption of said notes."*

He went on to offer the Plaintiff an opportunity to plead their case on the proper filing of their appeal by ruling; *"If the Plaintiff will file a brief on the Law and the Facts with this Court within 10 days, or if Plaintiff will file an application for a full and complete hearing before this court on the determination, a prompt hearing will set be set and if plaintiff can satisfy this court that said Notes are lawful money issued in pursuance of and under the authority of the Constitution of the United States of America: the undersigned will stand ready and willing to reverse himself in this determination."*

Needless to say, no application or pleading on this issue was forthcoming. The Plaintiff dropped all attempts at appeal because there is no legal argument to rebut Justice Mahoney's position!!

To allow the truth to emerge and law to prevail in this manner took a high level of character and courage. Martin Mahoney deserves a strong and heartfelt salute from all honest Americans. Here's to you Mr. Mahoney!!

Sadly Mahoney's court was a very low level court and not one which could set precedent.

Nonetheless, it is almost unimaginable that a modern era court would rule in this manner based upon the truth and against the money powers. This writer has information from people who know Mr. Daly personally. Justice Mahoney died very shortly after this ruling and Mr. Daly is far, far away from Minnesota. So much for lawful courts!

So the banks by law, cannot issue credit. They certainly don't issue lawful money as defined in the constitution, Article 1:10:1

Colorado Revised Statues (current)

11-61-101. GOLD AND SILVER COIN A LEGAL TENDER.

The gold and silver coin issued by the government of the United States shall be a legal tender for the payment of all debts contracted on or after April 5, 1893, between the citizens of this state. The same shall be received in payment of all debts due to the citizens of this state and in satisfaction of all taxes levied by the authority of the laws of this state.

The footnotes to the above tell us that "State statute on legal tender cannot prohibit acceptance of federal reserve notes." However, nowhere does the law "compel' us to use Federal Reserve Notes. They can't because by the supreme law (constitution) FRN's are not lawful money nor are they legal tender by state statute!

A multitude of books have been written on this subject alone which you can find, and we recommend you do. The point is, our so called 'money' is comprised of many things; legal tender, notes, credit, negotiable instruments, demand deposits (electronic computer bookkeeping), checks and many other forms of commercial paper. All of these are unlawful yet accepted by agreement. So called 'money' is created by the stroke of a pen and some creative bookkeeping entries by a private corporation (bank), the Fed. This is backed up by the public debt (your labor), everything you think you own or will ever think you own. You see, you never really own anything, because unless you pay with lawful money of substance (gold and silver) you merely exercise the privilege of the 'discharge of your debt' liability when you use FRN'S.

The debt never goes away, just the temporary liability. It never goes away because there is no lawful money to pay with. Only the current medium of exchange which is 'private credit'. This is why and how the government can seize your property without due process of law. They gave you the privilege in 1933 to discharge your debt liabilities with the fiat FRN's which were created to replace real redeemable money which was confiscated by President Roosevelt along with all the gold which backed it up.

The U.S. Supreme Court has ruled 'that which Congress creates, it can control.' Therefore, when it creates privileges that you accept or benefit from, you are under all the control of the issuer of that benefit. Most of this falls under the commerce clause of the constitution. They make everything an act of commerce from your 'birth' to your 'marriage' which then is subject to licensing and the Federal power.

You voluntarily give up your God given rights when you enter into voluntary contracts for *benefits* with the Fed and enter into commerce with them. Now your behavior is regulated by contract and the commerce clause and you have no 'so called' constitutional rights because you voluntarily waived them when you applied for the benefits of the contract. Some examples are: social security benefits, veteran benefits, FDIC insurance when you opened your bank account, drivers licenses, state auto registration, marriage license, bicycle license, dog license, licenses of all sorts: state and federal and on and on.

Now, ultimate power in this contest resides in the people. They are the principals of government, the sovereign. They created government as their agent to carry out their will for their own benefit. When we delegated the responsibility of creating money to Congress (our agent), that agent must complete the task. We the People do not give up our power just because we delegate it. When delegated, it is merely on temporary assignment. Furthermore, when we tell our agent (government) to do something, our agent must do the job. It has no authority to delegate its duty to someone else, i.e. the private Federal Reserve. Therefore, we the people still retain the power to create money even though our agent has overstepped its bounds of authority by delegating their task to the Fed. The people must find a way to exercise their authority and reel in the Fed to avoid ultimate slavery and the destruction of the nation.

Now, by statutory definition a 'bank' is 'any person or organization engaged in the banking business.' Colorado Revised Statutes (C.R.S.)

Family Farm had put all of this and much more research together and decided to enter into the private banking business. Since one private group (the Fed) was issuing credit under the public debt money system, Family Farm, or those people, as principals could exercise their sovereign authority to issue their own credit, backed up by promises and other assets, reduce it to negotiable instruments and use their "Private Credit Money" to help people who were in distress to the parasitic bankers who steal people's collateral without risking one thin dime of their own just like the First National Bank of Montgomery did to Jerome Daly. They'll get more into that process later in chapter fifteen.

Family Farm, through its established 'credit' would issue a certified money order (C.M.O.) to its client who would in turn tender it for the discharge of the debt to the bank. The C.M.O. was in fact a negotiable order to pay. The bank would clear (redeem) the C.M.O. with Family Farm (the issuer of the private credit) who in turn would issue back to the bank a certified banker's check payable in 'money of account of the United States' (which has never been determined in law) or in the alternative, 'credit money' as per U.C.C. 1- 201(24).

The bankers would do their usual bookkeeping and enter one of those deposited negotiable instruments as an asset to the bank which in turn would enhance their electronic demand deposits and thus allowed them to receive more cash or credit from the Fed.

So this private credit money plugged right into the public debt money system. Should the banker's refuse the private negotiable instrument for any reason and return it to the issuer, by law the debt is discharged anyway according to the U.C.C. (Uniform Commercial Code) wherein

'an offer to pay in full, which is refused, is a debt paid by law.'

Rex had seen several payoff letters from banks and mortgage companies and heard of many more. It seemed like a perfect way to help people who were in distress at the hands of the bankers. This knowledge was extremely powerful!

Based upon the thorough research of the originators of the program at Family Farm and some additional research Rex did on his own, he began setting up a system to assist people with the process. It didn't take long at all, once word got out, before people came knocking at Rex's door.

Some creditors were stubborn. Some were ignorant. These sometimes required a series of letters advising them of the legalities for processing the instruments which were tendered and the liabilities they might incur if they didn't. There were some instances where they had a standoff and threats were flying in both directions. All comers into this endeavor needed to be prepared for a fight.

On the other hand, several people got their payoff letters promptly and of course this stirred quite a bit of excitement.

This knowledge was catching on nationwide and it spread like a Kansas grassfire on a windy day. It wasn't long before the bankers figured out that their monopoly on the money system was over if this kept up. They knew they had to do something to crush their newfound competition. Since the peoples' victories were based on the truth of the monetary fraud of the Fed system, truth wasn't a weapon they could use.

They had to turn to their usual tactics of demonization through the media and intimidation through the law enforcement/judicial/government channels. Newspaper and magazine articles started appearing warning people about this 'money order scam' that was going around. People were being told through the prostitute media mouthpieces that they would go to jail for fraud if they got involved!

Local district attorneys' offices were sending out investigators and deputies to make personal visits to the participants in the program, (Rex's clients) advising them through thinly veiled threats of prosecution and of bad things that would happen if people didn't back off.

Of course, when challenged by the creditors, through lack of conviction and lack of knowledge some people using the system buckled immediately from fear. Several were approached by scared authorities and under threat of police action, agreed to try and set up the Family Farm people and induce them into doing something illegal to take a fall.

By this time another group had sprung up with a more professional information package. Their C.M.O.'s had routing numbers in magnetic ink at the bottom and they were reportedly working with a Panama Bank to back up their credit with gold reserves. This group was 'U.S.A. First' in Waxahachie, Texas.

As the hammer began to fall on these resourceful, self-reliant Americans both offices of Family Farm and U.S.A. First were raided by the F.B.I. Computers were taken along with all the files and paperwork the Feds could carry out. These so called 'criminals' were being put out of business.

A very interesting point remains today, if this was such a criminal enterprise, why were none of the people who were subject to the raids at Family Farm and U.S.A. First arrested and indicted on any criminal charges at that time? That's right! Before you start screaming 'scam', nobody was arrested! What does that tell you?

Their offices were ransacked and burglarized by the F.B.I. but nobody was arrested during the raid! The events more resembled a mob suppression tactic than anything.

Demonization Begins

On the local front, the controlled media was the initial weapon of choice to be used against Rex personally to stop this 'phenomenon'. On Rex's way in to the office one day he was jumped by John Ferrugia, an investigative reporter for the local Channel 7 TV news and his camera crew.

Ferrugia immediately jumped him in the parking lot and started asking him very biased and slanted 'attack' questions about 'bogus' money orders and stuck a microphone and camera in Rex's face in full ambush mode. Rex calmly and politely explained to him that if he would have the common decency to ask for an appointment, he would be happy to grant an interview and spend up to a couple of hours with him if necessary so he could get a complete grasp of the issues for his story. Rex told him specifically that the camera was not invited as these issues were too complicated to properly convey the truth in a few short sound bytes, which was surely all they would use.

Ferrugia declined the offer saying he didn't have the time and especially wouldn't do it without a camera. Well, so much for investigative news which is committed to bringing people the truth about a 'real story'. Evidently Channel 7, a division of McGraw Hill Inc., had their own idea about what this story was going to be about (before getting the facts) and Rex was going to be the cannon fodder for them to make their own point to protect 'the system'.

Ferrugia tried to salvage some respectability and honor for himself by telling Rex he would call him and review the facts with him, allowing him to give input on any incorrect facts before they ran the story. He said he wasn't sure if it would run anyway. Right! Ferrugia was there for a reason and it wasn't to 'find' a story. It did run and as expected, it was a 'hit piece' designed to smear Rex and discredit him in public. Of course Ferrugia never called as he promised. So much for the integrity and honor of this media minion!

It was the headline story done in segments, two nights in a row on the 10:00 o'clock news. According to Ferrugia this national phenomena of 'fraud' was solely instigated and perpetrated by Freeman who was selling 'bogus checks" to poor unsuspecting souls who sometimes had nowhere else to turn in their troubles. The implication was that by Rex's cold calculating criminal nature, he would take advantage of anybody for a buck.

This is what they do when the facts and the law don't support them. They vilify, castigate and marginalize you in the public eye so that you become an 'undesirable' and people shun you. It works! You see it all the time with whistleblowers and purveyors of truth who are not 'friendly' to the power structure.

One young couple was desperate and came to Rex with their last $500. They were prepared to give it to him for help. They were days away from eviction in a foreclosure proceeding. Rex refused to accept all but $100 which didn't even cover Rex's costs. His thinking was that if this didn't work; they would need money to move. Rex was not going to leave them penniless if his solution didn't work. He wouldn't do that.

On the other hand, if Rex's services did work to at least buy them some time, the agreement was that they would then pay the balance of the $500 which was less than one payment they already owed anyway.

Additionally, he recommended a low cost legal services plan they should utilize to enlist additional legal help as he didn't pretend to have all of the answers and he was dealing with real people in a critical situation. They didn't get the legal help he suggested, but Rex's efforts did buy them valuable time to save up and make alternate living arrangements before things did finally cave in on them. They were weak and not good fighters.

They were too desperate to make good decisions and didn't follow through on the process. They never paid him as agreed and Rex was out hard money costs and time for what he did, not to mention how he was ravaged on T.V. by their friend Ferrugia. But They were successful to an extent in buying them some time and he chalked it up to doing a good deed.

Ferrugia interviewed the crying spouse at her place of work and made it look like Rex was responsible for taking all their money and the loss of the house. That's what you get sometimes for trying to help people.

Shortly after this fiasco Rex learned that a District Attorney in Washington County was preparing a 31 count indictment for fraud against him. Rex called him and arranged for an appointment to come in to his office and set the record straight.

Rex showed up at the D.A.'s office with his fellow law student friend Kelly who was to be a witness for him. For backup, they placed a micro recorder in a small camera bag and let it run just prior to entering the D.A.'s offices. They were greeted by a stern looking, pudgy stiff who called himself a deputy District Attorney in charge of the investigation. They were led to a small conference room in the back.

They sat down; the camera bag was placed on top of the table between Rex and the deputy D.A. The mood was tense, with the District

Attorney on one side of the table, Rex's friend Kelly and he on the other. It was 50/50 that he could be arrested right there on the spot.

Rex established his purpose for the meeting which was to learn more about the basis for their investigation and set the record straight. The D. A. Neal, followed with his remarks. He was cleverly cajoling Rex for admissions and confessions. Rex wasn't giving any. Neal was cajoling him for indications of an unlawful conspiracy. Rex wasn't giving any. Since neither one of them wanted to talk, it was slow going.

Then, Neal challenged the camera bag. He demanded, "What do you have in the bag, a tape recorder?"

Kelly responded, "I have an expensive camera. I didn't want to leave it in the car." To call his bluff Kelly started reaching for the bag as if to offer it for inspection, and asked, "Do you want to see it?" The D.A. didn't respond affirmatively and Kelly stopped short of opening it. The bag stayed put with tape rolling.

Neal wasn't getting anywhere in establishing illegal conspiracy and he wasn't getting any closer to any breakthrough on a few key issues. Rex proceeded to set the record straight on the law versus the actions involved and the DA didn't agree with him at all. This meeting wasn't going anywhere so the only thing for him to do was to get up and see if he'd be able to walk out of there without getting arrested.

They got up. Rex dropped a stack of legal research papers on the table and said, "you might be interested in understanding the law before you proceed against me. I suggest you read it. This is your good faith notice. I'd hate to see anybody get into trouble for false arrest or worse". Rex held his breath as they started to walk toward the door and out of the enemy camp. You never know what to expect.

Neal was obviously agitated that he didn't control the meeting and that he was unable to intimidate either one of them. This in itself was worth making the visit, just for fun! They made their way through the office toward the exit. On the way out Neal followed them and made a comment, "We'll be in touch as soon as we get the grand jury indict-ment, you fraud!"

They stopped dead in their tracks and turned around. Rex took two steps back toward him and was standing nose to nose. Neal was smaller than Rex and it was like being at a baseball game watching the manager and umpire getting in each other's faces.

Rex replied, "We know you're not interested in justice when you can trump up a conviction using your machine. You just read that law of yours, and if you continue on this path, we'll be glad to raise all kinds of 'fun' issues in Federal court which you will then be famous for, around the world! Bring it on Neal! We'll get our justice in Federal Court. Consider this notice!" Neal shut up backed off.

Rex and Kelly got out of there in a hurry, looking over our shoulders for a sheriff's deputy the entire way.

Neal **never** pressed charges on any of those 'alleged' 31 counts in-volving the 'money issue' and the C.M.O.s.

PRIZE CAPTURED

Rex had met the dragon head on in the dragon's lair and walked away unscathed. The crusade for truth and for providing assistance to the victims of the bankers' debt virus continued.

However, Rex felt handicapped. He has always felt that any sort of 'preacher' needs to walk the talk and lead by example. Rex wanted to prove the system himself and lead by his own example. The problem was that he had virtually no bank debt to liquidate of his own.

It was time to get creative. For demonstration purposes it would be nice to have something tangible and visible for people to see and leave a visual impression. With some assistance from a new found friend named Bruno, he decided to find someone who wanted to get out from underneath the payments on a nice car. Rex needed a company car anyway. Rex's business was called National Consumer Advocates and he had assembled a portfolio of financial, credit, and legal services in what was primarily a credit and financial consulting operation.

He had established a nationwide customer base by buying out another small credit repair operation in Utah which had national advertising and calls coming in regularly on a toll free number. So travel was inevitable and a reliable company car a necessity. The strategy was now clear.

After scouring the papers for a week or so Bruno found a couple of situations that were appropriate. Bruno was German and had sold Mercedes Benz cars in Europe. Since he was partial, and now interested in backing Rex's new operation, they looked exclusively at Mercedes as a matter of preference. Bruno got no argument from Rex.

The first situation they looked at was from a young entrepreneur who was getting divorced and needed out from his banknote on a beautiful 4-door midnight black 550 SL. They entered into a contract to transfer the property only upon successful discharge of the debt. They tendered a private credit instrument to the seller's bank which was negotiable at U.S.A. First in Waxahachie, Texas. Surprisingly the bank actually followed the instructions for redemption and proper routing, which was NOT to deposit the instrument in the local bank, but to send the C.M.O. for redemption by FedEx to U.S.A. First. Unfortunately, the day that U.S.A. first received and signed for the Certified Money Order (CMO), they were raided by the Feds. The C.M.O. was confiscated along with the contents of the entire office in Texas. They didn't realize it at the time but it was a dead letter issue. Several inquiries were made at the Seller's bank as to the delay. Finally after Rex and Bruno discovered the mud, they decided to abandon plan A on that particular car. Later the seller of the car was able to say that the CMO was bogus because the attempt at redemption was never honored. What could they do?

Since no arrests were made during the raid, despite the handicap of being without their computers, etc., U.S.A. First was back in business the next day. Files had to be reconstructed with the help of U.S.A.'s clients but that was a minor speed bump.

Rex and Bruno moved on to plan B, a beautiful 'signal red' four door 190 E with leather seats, sun roof, great tunes and all the extras.

Rex drew up another contract with the seller. It was agreed upon and signed.

They tendered a CMO as per the agreement, to the clients' finance company which was Mercedes Benz Credit Corp. They received the CMO with specific instructions and accepted it. They then released the lien, sent clear title, and all related paperwork to the seller who lived in Kansas. The seller called Rex up and told him he'd be over to Denver in two days with the car and the papers according to the agreement.

BINGO! They not only had a beautiful company car, but proof positive that the People could in fact break the Federal Reserve's monopoly on the money system. Private credit and private banking would free America from the usury and financial slavery of the elitist international bankers. They were beating the big boys at their own game. It could only be divine providence!

Sneak Attack

The revenue enforcement agents for the bankers tried to use the media to demonize and vilify Rex with manufactured public opinion. That didn't work. Rex's clientele kept growing. They used threats and intimidation against him with the local District Attorney. Rex knew the truth, stared down the D.A. and didn't budge. As an old middle linebacker who conquered the commercial jungles of West Africa, he looks forward to a good fight now and then, especially when he knows he is properly equipped to win!

The next effort from the cabal was to contact some of Rex's clients, intimidate the hell out of them and get them to roll over and come against Rex with testimony, be it real or imagined. There were several clumsy attempts to lure Rex out of the office to meetings in a 'controlled environment' which was set up where he would be tricked into saying or doing illegal acts. Rex could always see them coming and he stayed clear. That didn't work. Of course these clients were the ones who paid the big bucks for a quick fix and were looking for freebies. They came to him based on greed, not need and didn't grasp the big picture in the first place. They had used up a majority of Rex's support services (and expense) and then bailed out in the middle of the process before seeing it to its proper conclusion.

These clients 'quit' and all wanted full refunds of what they paid before fulfilling their obligations to follow through. It wasn't right. It didn't make sense. They didn't deserve the refunds and the funds were used so he didn't have the money to pay them at the time anyway. However, under the circumstances, it was the only thing to do. Surely Rex's enemies anticipated Rex's reluctance to cave in to the client demands, what with him being a somewhat stubborn fighter and having strong principles. So they figured the deal would go down like this: he wouldn't give the refunds and they would try to nail him on some sort of deceptive trade practices charges just like they did Phil & Marlene Marsh. Rex saw that one coming.

So he sold the beautiful red Benz for F.R.N.s and made arrangements to pay the suckers for the refunds that they didn't deserve. But he got the last laugh. Once again, he thwarted the enemy using the law on 'money' and 'private credit' and was still loose on the street recklessly spreading truth and justice to anyone who would listen.

"Throw that noose around the stump boys, there'll be no hangin' today. I'm going home!"

CHAPTER 10

AID AND ASSIST

ABOUT THIS SAME TIME, REX had met and developed a close friendship with a Gary Woodland. Gary is a fervent brother in Christ who founded an educational self-help organization similar to A.L.C. called American Freedom Resources. While he was involved in helping people on many issues including personal sovereignty, travel, taxes, allodial ownership to private property, etc. His primary focus was on spreading the news on the '*farm claims program*' and helping people who wanted to participate, complete their paperwork.

Let's review a little background on the Farm Claims Program. The following was Rex's understanding of the history of the farm claims program which has evolved into NESARA (The National Economic Security & Reformation Act) which you can research yourself online.

Two farmers/businessmen, J. B. Foster and William Baskerville were being foreclosed on back in the early eighties by one large bank and the Farm Credit System (FCS). The defendants naturally fought to save their farm. In the process they uncovered some surprises which turned out to be fraud and the 'defense' against foreclosure then turned into an 'offensive' against the perpetrators.

Congress established the Farm Credit System in 1916 to provide a reliable source of credit for the nation's farmers and ranchers. Today, the FCS provides more than one-third of the credit to many of those who live and work in rural America.

When Foster and Baskerville ran out of money the attorneys abandoned the case leaving them to continue on their own.

They were in and out of court during most of the eighties with various ups and downs along the way.

In the early 1990s they met up with Roy Swasinger who began to help them in their cause. With his help they then began to make some progress. At some point they filed a new action to force an involuntary chapter 7 bankruptcy on the Farm Credit system after previously winning damages that were not paid.

The Farm Credit System defended themselves in the action by saying that they were not a private business, but were instead a Federal Agency and therefore not eligible for bankruptcy and liquidation. The Judge agreed and dismissed the forced bankruptcy case.

The judge was right, you will not find the Farm Credit System registered to do business as a private corporation in any State or with the Federal Government. They searched the records for the numerous names which the FCS has used in its business dealings with their borrowers. They found nothing. They searched the Secretary of State offices in a number of states. The Farm Credit System is not filed in any of them.

This would mean that in law, they had no legal standing to bring a case in any of these jurisdictions and should not have been able to use any State Court to foreclose on anyone, which was done on numerous occasions. Any foreclosures they caused were illegal and null and void. Imagine the damages!

This, however, is not the issue we are discussing here. According to information in the Congressional Record, when the FCS was created by congress they were to be *only* a loan *guarantor* to the bank making the loan. They were *never* to loan money directly to the farmer. This was never changed by congress.

Once this was determined and well established the people involved in the original FCS cases went to court with these and other documents to seek significant damages.

All these cases to date were civil cases. No one involved on the farmers' side ever filed or attempted to file a criminal case. *However, the District Court Judges had evidence of a crime before their bench and they caused a criminal case to be filed.* That case number is 93-1308-M. There was another civil case filed at the same time as the criminal complaint.

The 93-1308-M case was huge with several hundred pages in the docket sheet (index of the case).

During the time that all this was going on, the government had lost several of the earlier cases which had been appealed and they lost the appeals as well. They saw the writing on the wall and came to the table with an offer to settle.

So let's look at what was agreed to in the settlement and why:

When the fourteenth amendment was adopted there were two attachments to it that most people are not aware of.

One of those attachments was a onetime payment to anyone who filed from either side of the civil war that had suffered damages to their property as a result of the fighting. Obviously the cause for filing on this attachment is long passed.

The second attachment was a one-time filing and payment to anyone who suffered damages as a result of our Federal Government failing to protect the citizens of the several states from harm or damages by a foreign government. This is the attachment that 'the claim' is based on. Most people are not aware of these attachments and that is due to the fact that President Grant at the time had the two attachments sealed.

By an act of divine providence they were led to this discovery. Just because they are sealed does not mean they are still not valid. So the claim was based on the fact that a foreign government had damaged us as citizens of the several states. That foreign government is the corporate UNITED STATES which we've discussed previously.

When the *Trading with the Enemy Act* was modified and signed by President Roosevelt on March 9, 1933 the citizens of the several states were classified as enemies of the Federal corporation called the UNITED STATES.

That was the basis of the claim and the agreement by the Federal Government to the claim is proof that they agree to the premise.

Since an agreement was reached by the parties in an out of court settlement, the Judge had to agree to the claim. He did and then the resulting agreement was sealed.

That means we can talk about the settlement and show the claim which is the result, but we cannot show the court record of this without violating the terms of the agreement.

The result of all this court action was that we now had an agreement on a claim that could be filled out by the claimant. Claimants were able to seek recourse for damages caused by: 'foreign law', any interaction in the banking system due to the false weights and measures of the Federal Reserve system and the fiat currency, any foreclosures, judgements, penalties, jail time, loans at usury, and the list went on and on. The sums claimed for damages were huge.

One of the items that had been negotiated away when reaching the settlement was the right to put this information on the major TV networks, which was what was originally planned.

Therefore, the only way to publicize this agreement was to have meetings across the country. It was in this process that Rex became actively involved and met Gary when he was involved in the meetings and helping folks prepare and submit their claims.

The claims process had three major objectives.

First, the banks would be required to go back on lawful currency (gold and silver) as the Constitution requires. This had to be done because the agreement required that the claim be paid in lawful currency not legal tender. Please do not say there is not enough gold because that is not true. What this will do though is eliminate all inflation.

Second, the courts would all be required to go back to common law (versus the gold fringed flag Admiralty Law) as the Constitution specifies. This would mean that we get back to the idea that if there is no

*damage or harm there is no violation of law and much of the creation of
millions of laws to control people would be eliminated.*

*Third, the IRS would be disbanded and a constitutionally proper
tax (sales or transfer tax) would be created and implemented. The people
who were involved in the court cases and the settlement of the details of
the farm claim knew that if these three things were accomplished then the
Federal System would soon be brought back under control and its size and
power reduced to what is prescribed by the Constitution.*

Now with the facts, the law and the fraud established, the stage was
set for the **Farm Claims Program** to get 'legs'.

In addition to the large regional meetings being held by some of the
leaders like, Scott Hildebrand, Joe Mentlick, Roy Swasinger et al, Gary
began holding his own meetings for education and support on a local
basis. Gary's local meetings would generally attract groups of twenty or
thirty or more and they were gaining in popularity.

Of course this activity is nothing more than a peaceful and lawful assembly. Its only purpose was to petition (file a claim) for redress
of grievances against our agents in government for damages incurred
against the people by way of fraud and the exercise of extra jurisdictional, 'ultra-vires' (lack of) authority. It is fully protected by the First
Amendment to the Constitution.

Now the claims writers, who made themselves available to assist the
people, were required to go through a training and certification process which gave them the required technical knowledge to do their job
properly.

The filing of a claim was also very time consuming and required
hands on consulting by a claims writer. In view of this commitment of
time and energy by the claims writer and the supporting organization,
voluntary donations were accepted. The suggested donation was $300
from which the actual claims writer kept only $100 which was nomi-
nal for the time and energy put in. The balance was split between the

regional coordinator and the national organization for educational seminars, travel and a myriad of operating expenses. Nobody was getting rich doing this, that's for sure.

Rex knew many people personally who had put in a claim and he was one himself. The prevailing attitude was that this whole program was a $300 lottery ticket. It might pan out. It might not. In any event, most people felt that the education gained in the process made the fee worthwhile regardless.

However, there were many people who didn't have the $300. Yet the claims writers he knew, helped them with their claims anyway. They expended a lot of time and energy in doing so because they believed in what they were doing; helping people and building a mandate to return this country back to an honest representative form of government.

This single fact alone, being one of many, dispels much of the controversy and all the cries of fraud surrounding the Farm Claims Program. Of course whenever sensitive issues of truth threaten the house of cards built by personal privateers in public capacity, the investigations, public demonization and intimidation begin.

Infiltration & Fraud

The Attorney General's Office for THE STATE OF COLORADO began an investigation which included sending an investigator named Bob Clayman as an undercover agent with the assumed name of Bob Carson. He mixed in with Gary's group and ultimately ended up in Gary's home to file a claim.

Of course the entire investigation was commenced without a single complaint from the public, thereby making it unlawful from the beginning. You see, in organic (common) law, there can be no crime without a damaged party (corpus dilicti). In this case they were dealing with statutory (corporate) code and the alleged crime was a 'victimless crime against the state'. Threatening them with 'truth' was the apparent crime.

Clayman and his cohorts assembled a Multi-Jurisdictional Task Force (M.J.T.F.) consisting of sheriffs' departments from Washington County, Adams, Arapahoe and Douglas Counties, the Colorado Bureau of Investigation (C.B.I.) and the local Parker Police among others. Clayman had all he needed to close in, which was nothing. He had Patty Putin write up what they called an affidavit in support of a search warrant which was bogus from the 'get go' due to false and erroneous precepts of 'probable cause'.

First of all, Patty Putin is a sheriff's deputy from Washington County which is fifty miles and three counties removed from Gary's home in Douglas County. Washington County, its court and deputies have absolutely no jurisdiction in Douglas County.

Secondly, Putin's affidavit was not sworn to under the penalties of perjury. An ancient maxim of law states that with 'no risk' a statement carries no authority.

Third, it was not sworn to in accordance with the three point oath, being; true, correct and complete. Telling deceptive half-truths is the equivalent to telling whole lies.

Fourth, she had no 'firsthand knowledge' of the facts she alleged. All the information came from Clayman, not Putin who signed the so called, affidavit. If it's 'hearsay' it's not an affidavit, it's 'gossip'.

Fifth, she had no legal grounds which established any probable cause for suspicion of criminal activity. She merely checked off a box on a form saying 'grounds existed' for probable cause of criminal activity but no facts or supporting information were established.

Sixth, the so called warrant didn't contain a bona fide, original signature from a judge. It appeared to be a rubber stamp which could have been used by a clerk, a janitor or possibly even a deputy. Sakes alive imagine that!?!

Seventh, when the warrant was served the alleged affidavit was not attached which would show its subject or occupant the probable cause and legal grounds for the search. A warrant without affidavit is like a shoe without laces. It doesn't work!

In other words the search warrant was issued unlawfully due to a defective "affidavit' and insufficient grounds with incomplete law, incompetent jurisdiction and no firsthand knowledge of any alleged crime. In fact it wasn't even qualified as a poor affidavit. It was nothing more than an unsworn declaration of hearsay information, which even if accurate, did not establish any reason to believe that a crime had been, or was about to be committed. This is how they operate these days.

If this wasn't appalling enough, Clayman and Putin got it issued as a 'no knock' warrant. This classification authorized the goon squad to bust into the house unannounced with heavily armed jack booted thugs to terrorize the occupants with force and the element of surprise. No knock warrants are used typically in dangerous situations against known criminals who are armed and dangerous.

Now Gary is a humble Christian man and he is also quite small. He is lucky to stand four feet six inches tall. He had no criminal history whatsoever. His quiet wife and two sons of five and seven years old hailing from rural Indiana certainly fit the profile of a dangerous terrorist gang, don't they?

So good ol' gung ho Patty Putin took a nice little afternoon drive over to Douglas County with her *warrant*. She marshalled her M.J.T.F. troops in Parker and prepared to move in with a frontal assault to establish a Beachhead at 4643 Applewood Court in Parker. She was determined to take down the infamous and certainly troublesome 'Gary Gang' no matter how much firepower and manpower it took! Who knows, she and Clayman could earn themselves the distinguished Washington County medal of honor for heroic valor in such an intricate and risky operation!

The goon squad of twelve or more backed Patty up when she served the warrant. Gary had guests in the house at the time. The M.J.T.F. proceeded to forcefully enter and ransack the house taking anything that wasn't nailed down or perishable; computers, files, address books, phones, books, business equipment, research papers, pamphlets, flyers, lists, disks, manuals, personal files and papers, family pictures, private family documents, finance statements, bank account documents, correspondence, note pads, blank forms, office supplies, etc., etc., etc.

Fortunately for the search party, they found some cash and jewelry in one of the guest's private purse so the booty made their time a little more worthwhile. The Woodlands were told it was probably *unlawfully obtained* even though the guest wasn't a subject of the search warrant. Who worries about details when you have a bogus warrant, a badge and a gun? The pickings don't get any easier than this!

After several hours of sorting and boxing their loot, the M.J.T.F. packed up and headed out without pressing any charges! Now think about it. If they seized property then there must be evidence indicating probable cause to suspect criminal activity, thus warranting an arrest. If no arrest, then it would follow that there was no probable cause for seizure. What's missing in this picture? Logic leads us to only one conclusion: the only purpose for the pirates' raid was to put Gary out of business by wiping him and his family out under 'color of law'.

Of course the Woodlands were left in fear, shock and total dismay. One can only imagine the lasting emotional trauma this left on the young children having just witnessed their parents being held at gunpoint while a gang of strangers hauled out nearly half of what they owned. So much for that comforting sense of security in house and home.

It is a sad commentary on the state of our once great land of liberty when the citizens of America have become so comfortable in our ignorance and indifference that we have allowed this blatant abuse of power and authority to become such a common *modus operandi* for our public servants.

The question is then raised: Who is the government? And also: Who are the real terrorists that affect us day in and day out?

Gary knew full well what the answers were and immediately went to work. He called Rex and several others on the phone and after apprising him of the gory details of the atrocity, they agreed to meet with him and his brain trust to develop a plan of action.

Pursuing Lawful Recourse

The first thing they did was to try to get a copy of Putin's so called affidavit, which of course was not attached to the warrant nor was it freely given to Gary as it should have been. Since there was no case yet in the courts it was not available there. It took some doing but it was ultimately obtained. Once they examined it they found the obvious flaws. If it weren't such an affront to American jurisprudence and freedom it would have been laughable.

Once they had determined the unlawful nature of the seizure, a petition for a 'writ of replevin' was prepared for the return of the unlawfully held property. Gary filed this in Douglas County court since the raid was done under the supervision of local police and this should have been the court to issue any warrant in Douglas County in the first place. It had the proper jurisdictional authority.

Instead of assuming its lawful jurisdiction over the matter, the Douglas County court judge backed off and dismissed the petition for writ of replevin, without lawful cause. One can only speculate but it appeared that as soon as the judge saw the M.J.T.F. "Made in the Colorado Attorney General's Office" label, he timidly allowed his jurisdiction to be usurped in deference to Washington County. Whatever happened to our bold, courageous and lawful judiciary? My God! What a sad state of affairs.

Gary continued in his efforts in Washington County (WashCo). He was shut down again. He sent letters, demands, requests and notices of unlawful seizure to everyone he could think of including the Attorney General's office, all to no avail.

If he couldn't get the replevin heard by a county judge he certainly would never get a district attorney to follow through on a criminal complaint filed against their own 'business brokers' and 'marketing agents', the police, sheriff's and/or A.G. This is what is known as 'selective prosecution'.

The net result was that Gary had been shut out of the state court/legal system. He was denied his rights to lawful redress of grievances and basically was finding out that he had no legal recourse to defend his rights, property and peace for his family.

After numerous good faith attempts at reason, logic and good law, it was time to crank up the heat. With a little input from several corners of his camp, Gary decided on a pincer movement. (military strategy for hitting the opponent from two opposite sides at once.)

Since his constitutionally protected, God given rights had been violated under color of state law by actions of the state Attorney General, a federal civil rights lawsuit under Section 1983 of Title 42 of the U.S. Code was appropriate. It is ultimately the responsibility of the citizens to ensure that our public servants in law enforcement are also law abiding as we see in the case decision in Wood v. Breir 54 F.R.D. 7 (1972) which elaborates on the concept that citizens are able to act as a 'Private Attorney General' to bring cases which are in the public interest more so than just in the interest of the plaintiff. Correcting illegal behavior by public officials would qualify, don´t you think?

With a little teamwork Gary put the complaint together and filed the lawsuit in U.S. District Court, 10th Circuit in Denver. This was the hit on the left flank.

The pincer hit on the right flank was to come in the form of a standard presentment in commerce. To understand this, let's look at an example of a common commercial presentment.

Example: When the I.R.S. sends you a NOTICE OF TAX DEFICIENCY. They give you NOTICE in GOOD FAITH of what they think you owe. You then have a GRACE PERIOD, usually 90, 30, or 10 days to do one of three things:

1) Agree and make arrangements to pay, or
2) Dispute the amount and demand a hearing where you would bring your evidence to support your position and have the dispute adjudicated, or
3) Do nothing and default on the grace period. Your silence, or failure to object, by the end of the grace period is construed as consent to the amount owed and they proceed to collect regardless of what you may say afterwards. In law, *silence is consent* and *failure to object is fatal*.

This process embodies the common law doctrine of NOTICE & GRACE. When a person says nothing in his own defense' this is what's known as 'nil dicit' (Latin). In this case a *judgment nil dicit* occurs and the defendant convicts himself by his silence when he should have said something in his own defense. This doctrine is embodied in the U.C.C. (Uniform Commercial Code) and is used every day in commerce by bankers, collectors, attorneys, etc.

Gary's presentment to the A.G. and a list of other co-conspirators amounted to $25,000,000 in actual, compensatory and punitive damages based primarily on violations of rights, violations of oath of office, breach of public trust, etc., multiplied by the number of occurrences for each violation times the number of people involved times the specific dollar amount attached to each offense. It adds up quickly.

Each person Gary named in his presentment would be attached in his/her personal capacity should the presentment mature against them. Since the U.C.C. allows the parties to a contract to choose the law applicable to the contract (U.C.C. 1-105) Gary chose the common law or the court of public opinion wherein any rebuttal by the A.G., et al, would have to be by an affidavit sworn to under the penalties of perjury addressing each allegation point for point. Anything less is default. Of course when your original presentment/complaint is legitimate they can't meet the burden of proof and always lose by default. So typically errant officials either just;

a. Laugh it off out of ignorance or arrogance,
b. Hope it goes away, or
c. Attack with threats, intimidation and various forms of coercion to get you to back off.

As per our expectations, all of the defendants/debtors in commerce defaulted on Gary's presentments and judgment nil dicit occurred. Gary sent each party a *Notice of Default* and in good faith offered another grace period for them to correct the problem which they could do by simply returning the stolen property and restoring him to whole again, or citing the law which supported their position (impossible). They refused to respond and defaulted again despite Gary's good faith effort.

Gary was then forced to start initiating the lien process. He now had a bona fide 'judgment nil dicit' for $25,000,000 on numerous individuals from the local police department in Parker through several judges, sheriff departments all the way to the state Attorney General. He went down to the County Clerk and Recorder office to file, not an actual lien itself, but a 'Notice of Lien' to publicly record the fact that these events have occurred and that further action was pending.

Meanwhile back in Federal Court, with the Title 42 lawsuit filed, the defendants returned the volley. They filed a rule 12(b)(6) motion to dismiss which is a standard knee jerk reaction by governmental agents who try to assert that the plaintiff has failed to state a complaint upon which relief can be granted. It is essentially a trick to get you arguing their case instead of your own. If you traverse to their argument the judge has the authority to roll them both into one and dismiss the whole thing.

The ball was now back in Gary's court and he needed to respond to the 12(b)(6) motion in his Federal suit. He also was in the process of preparing to file his remaining paperwork to complete the lien process. He was in a strong position and the pincer move was looking formidable and likely to be effective.

A Second Assault

That was until Patty Putin, the M.J.T.F., the A.G.'s office et al, decided to launch another assault. They raided the 'Woodland Gang' a second time without warning. As they forced their way into the house little 5 year old Matthew ran upstairs to his dad, screaming in a panic, "Someone's broken into the house daddy, someone's broken into the house!"

As any responsible father and head of household would do, he grabbed a shotgun out of the closet and started downstairs to protect his home and family. As he started downstairs, because he ' hadn't had time to put in his contact lenses, he grabbed the stairway banister with his right hand. He held the shotgun in his left hand by the pump grip on the barrel and it was pointed straight up at the ceiling in a non-threatening fashion as he made his way down the stairs.

Of course, by this time the first floor was crawling with the same goons from the first raid that calls themselves law officers. As Gary descended the stairs, he was nearly blown away in front of his family by up to six lethal weapons all cocked and aimed right at him. Of course, as these scenarios usually come down, there was a tremendous amount of screaming, yelling and confusion which just added to the terror of the poor family standing by helplessly in horror that 'Dad' was about to be riddled with bullets. The screams came from the goons, "Put down the gun or we'll shoot!" "Police!" "Drop it," from one and "lay it down gently" from another.

Now, finally realizing what the situation was, Gary thought to himself, "here we go again." As soon as he submitted, several goons pounced on him and threw him down face first on the floor with a knee in his back. It was here that he remained while the government thugs proceeded to ransack his house, once again.

They stole virtually everything Gary had in the first raid. What could they possibly want now? You guessed it, they came back to cripple his lawsuit and lien by stealing anything and everything related to his lawful efforts to pursue justice and obtain some peace. They got all of his original documents, legal research, rule books, sample templates, etc., Gary had gotten a nice new computer to replace the first one they stole from him. They took that and a whole lot more.

Of course Gary had done nothing wrong to justify an arrest warrant, again, and since Gary had demolished their previous attempt to create a bogus warrant, they didn't even bother this time around. So they didn't have anything to even present.

While the family was sequestered as the MJTF team ransacked the house again, Karen needed to take the kids someplace and she asked if she could go. They said "yes". She then asked, "Is everything all right?" Will Gary be here when he get back?" They responded, "'Yes, everything will be fine They just need to complete our inventory and we'll be going on our way." So Karen left with the kids with a little peace of mind, very little.

While Karen was gone Gary heard Pat Putin tell another officer saying, No, you didn't see it that way, what you saw was Woodland aiming the gun at us in the ready position. Got it?" Once they got their story straight they arrested Gary for six counts of felony menacing on the basis that he threatened the officers with a deadly weapon (six officers were on the scene). How convenient. That's what you get these days for trying to protect your own home and family.

Karen came back home. The house was empty. Gary was gone. They lied.

While they now had Gary in custody they decided to go to the wall with him. The A.G.s office clearly manipulated a grand jury to extract a sixteen count indictment against him for filing false documents relating to the Notice of Lien and attempting to influence public officials.

Rex later obtained the minutes of the Grand Jury hearing. What they found was blatant distortion of the facts, half-truths, and manipulation of the jurors by an unlawful limiting of the scope of questions they were allowed to ask, and of course Gary was never invited to testify or present his evidence nor was anyone on his behalf. This type of misuse and abuse of our sacred checks and balances should make every red blooded American just absolutely sick to his stomach.

Think about it for a minute. If the people are prosecuted now for attempting to influence public officials to urge them to follow and abide by the law, only one question remains, to what level will the resulting tyranny and oppression rise to? Isn't threatening to use your vote one way or another an 'attempt to influence a public official'? Or how about calling your congressman to express your views on an issue? When did this become illegal?

Furthermore aren't our public officials actually our agents to do our bidding? As principals (We the people) it is our duty and ultimate responsibility to influence our agents. So now Gary is facing sixteen felony counts for doing his civic duty and trying to use all lawful means for redress of grievances? This doesn't include his six counts of felony menacing or the half dozen or so additional counts of fraud they were preparing for his involvement with the Farm Claims process.

Benjamin Franklin once said: "Man will ultimately be governed by GOD or by tyrants." Question: Which is it that governs us today?

POKING HIS HEAD UP

Gary was now in a very deep and dark hole. A series of advisement and preliminary hearings were set in both Douglas and Washington counties. The first one was on his felony menacing charges in Douglas County. Rex showed up for the hearing in the courtroom in Castle Rock to observe and be a first hand witness of any shenanigans that might go on there. We all know that once you start a story with a lie you can do nothing else but perpetuate it with more lies and deception. This was going to be interesting.

Gary was brought into the courtroom through the prisoner entrance was uncuffed by the deputy and sat down at the defendant's table. While they waited for the judge to enter the courtroom Gary saw Rex in the public gallery and signaled him to come up and talk to him which he did. While they discussed several procedural issues at the defendants table the judge suddenly entered and the bailiff commanded, "All rise." So Rex did, not attempting to move from the defendant's table. As they sat back down again the judge announced the case and the prosecutor entered his appearance for the record and announced himself as district attorney representing the state on this case and he introduced his associates at the table, of which there were several.

Gary entered his appearance for the record not as defendant but as the 'falsely accused' *sui juris,* (acting on his own behalf) not wishing to accept the premises established by the complaint to begin with.

Suddenly everyone was looking at Rex. He stood up and identified himself as Rex William, which was his given name, without Rex's family name and was consistent with the only I.D. that he carried which was his 'Sovereign Authority to Travel' card. After having done this he explained, "Judge I am here as assistance in counsel to Mr. Woodland." The judge replied, "'Mr. William, Are you a licensed attorney?" "No sir," he said. The judge came back, "Well if you're not a licensed attorney he can't allow you to act as counsel for Mr. Woodland, we'll have to ask you to leave."

This wasn't going very well and he objected. "Judge, I am not his 'counsel'. I am not here to represent Mr. Woodland nor to act in any capacity on his behalf. But as Mr. Woodland has no legal representation, I believe he is entitled to assistance whether it is administrative or otherwise."

By this time the deputy D.A. started into a loud tirade. They hate it when a foreigner (non-bar member) comes in to challenge them at their own game. "Judge, he can't be here, he's not a licensed attorney, We haven't been notified, he has no business being here, he's not a party to the action..." and he went on and on.

Rex looked over at his table and he had three or four assistants with pads, files, stacks of books, etc. Rex interjected into his little temper tantrum, "Judge, does the deputy D.A. complain because he only has Mr. Woodland outnumbered four to one on assistants? I believe that as a matter of right Mr. Woodland is entitled to at least one assistant to help him take notes, keep track of his papers and help keep him organized in order to help keep this not only an efficient hearing but also to preserve the appearance of an unbiased court that operates on a level playing field for all parties. The prosecutor is clearly being overzealous and unfair."

The judge responded, "You're right Mr. William, you may stay." Rex sat down and Gary and he exchanged low fives under the table. You could almost see the steam rising from the prosecutors table!

This was a preliminary hearing which is like a mini-trial where the prosecution needs to establish probable cause to the judge in order to proceed further toward trial. As a result, our friend Patty Putin and a series of Parker police officers took the stand to tell the 'story' of how

Gary had threatened all of their lives. The A.L.C. court observers made notes of the lies and gasped in disbelief, but it was the word of numerous law officers against Gary's. He had no witnesses on his behalf.

It went about as expected. By this time, they all had their story pretty tight. Gary did all he could do to set the record properly on all the issues. The bottom line was that the case was bound over to district court for trial.

A week later he was transferred to WashCo (Washington County) where they went through the same scenario all over again in his 16 count indictment case. This time he added a twist. Since WashCo jail only allows two normal visits from the public per week to inmates, Gary needed special dispensation if he was going to try to help him in any way. Rex needed unrestricted access to him.

Events unfolded almost identical to what happened in Douglas County. Rex was emboldened by that experience and requested that the judge issue an order to grant him unlimited attorney/client visiting privileges the same as any attorney would have. This sent the prosecutor into a very vocal, high energy tailspin. However, Rex stayed 'on point' with the argument focusing on Gary's rights to have assistance in his own defense. The judge graciously granted a court order for Rex and instructed the clerk to prepare the written court order for unlimited 'professional' visits for him, after the hearing.

Rex was an upstart and an unknown factor in the equation of oppression against Gary. Since he was not a licensed attorney they could not control him with threats against his license or the 'code of ethics' and all the standard 'protocols'. If the persecutors were unhappy with him sitting with Gary in the courtroom before, now with a court order in his hand allowing him to intervene at will, things were escalating in Rex's favor. He was putting unusual pressure on the operatives of 'the machine' and they weren't used to it!

This was to be the beginning of a whole new series of events. A new investigation was begun by Putin's cohort in the WashCo Sheriff Department, Mr. Don Esters.

AN INVESTIGATION BEGINS

After the hearing in WashCo Rex went to the clerk's office and waited for her to prepare the court order for visiting privileges. He immediately took it down to the jail to have a copy filed with the deputies at the visitors' entrance. He then went in to see Gary to help sort things out with him. While doing so, Esters was out in the parking lot inspecting Rex's car for defects hoping to find probable cause to pull him over on the way out.

This raises an interesting question. Isn't probable cause or at least reasonable suspicion of a crime required to begin an investigation as opposed to beginning an investigation with the purpose of trying to obtain some form of probable cause or reasonable suspicion?

Esters found what he was looking for, a cracked windshield. This would enable them to make contact with him and start putting some heat on Gary's 'mystery advocate'.

INITIAL CONTACT

When Rex came out of the jail from the visit and tried to leave the visiting area, it took an unusually long time for them to return the I.D. he gave them. You see, he had previously canceled all his contracts with the state, including Rex's state issued drivers license. Instead, he carried a very nice looking, private, 'Sovereign Authority to Travel' I.D. card which was nothing more than a statement of fact and law pertaining to Rex's rights to travel freely. It contained the usual photo and I.D. information on it. However, this I.D. only carried Rex's given name of Rex William. There was not enough room on the card for Rex's family surname and so he left it off. He did some legal research and was quite satisfied as to the lawful use of his unique given name and used it as such. It was truthful and not misleading.

While he waited in the jail reception, he knew there was a conversation going on in the back office regarding the issue. He could just feel it in his bones.

When they finally did come back and return it to him he was highly suspicious of a set up. He didn't go directly to the car. He stood outside and walked around for awhile as if waiting for a ride. He expected to see a police cruiser come sneaking up but it never came. He walked over to the bus stop and stood there for awhile. Nothing still.

Well, he had to go sometime. He thought to himself, 'now was as good as ever.'

He got in the car and drove down the hill. So far so good. He turned on the access road and then onto the street leading to the highway keeping an eye on his rear view mirror. It looked like he was in the clear as he got on the highway. Then all of a sudden, a cruiser appeared behind him out of nowhere and sure enough, on went the emergency lights. Rex pulled over, prepared his little electronic witness, mini-cassette recorder and prepared to have some fun!

What ensued was a 45 minute verbal volleyball game. The deputy who pulled him over was very open to what Rex had to say to him. He was a good guy, very professional and courteous which surprised and impressed Rex. He was actually expecting some jughead who was more interested in busting him up than anything, so it was a nice surprise to encounter a courteous professional. Through Rex's training in the club 'sessions' he was very adept at verbally maneuvering the officer into a position whereby he has a choice to make: either back off of the ticket and stop impeding Rex's liberty, or proceed to violate Rex's rights and leave himself wide open for damages in a Federal Title 42 civil rights lawsuit.

It was twenty minutes into the exchange and the deputy still had not gotten any documents from him. Rather than blindly produce all the paperwork they usually ask for, Rex wanted to know a few things which was his right to know. He started by asking very politely and with all due respect, who was he dealing with? In fact there was a sensational article in the news just the previous week about a criminal pulling cars over with an emergency light and then the criminal was impersonating an officer to rob the victims.

Rex also wanted to know: 'what was his authority?' He did request and receive his name and badge number which he provided him like a professional would be expected to. The deputy asked again for license, registration and insurance papers. What he got from Rex was another question: 'Officer what is your R.A.S.?' An officer must have 'Reasonable Articulable Suspicion' that a crime was committed or was about to be committed as the necessary threshold to have the basis to 'detain' anyone and impede their liberty. Rex learned this directly from the POLICE OFFICERS HANDBOOK published by the Colorado Law Officers Association. He had a copy in the law club! The deputy asked Rex curiously, "Are you an attorney?" Rex tried hard to keep from smiling because he knew he had the deputy 'on notice'. Whatever he was, he was not your normal 'sheeple' citizen and this was not a normal traffic stop.

Rex knew full well that this was an illegal 'pre-textual' stop. In other words, there was no valid basis to pull him over other than to poke around and see what they could find out. Rex wasn't playing along.

After some time of going around and around, Rex still had not produced his documents and had the deputy on the defensive. He could sense that the deputy was getting a little nervous or maybe just worn out and was coming close to his wits' end. To his credit, the deputy did maintain his professional posture at all times, which Rex respected him for. He went back to his car again to radio in probably the 'umpteenth question' and dispatch finally sent out a couple more units to the scene to put some weight into this situation and try to bring it to a head. Soon he had three units behind him and it was near dusk so the flashing lights lit the sky and it looked like a pretty big scene from the passerby's perspective.

Finally, after much friendly bantering with the newly arrived senior sergeant, he was satisfied that he had set the stage sufficiently to nullify whatever they wanted to do and Rex gave them his private Sovereign Authority I.D. card. which they just copied in the jail. He told the sergeant to read it carefully and check with his dispatch if he had any questions. (God no! Not the dispatch again!) Both deputies looked at it, looked at each other and had another discussion.

When the original officer finally reappeared he was prepared to issue him a ticket for driving without a license which he had all prepared and he presented it for Rex to sign. Rex asked him, "what is this, an invitation to a party?" He smiled, 'yeah, we just need you to sign to RSVP so we know you can come!" he replied, "Great! and what happens if I don't want to sign right now?" The deputy paused again. It seems nobody ever asked him this before. He came back with, "Well, I'll just sign it for you then", he said, Rex responded, 'Great! Please do!' He did and handed him the ticket with the deputy's signature, which under those circumstances, Rex agreed to take it. Fine! Done! In the end they had a very pleasant discourse which was amusing for both sides. The deputy made the comment directly to Rex: "This has probably been my most interesting stop". They parted cordially with mutual respect and Rex thanked the deputy for his patience. "See you at the party!" They both smiled and went on their way.

To back up a little bit, Rex's normal tact with the question: 'and what happens if I don't?' (sign) is to get them to threaten him or intimidate him with some comment like, 'I'll arrest you', or 'I'll impound your car' or something like that. It's better when they use flagrant language in an emotional manner like 'then I'll throw your ass in jail mister!". You can see the value in that on the tape recorder and possible future transcripts.

Then, with such **threats of force**, he can sign under 'threat and duress' and according to commercial code it is not a voluntary or willful signature so the intended contract (ticket) is not binding. With Rex's tape recorder going he would really play this up so it was very clear and repeated several times with no uncertain terms. The more emotion the better. Sometimes you can really get the young power-hungry jug heads going!

You see, since all 'traffic' is *commerce* and commerce is regulated by contracts, by signing the traffic ticket you would automatically be admitting jurisdiction for them to regulate your person in the realm of commerce when you aren't involved in commerce and they have no jurisdiction over your private, non-regulated activities. Further, once you sign the contract (ticket) you are accepting all kinds of stipulated assumptions and presumptions in the contract which you do not want sticking to you because they are usually not true.

The net product of the stop was twofold;

a) They issued a non-binding ticket (contract) on a private party for driving without a license (commercial activity) which is outside their scope of authority and jurisdiction and which was only signed by the issuing officer, (not Rex) therefore there was no agreement to its terms and they had imposed no new legal obligations on Rex whatsoever.

b) Rex had a cassette tape recording of the entire event!

Rex never traveled anywhere without his handy little electronic witness! You'll never guess what the topic of Rex's next radio show was going to be!   He was very excited and laughed all the way home.

The following Saturday Rex was in the studio. As the intro music drifted off, he came on the air, "'Ladies and Gentlemen, today we will explore techniques on how to render that traffic ticket NULL and VOID before the ink on it is even dry". He set the scene and prepared his listeners to pay close attention and take notes. He then went on and replayed key segments of the tape of his recent stop, on the air and often paused it to interject his comments and instructions throughout.

It wasn't until afterwards that he really realized the importance of what he had just done. He had just exposed to the world, on the broadcast airwaves, how to render law enforcement, or should he say 'the revenue enhancers' impotent in issuing traffic tickets and he used the proud N.W.O. WashCo as a crash test dummy for all the world to see. Visions of the sitcom character "ERKEL"' came to mind, "Oops, did I do that?"

With all Rex's travels to WashCo to help Gary, the cabal soon tagged him with another ticket for driving without a license, perhaps to send him a message that he was a marked man. When offered the U.C.C. presentment by the officer he immediately 'refused it' in writing 'for cause' being that it falsely implied a contractual liability with the presumptions that come with a traffic ticket i.e. that he is a member of the state corporation being *'resident'* or *'doing business in'* THE SATE OF COLORADO (corporate entity). Rex later returned his copy of the tickets back to the respective issuing officers along with his 'refusal for cause' letters pursuant to U.C.C. 3-501, and the written 'word for word' transcripts off of the audio tapes of the stops. This showed the federal liability of the officers for clearly violating constitutional rights. He beat both tickets.

To the corporate (state) revenuers this situation was intolerable! Here was this radio jock, 'Patriot', 'Johnny come lately' running circles around the so called 'professionals' and doing so very publicly. Something had to be done!

WORKING FROM THE INSIDE

The next time he showed up in court with Gary, as soon as the hearing was over the prosecutor announced to the judge, in the courtroom, that she had an arrest warrant for Rex and that they were going to arrest him there. The judge was very upset that she would bring that business into his courtroom and he started chastising her in public which Rex enjoyed. During their discourse, Rex quietly shoved his private papers and personal things over to a friend sitting nearby so they wouldn't fall into the wrong hands upon Rex's capture.

Rex stood up and approached the prosecutor and asked to see the warrant. What she handed him was a small slip of paper which was nothing more than a computer printout of two or three lines of computer printed text. It certainly was NOT a 'bona fide' warrant. And they were doing this right in the courtroom? Rex objected to the judge, but by this time the judge wanted nothing to do with this nonsense. The judge gave the prosecutor a tongue lashing for making such a scene in the courtroom and he then scurried out of there so as not to be seen as being complicit in an unlawful activity in his own courtroom! He knew what was going on and wanted nothing to do with it.

Surrounding the prosecutor were half a dozen deputies who were all standing at the ready by her side and in front of the door to block Rex's exit. They were trying to look very tough and formidable all standing very purposeful and rigid. They were ready to pounce on him in an instant given the slightest excuse.

Rex proceeded to advise the prosecutor and the deputies the problem they had with this so called warrant and the Federal liability they might incur if they tried to arrest him under 'color of law' without due process including proper paperwork.

They didn't care. They were on their turf and felt very comfortable. He was arrested on the spot for (drum roll) 'criminal impersonation.' he asked, "who am I impersonating, myself?" He didn't have much choice but to allow them to cuff him and put him under arrest. He was taken out the side door of the courtroom into the underground tunnels to the jailhouse to be processed.

He refused to submit to jurisdiction and did not cooperate in the booking process. They asked him to take off his clothes and get into an orange jump suit. He asked to see a proper arrest warrant and he verbally denied and challenged that they had any lawful authority to request anything of him and he respectfully and quietly refused. They had several deputies come over and physically restrain him while they removed his clothing against his will. They then wanted Rex's mug shot and finger prints and he again refused.

Rex would not voluntarily submit to an unlawful kidnapping without due process and he refused to take the mug shot. Realizing that the mug shot wouldn't do much good if they had 6 or 8 hands around Rex's face and head to hold him straight for the camera, they gave up on the idea and put him into a solitary holding cell. It was a concrete enclosure of about 8' by 4' and -contained nothing more than a hole in the floor to urinate in. It was a concrete box.

After some time they would check with him periodically to see if he was ready to complete the booking process. They figured that after enough time in solitary confinement without so much as a toilet to use, Rex might soften up. Rex continued his holdout. He wasn't going to volunteer into their jurisdiction without due process.

At that time of Rex's life he was in the Colorado Choir made up of mostly music professionals and it was an excellent choral group which he was honored to be a part of. So he started singing in the concrete box which echoed and reverberated throughout the entire section of jail there. He did the star spangled banner at the top of his lungs which filled the entire booking area as the sound penetrated the concrete walls and steel door. Then he did a great Negro spiritual he had been practicing and really got into the rhythms.

And he continued singing as he paced his eight feet of space, back and forth. The deputies were a bit curious as to how he could be having so much fun, given his circumstances. Rex was having a one man party! They would come over and check on him from time to time to see what all the ruckus was about.

Finally, after several hours of this, they came over and threw him a bologna sandwich and an apple in a brown paper bag, asking him again if he was ready to come out. Rex said, "show me the warrant and surely!" The steel door closed again.

It was almost 24 hours in this circumstance and they didn't know what to do with him. Several times a clerk from a judge's office would come down and try and convince him that the judge understood Rex's situation and wanted to 'help', (B.S. tricks and traps) but that he'd have to 'book in' before they can get him to his courtroom. He thought to himself, 'sure thing buddy', and continued to hold out for a lawful warrant.

Once they finally realized Rex's resolve on the issue, they finally took him out of the holding cell and skipped the booking process entirely putting him in general population in the jail which is not only contrary to protocol but entirely illegal.

Bond was later set at $50,000. They didn't want him to get out easily. They wanted him out of the way and silenced. The charges *criminal impersonation* are class six - felonies and each carried a maximum term of 24 months per each of the two counts. Evidently he was impersonating himself (joke) when he told each of the officers in the traffic stops that he was Rex William (his real name).

As they processed him in the WashCo jail he realized that he was given exception. They routed him through jail differently than the others who were going in with him. Specifically, they didn't want him to come into contact with his good friend Gary, who was in the same jail of course.

They were to be kept apart, as they didn't want these two communicating to each other, which was an integral part of the plan. Rex was routed upstairs to general population on the 7th floor while Gary was downstairs in the basement classification section.

It was midweek and he had to figure out what he was going to do about his radio show on Saturday. He needed to find a replacement, or something. As he thought about it, he didn't want to miss it. Could he possibly do the show from jail? The thought intrigued him.

He went to work talking with all the guys in his 'pod' to work out how he could access the phone for an hour to do a remote broadcast. There was a phone in the pod but it had to be shared between 'all' the guys there. You could only make outbound collect calls. As you might imagine, some of the guys in there were none too friendly. Rex told everyone about his situation and they all shared Rex's enthusiasm for the 'project'. It was soon arranged. He was set on calling the station remotely by phone, collect, from the jail. He had to explain to Dana, Rex's board operator, and hope she would go along with him. It was Rex's only shot.

Next, he had to arrange for a guest. What about Gary downstairs? It was an intriguing thought. Of course, Rex's jailers were doing everything possible to keep them apart so there would be no way they could do the show together. Could he possibly get word down to Gary downstairs, to access a phone like he did, and call the station at the right time so they could be patched through to each other? This was a scintillating thought. Regardless of the long odds, he had to try. This would be just too good!

In the jail there are what is known as 'trustees'. These trustees are inmates who move around the jail with a higher level of free movement. They serve meals, collect laundry, do odd jobs, maintenance, etc. Everyone knew who Gary was. He had been there awhile and was a unique character. Rex put the word out through the trustees and tried to get the message to Gary to get to a phone on Saturday and call in to the station. He wouldn't know for sure until it actually happened, if it did at all.

The next couple of days were interesting. This whole 'jail experience' was new for him and he was in a whirlwind. Rex had his preliminary hearing and watched guys charged with 'hit and run' get out with only $6000' bail. One guy was charged with murder, and he was out on $15,000 bond. Rex 'impersonated himself' and was hammered with a $50,000 bond. It was clear that he was a 'priority'!

Saturday came around quickly and the clock soon struck 10 A.M. Showtime! He was on the phone to the station and Dana took Rex's call! He was thrilled. Rex heard the intro music begin and he was on the air! This was great! He started out, "Ladies and gentlemen, I am broadcasting today live from module 7D of the WashCo jail and it's not by choice!" He was 'live' on location with, shall we say, a 'captive' audience.

He started the show talking about the abuse of rights and violations of due process and then proceeded to interview several of the inmates who were with him. He wanted to expose the horror stories and abuse by the prosecutors and court system there with first hand testimonies.

This was a 'hands on' expose! There were a litany of abuses and they quite frankly didn't have time for all of them. He was doing this live from the dungeons of the witch's castle before a worldwide audience! Does sardonic humor get any better than this?

Then about 20 minutes into the show Rex's board engineer interrupted an interview, "Rex, you have a caller. Gary from Golden, Colorado is on."

It worked!

Rex was in jail to be silenced; Gary and he were deliberately kept apart from each other so that they could not 'collude' with each other to thwart the conspiracy to suppress his case. Here they were, both in the WashCo jail being kept under wraps, talking to each other 'On The Air' for all the world to hear. It was great hearing Gary's voice again. Despite the most devious plans against them to put them down and shut them up, here they were in full communication sharing their stories and complaints on the air with KHNC, being broadcast through affiliates nationwide and worldwide on shortwave radio. The old saying is true; you can't keep a good man down!

Poetic justice doesn't get any better than this. It was a good day.

They proceeded to continue the expose of abuse of power and blatant treasonous injustices against the people (Gary's case) by Washington County and the N.W.O. & M.J.T.F. gang. It was scathing and they had some very good laughs along the way.

Rex was able to pull off the same escapade again the following week. Then, after a long fight, he finally got the bail reduced and got out to continue his expose of the criminals hiding behind black robes and badges.

Rex wasn't the least bit concerned about the charges of criminally impersonating 'himself'. All along, included in his refusal letters and other communications which he sent to the courts, the prosecutors, the officers and everybody, he clearly identified himself as Rex William Freeman so they would know exactly who they were dealing with and there was no attempt to 'hide' anything.

Not only was he acting in good faith with full disclosure but he had done his research and knew that, had he wanted to, he could use any fictitious name so long as there was no fraudulent intent. Why would he try to hide his identity to get out of a ticket when he can beat it hands down anyway? Knowledge of the truth would be Rex's escape route.

It took about three weeks of maneuvering, but he finally was able to raise bail money from friends. He was back on the streets.

The joke today still is: If you see him on the street hide your children and run for cover. He's likely to 'impersonate himself' again at any time and right in public even!

The state was deadly serious about taking Rex down.

They couldn't stand the fact that Rex was having fun with them and broadcasting it to his listeners!

CHAPTER 11

WASHCO & J.C.

DURING GARY'S INCARCERATION IN WASHINGTON County (WashCo) jail, things took an interesting turn. He met another inmate whom the deputies knew as Buck James. Buck already knew a lot about Gary and the 'claims' program. They hit it off well with common knowledge and interests. Once confidence was established between the two, Buck revealed some startling information.

He was not 'Buck James'. His real name was James Calvin Black or J. C. for short. J.C. revealed himself to be an ex-C.I.A. operative who had a long history of activity in very sensitive operations including the 'claims' project. During his years with 'the company' J.C. had top security clearance.

He had often roamed the halls of the White House and was so well known there that he could do so without even being questioned. He had been involved in training Mid-East terrorists and was also on the security team during Nixon's historic visit to China. He was a trained 'hit man' who used his training on more than one occasion even though the politicians and media say they don't do that sort of thing anymore. With a career spanning almost 30 years, he saw a lot.

Through Gary, Rex got to know him fairly well. J.C. started his career with a sense of duty and good patriotic intentions, figuring he would be helping his country. He was soon involved in things that turned his stomach. Not only was he not proud of his own activities, but he was appalled by government operations and policies which were inimical to the interests of its own people. However, since he was then an insider with dirty hands, he didn't like his chances if he tried to bail out too soon. He knew too much about how things worked.

About mid-way through his career the flames of patriotism still burned within him and he was determined to be the public servant that he started out intending to be. J.C. devised his own plan and started accumulating critical and very sensitive information and evidence which he stashed in various places around the world for possible future use and leverage when the time might be right to bring it forward.

Years later, shortly after his eventual retirement, 'the company' discovered his plan. J.C. was living in South America when he got word that a close friend had died in Washington state. He thought about the risks of returning to the USA and after careful consideration he decided he had his 'insurance' well placed if needed so he come back for the funeral.

That was a mistake. By the time he arrived for the funeral, the web had been woven. J.C. was apprehended with the help of local officials in Washington state.

At the time, there was a common criminal in jail there for burglary. His name was Buck James. At the same time that J.C was brought into the jailhouse after his apprehension, Buck was quietly released informally and J.C. was put in his place under Buck's 'jacket' with an active file. J.C. was never processed as a new inmate going through the intake and booking process. He was now officially Buck James as far as the system knew.

What ensued was a heavy dose of *diesel therapy*. Diesel therapy is a term used when, as a prisoner, you are constantly moved from one jail to another. This way nobody knows for sure where you are and as a transitory, temporary prisoner, the jails/prisons housing you at the moment don't bother with much information or questions. It's a nice way to hide somebody for an indefinite period of time. J.C. ended up in WashCo, right in Gary's lap by divine providence.

PRESSURE ON J.C.

Through Rex's contacts with Gary, and now J.C., he learned that J.C. was getting regular visits by the Feds in the middle of the night. They were trying to coerce him into turning over the information he had stashed away and to give up his plan. The people in high places of the cabal were at great risk with this information just floating out there.

J.C. held out. But as the pressure increased, his health began to fail and he became concerned about his safety. He mysteriously went into convulsions one day and had to be taken to the hospital. This had never happened to him before and it raised suspicions. He figured he had to go public now and bring the spotlight in on his situation to preserve his safety and wellbeing, or this could be his final act.

By this time J.C. knew about Rex and his radio show but J.C. warned Rex not to get involved for obvious reasons. It was a tar pit. Rex already had his own battles brewing and knowing what a hot potato he was, J.C. didn't want him getting in any deeper than he already was. Neither did Rex!

So Rex helped arrange some visits by a couple of other media groups. They had the CBS 60 Minutes crew all set up to come and interview J.C. They had advance authorization and everything that they needed. It was all set and ready to go. It was canceled at the last minute. The same thing happened with a local network affiliate. Apparently the word had come down to the media, "hands off Buck James!" He was too hot to handle and the media minions were to stay away from the story!

Rex tried to get Scott Wheeler interested. Scott was an investigative reporter working with him at KHNC radio at the time. Scott said he was too busy and focused on Clinton's drug and guns operation in Mena, Arkansas and was spending a lot of time down there. He wasn't interested in diverting his attention. Scott is now making a name for himself as Executive Director of THE NATIONAL REPUBLICAN TRUST, a political action committee and is a frequent guest on national news shows. But 'The Mena Cover Up' was an interesting story in itself.

J.C.'s Plight Exposed

At this point Rex felt that he had no choice but to get involved. J.C. agreed to start telling his story on Rex's radio show, the 'Citizens Rights Forum'. He was able to arrange his dayroom time when he could access the phone and coordinate with Rex's Saturday morning show. J.C. became a regular call in guest.

Among other topics, J.C. discussed Henry Kissinger's involvement in smuggling a '$100 bill' printing plate out of the country and how it ended up in the hands of the Iranians who have been active counterfeiters ever since. The media said that the counterfeit bills are 'nearly' flawless. Actually they 'were' flawless because they're made with Fed plates, not to mention our own Treasury Department printing presses which were given to the Shah before the 1979 Iranian revolution. Once again the American People don't get the whole truth from the media.

They discussed operation 'Kingfire' which was an international ring of national leaders involved in running drugs, guns and death. They discussed J.C.'s involvement and presence in the Branch Davidian compound the day before the Waco siege began. They discussed some White House secrets and J.C.'s insights on the Oklahoma City bombing which were quite revealing. His information was corroborated by Brigadier General Ben Partin and other sources. They discussed his long time involvement and research into the 'claims' program and of course much more. They also had a number of private discussions off the air on many matters and developed a nice friendship.

What was interesting on a local level was J.C.s knowledge of the scams, politics and money trails in the new Denver International Airport debacle. J.C. started his own personal investigation when, as a private bond investor, his investment went south when the bonds were downgraded to a junk bond rating. This happened, perhaps not so coincidentally, immediately after then Denver mayor Wellington Webb returned from a trip out to New York and Washington. What J.C. turned up involves a scoop on some very high profile public officials and cases which have yet to be brought to the forefront. Let's just say that his bond losses were not just natural 'market fluctuations'.

Renewed Energy

The strategy of going public was working perfectly. Through the broadcasts on worldwide shortwave, satellite and A.M. band Rex had developed some interesting listeners. J.C., through this exposure, had now reestablished contact with a part of his old network. Some old friends began writing him and he could then contact them by phone and take care of some business.

In addition to some old friends, he started getting mail from many new ones. J.C., through his own bravery in disclosing treasonous acts by government officials on the radio and then through some correspondence, prompted a Navy Admiral to do the same. His new Admiral friend would regularly gather his officers together on board his ship while out in the Mediterranean, to listen to the show on shortwave.

Being in the top brass, the admiral had accumulated his own 'goodie bag' and started bringing it forward with J.C.'s encouragement, help and backing. It's amazing how contagious a little courage can be!

Another new friend who had started writing J.C. as a result of our broadcasts was a retired state Supreme Court Justice from Florida. He was fully supportive and agreed something must be done. He helped James by providing some names, numbers and ideas. There were many more interesting stories too numerous to mention related to this guy.

When Gary and Rex first knew J.C. he was terribly ill, dejected, brow beaten and was essentially resigned to dying in prison either by natural causes or otherwise. His new found friends and notoriety were a tremendous injection of new life and hope for him. J.C. was not a Christian, yet he felt bad about many things he had done in his past. It was on this platform that Gary showed him how God was working in his life and led him to the Lord where he became a born again Christian. They had us a new man! Praise God! Gary's incarceration served a tremendously valuable purpose right here.

"And They know that all things work together for the good to those who love God, to those who are called according to His purpose." - Romans 8:28

With this injection of new energy, J.C. was back on his feet and in business. With the help of his friends, both old and new, he was making contacts around the world, confirming the availability of his stashed armory of information and evidence.

Rex Becomes a Mule

J.C. needed to relay some very sensitive information to his friends on the outside and he couldn't risk sending it out through his monitored mail or phone calls. By this time he had friends on the inside and key personnel knew who he was and what was going on. Somehow, he had arranged to have this private information quietly put into his property bag in the property room of the jail with an authorization to release it to Rex, of all people.

The plan was for Rex to come to the jail, present himself and claim this special item which would be waiting for him with help from the inside. The 'item' was a paper with highly sensitive and confidential instructions. Rex was to arrive at a specific time on the evening shift which would have certain "logistical advantages' close to closing around 10:00 p.m. Once the papers were in hand, he was to get out fast and deliver the information to the proper parties A.S.A.P. One party was a Saudi sheik.

Understanding the importance of the mission and its sensitivity, Rex didn't want to take any chances. He was already not the most welcome person in the county complex. To confound any potential observers, on the way in he parked about 3 blocks down the road from the jail and was out of sight, yet still inside the county government buildings complex.

This way he could approach the building a bit more nimbly emerging from the darkness on foot.

He passed through the initial checkpoint in the visitors' reception area with his now famous Sovereign Authority to Travel I.D. and he proceeded down to the property room. He presented himself to the clerk who was very cordial and cute. After some innocent flirting the item was ready for him. The clerk made the transfer with a smile and a wink and all Rex had to do now, was get out of there!

With the information in hand, he folded it up and tucked it in his pants. He then retraced his steps back out the front entrance quickly and quietly. He was fully aware that this too, could be a setup, just like last time.

Outside, he was just across the road which runs in front of the jailhouse and was well lit. Beyond the street lights was a large open field which stood between Rex and his car. It had a pronounced depression in the middle. It was unlit and very dark beyond the streetlights.

No sooner had he disappeared into the shadows of the field, did a Sheriff Dept. cruiser come racing out of the garage from the side and back of a nearby building. His velocity startled Rex. The cruiser screeched to a stop very abruptly in the exact spot where Rex had just been.

Had Rex been in a car, the deputy's timing would have been perfect. He would have been right on top of Rex. But that wasn't the case. Rex could tell the deputy was confused because he should have been able to see Rex's tail lights somewhere. But now in the shadows, he was nowhere to be seen.

Realizing the situation, the deputy acted quickly. He turned on his side mounted spotlight and scanned the field. By now, Rex was already lying face down on the ground in the shadows cast by the depression in the field. The spotlight was scanning the field and went right over the top of him. So even though the light was aimed right at him, he was out of view yet in plain sight. The spotlight went back and forth a few times. Surely the deputy was baffled 'knowing' he had to be there. People don't just disappear into thin air! He very slowly moved on in search, like a cat on the prowl on high alert.

Rex waited awhile until he saw him head the other direction. He then bugged out, scrambling to his car and quickly blended into the normal night time traffic out on the main road. J.C.'s information was on its way!

The fraud of J.C.s incarceration was exposed. His mail was increasing from sources worldwide and pressure mounted on his keepers. By this time Rex had suggested to Gary that he put James Calvin Black on his witness list on his case in WashCo, which would really put the screws to the works on several levels!

1. it would blow the lid off of the diesel therapy 'Buck James' was getting!
2. it would add a 'ringer' of a witness for Gary's case
3. it would send a message loud and clear to the cabal that Rex also had interesting friends who could raise the ante to this poker game up a notch or two.

J.C. was now listed in court documents as an expert witness for the defense in the government's attempt to stick Gary for fraud on the claims. He was now obligated to appear in local court which added a whole new dynamic to both Gary and Rex's battles.

Due to the fact that it was now public record that James Calvin Black was alive and well and living in WashCo jail. They exposed what the cabal was doing to him. Once again, truth prevails.

J.C. had now filed an affidavit in Gary's fraud case in regard to the claims program. This affidavit blew the lid off the prosecution's case and exposed them all to great liability for evident crimes and cover-up, but J.C. would need to take the stand to get his affidavit entered as evidence.

If Rex was getting the wrong kind of attention by stepping on some people's toes with his radio show *before* J.C. hit the scene, they were getting hit in the head with a sledgehammer now!

"What? Me worry?" - Alfred E. Newman, MAD Magazine.

CHAPTER 12
THE MONTANA SEVEN

I<small>N THE NORTHWESTERN PLAINS AND</small> badlands were some of America's last vestiges of true frontiersmen. They were called 'The Montana Freemen'. They fought to preserve law and order out on the vast expanses of the Montana range. Their weapons were their acute knowledge of history, law and commercial processes. Their ammunition: tremendous research and historical findings in the archives of the Montana code and constitution. The varmint outlaws they chased were corrupt legislators, politicians, bureaucrats and law enforcement just to name a few.

The 'Montana 7' consisted of Leroy Schweitzer, Dan Petersen, Rodney Skurdall, Frank Ellena, Dale Jacobi, Emmett Clark, and James Hence... These men had taken tremendous time and effort to perfect the research on commercial processes from the likes of Hartford Van Dyke (mentioned previously) and advanced it by several leaps and bounds.

They had, in essence, broken the bankers' code in such a way as to have the capability to reclaim our nation from the clutches of the Federal Reserve and its private international bankers. This is certainly no small feat. If they ever got around to writing a book it would be fascinating. However, it would certainly not be called 'How to Win Friends on Capitol Hill and Pals in the Banking Community'. We'll explore this issue more later.

On the local front, in Montana, the 'Seven' had discovered some mind boggling legal secrets. These secrets exposed fraud found in the archives of the Montana Code Annotated (MCA-state statutes).

Just a few of their findings were as follows:

Many of the words in the original statutes of MCA have been changed, deleted and replaced with others. For example, a law addressing the responsibility of the Governor interchanged 'Department of Commerce' for the word "Governor". This type of activity was a common occurrence.

The constitution had been rewritten without due process and the geographic boundaries of the state were omitted among many other wholesale changes. This is hugely significant because without boundaries there is no 'state' to which the constitution applies. Without a state there is no constitution or ultimate self-rule along with many other very serious implications. This is part of the move toward 'Regionalization' to implement and administer the N.W.O. (New World Order).

This is a common ploy by the N.W.O. to dissolve the boundaries of sovereign political entities so that they can be more easily merged into regional control and the consolidation of power which removes local self-determination, i.e., NAFTA & GATT among many others you can name. We can see that clearly with Obama's 'open border' policy to the south. North America is being homogenized into a 'multi-state regional entity'. Forget about local rule!

The legislative intent of much of the original MCA had been changed by attorney/legislators who also rewrote the Sessions Laws, which were the organic legislative acts. If you understand law, you know that the original intent of the ultimate codified statutes is derived from the Sessions Laws. So in rewriting the Sessions Laws, the perpetrators were hiding the original intent of the legislators so that they could pull off any form of abomination they liked without the proper legislative process done by the representative government. This of course then supported the fraud they were creating in the statutes and they could get away with whatever they liked.

For those not familiar in such matters, this is pure treason and sedition in the highest degree. It is tantamount to having the people pass a referendum by overwhelming mandate and their representatives then change it and put into law something entirely different in the final version. It is the equivalent to a hostile takeover by a foreign power. The implications for the traitors are far reaching and very, very serious.

What was truly amazing was that the attorney/legislators flaunted their arrogance by signing a statement taking credit for their work (fraud)!

NOTICE OF FRAUD GIVEN

Frank Elena, aka, "Max", held a meeting with many of the Montana state legislators to put them on 'Notice' of the fraud and to ask them what they were going to do about it. He also warned of serious consequences if they continued to cover up the fraud which included acquiescence by silence and doing nothing. Seeing the implications, several freshmen legislators resigned almost immediately.

The others, although terrified, did nothing. They were caught between the people and the powers that be. By doing nothing they made their choice to ride on the dark side.

This was the basis for some serious confrontations to follow. As you will soon see, the 'Montana 7' who were later to become known as the 'Montana Freemen', had previously become a burr under the saddle of the establishment for other reasons.

The primary reason was this: through intensive legal research in the archives of Montana jurisprudence, they had rediscovered the People's *'one supreme Court'* of the county which operates in common law with jurisdiction exclusive to the people. This means no attorneys ('esquire' is a title of nobility) or black dress judges (corporate government) allowed. Our *one supreme Court* is 'the court' of first and last resort vested with more authority than any of the municipal courts in the appellate jurisdiction, the so-called government courts. This momentous discovery, once again, had been deliberately hidden and written out of the law books and archives by the self-imposed monopoly on 'law', the minions of the Bar Association.

THE COMMON LAW COURT – SUMMARIZED

To gain a better understanding of this you can look to a brief, written by Jerry Wilkenson, a rare honest attorney from Texas who acknowledges and supports the truth based on those findings. Much of his instruction on the common law originated from the Montana Freemen's research findings which he corroborated.

This brief was used in support of a successful motion to dismiss a suit brought against his client by a T.V. station. His client had placed a very large Common Law/U.C.C. lien (a la Hartford Van Dyke) against the T.V. station for damages in running news stories which were very biased, untrue and damaging to his client's name and reputation.

The T.V. station sued to get the lien removed. However, the lien had previously been adjudicated by the People's common law court and the case was already *'res judicata'* or, a thing already decided. The district court recognized this and dismissed the T.V. station's suit for lack of jurisdiction pursuant to the seventh amendment to the national constitution. The lien was valid. More importantly so was the 'peoples common law court'!

The seven proceeded to lawfully establish their own township. Their township is named "Justus Township" which has a significant double meaning if you think about it. One significant point however is that it is not set up as a 'municipal corporation'.

What does this mean?

It means that Justus Township was NOT subject to the police powers and taxation powers of the **'Buck Act'** which essentially superimposes the Federal bureaucracy over the states and overlays the federal emergency, bankrupt corporation otherwise known as THE STATE OF MONTANA. This entity is not the constitutional member state of the republic but is an agent minion of the bankrupt U.S. Inc. which subjects all the sovereign people who don't know otherwise to its legislative compelled performance statutes and granted privileges rather than the God given, inherent, constitutionally protected rights.

This is a very deep subject and cannot be given proper treatment here. So let's review the basic idea briefly before we continue, before you discount this as pure 'nuts'.

It is well established in law that a bankrupt entity has no sovereign authority to pass title or judgment upon anyone or anything. The 'bankrupt' is merely a vassal to the 'trustee' and to the creditors of the bankruptcy.

With this in mind, let's take a look at what former congressional house representative James Traficant, Jr. (Ohio) said on the floor of the House which is recorded in the CONGRESSIONAL RECORD, vol. 139, No. 33, Wednesday, March 17, 1987 @, page H-1303 wherein he states:

"Mr. Speaker, We are here now in Chapter 11.

Members of Congress are official trustees presiding over the greatest reorganization of any Bankrupt entity in world history, the U.S. Government.

We are setting forth hopefully, a blueprint for our future. There are some who say it is a coroner's report that will lead to our demise.

Further, he continues and this is important for everyone to understand;

"It is an established fact that the United States Federal Government has been dissolved by the Emergency Banking Act, March 9, 1933, 48 Stat. 1, Public Law 89-719; declared by President Roosevelt, being bankrupt and insolvent. H.J.R. 192, 73rd Congress in session June 5, 1933 - Joint Resolution To Suspend The Gold Standard and Abrogate The Gold Clause dissolved the Sovereign Authority of the United States and the official capacities of all United States Governmental Offices, Officers, and Departments and is further evidence that the United States Federal Government exists today in name only.

The receivers of the United States Bankruptcy are the International Bankers, via the United Nations, the World Bank and the International Monetary Fund. All United States Offices, Officials, and Departments are now operating within a de facto status in name only under Emergency War Powers.

With the Constitutional Republican form of Government now dissolved, the receivers of the Bankruptcy have adopted a new form of government for the United States.

This new form of government is known as a Democracy, being an established Socialist/Communist order under a new governor for America. This act was instituted and established by transferring and/or placing the Office of the Secretary of Treasury to that of the Governor of the International Monetary Fund.

Public Law 94-564, page 8, Section H.R. 13955 reads in part:

"The U.S. Secretary of Treasury receives no compensation for representing the United States."

Gold and silver were such a powerful money during the founding of the united states of America that the founding fathers declared that only gold or silver coins can be "money" in America. Since gold and silver coinage were heavy and inconvenient for a lot of transactions, they were stored in banks and a claim check was issued as a money substitute. People traded their coupons as money, or "currency." Currency is not money, but a money substitute. Redeemable currency must promise to pay a dollar equivalent in gold or silver money.

Federal Reserve Notes (FRNs) make no such promises, and are not "money." A Federal Reserve Note is a debt obligation of the federal United States government, not "money?"

The federal 'United States' government and the U.S. Congress were not and have never been authorized by the Constitution for the united states of America to issue currency of any kind, but only lawful money, -gold and silver coin. It is essential that we comprehend the distinction between real money and paper money substitute.

One cannot get rich by accumulating money substitutes, one can only get deeper into debt.

We the People no longer have any "money." Most Americans have not been paid any "money" for a very long time, perhaps not in their entire life. Now do you comprehend why you feel broke?

Now, do you understand why you are "bankrupt," along with the rest of the country? Federal Reserve Notes (FRNs) are unsigned checks written on a closed account. FRNs are an inflatable paper system designed to create debt through inflation (devaluation of currency) whenever there is an increase of the supply of a money substitute in the economy without a corresponding increase in the gold and silver backing, inflation occurs.

Inflation is an invisible form of taxation that irresponsible governments inflict on their citizens.

The Federal Reserve Bank who controls the supply and movement of FRNs has everybody fooled. They have access to an unlimited supply of FRNs, paying only for the printing costs of what they need.

FRNs are nothing more than promissory notes for U.S. Treasury securities (T-Bills) - a promise to pay the debt to the Federal Reserve Bank.

There is a fundamental difference between "paying" and "discharging" a debt. To pay a debt, you must pay with value or substance (e.g., gold, silver, barter or a commodity). With FRNs, you can only discharge a debt.

You cannot pay a debt with a debt currency system. You cannot service a debt with a currency that has no backing in value or substance. No contract in Common Law is valid unless it involves an exchange of "good & valuable consideration." Unpayable debt transfers power and control to the sovereign power structure that has no interest in money, law, equity or justice because they have so much wealth already.

Their lust is for power and control. Since the inception of central banking, they have controlled the fates of nations.

The Federal Reserve System is based on the common law and the principles of sovereignty which are protected by the Constitution and the Bill of Rights. In fact, the international bankers used a "Common Law Trust" as their model, adding stock and naming it a "Joint Stock Trust." The U.S. Congress had passed a law making it illegal for any legal "person" to duplicate a "Joint Stock Trust" in 1873. The Federal Reserve Act was legislated 'ex post-facto' (back to 1870), although ex post-facto laws are strictly forbidden by the Constitution. [1:9:3]

The Federal Reserve System is a sovereign power structure separate and distinct from the federal United States government. The Federal Reserve is a maritime lender, and/or maritime insurance underwriter to the federal United States operating exclusively under Admiralty/Maritime law. The lender or underwriter bears the risks, and the Maritime law compelling specific performance in paying the interest, or premiums are the same.

Assets of the debtor can also be hypothecated (to pledge something as a security without taking possession of it.) as security by the lender or underwriter. The

Federal Reserve Act stipulated that the interest on the debt was to be paid in gold. There was no stipulation in the Federal Reserve Act for ever paying the principle.

Prior to 1913, most Americans owned clear, allodial title to property, free and clear of any liens or mortgages until the Federal Reserve Act (1913.) "Hypothecated" all property within the federal United States to the Board of Governors of the Federal Reserve, in which the Trustees (stockholders) held legal title. The U.S. citizen (tenant, franchisee) was registered as a "beneficiary" of the trust via his/her birth certificate.

In 1933, the federal United States hypothecated all of the present and future properties, assets and labor of their "subjects," the 14th Amendment U.S. citizen, to the Federal Reserve System.

In return, the Federal Reserve System agreed to extend the federal United States corporation all the credit "money substitute" it needed.

Like any other debtor, the federal United States government had to assign collateral and security to their creditors as a condition of the loan. Since the federal United States didn't have any assets, they assigned the private property of their "economic slaves," the U.S. citizens, as collateral against the unpayable federal debt. They also pledged the unincorporated federal territories, national parks forests, birth certificates, and nonprofit organizations, as collateral against the federal debt. All has already been transferred as payment to the international bankers.

Unwittingly, America has returned to its pre-American Revolution, feudal roots whereby all land is held by a sovereign and the common people had no rights to hold allodial title to property. Once again, We the People are the tenants and sharecroppers renting our own property from a Sovereign in the guise of the Federal Reserve Bank. We the people have exchanged one master for another.

This has been going on for over eighty years without the "informed knowledge" of the American people, without a voice protesting loud enough. Now it's easy to grasp why America is fundamentally bankrupt.

Why don't more people own their properties outright?

Why are 90% of Americans mortgaged to the hilt and have little or no assets after all debts and liabilities have been paid?

Why does it feel like you are working harder and harder and getting less and less? We are reaping what has been sown; the results of our harvest are a painful bankruptcy and a foreclosure on American property, precious liberties, and a way of life.

Few of our elected representatives in Washington, D.C. have dared to tell the truth. The federal United States is bankrupt.

Our children will inherit this unpayable debt and the tyranny to enforce paying it. America has become completely bankrupt in world leadership, financial credit and its reputation for courage, vision and human rights. This is an undeclared economic war, bankruptcy and economic slavery of the most corrupt order!

- Quoted from: <u>Wake up America! Take back your Country</u>."

You might understand that the original speech above, was modified for the record to conceal the truth. But what 'is' on the record says enough without having to elaborate on now what is public knowledge.

This public acknowledgement was merely confirmation of our national state of affairs since House Joint Resolution 192 was passed in 1933. H.J.R. 192 was a ruling by Congress that made it against public policy to require payment of an obligation in a particular kind of coin or currency.

This had the effect of denying the requirement of payment in substance of intrinsic money value, therefore allowing payment in non-substance or pure credit backed by 'no consideration'. (See U.C.C. 3-408.) Among other ramifications, this was the beginning of the end as it relates to the unending piling on of national debt as we just create more 'credit' without ever considering the need to actually have to 'pay' substance for our obligations.

This was done to cover for the fact that F.D.R. made it illegal for the people to own gold whereupon it was turned over to the authorities and given to the private corporation known as the Federal Reserve banking cartel which precipitated our bankruptcy.

Now, back to the Montana boys: The creation of Justus Township was the first sign of a constitutional republican form of government this country has seen since March, 1933 when the crime of F.D.R.'s 'New Steal' occurred. The Montana 7, by reclaiming their common law heritage, in the formation of 'Justus Township' had, in effect, seceded from the corporate Federal UNITED STATES (de facto) and recreated a toe hold for the republic of the united States of America (de jure)

These guys, through diligent research and application of the organic law had, between themselves, reestablished the U.S. of A. They had formed their own township, were operating their own courts, all in accordance with the supreme law of the land which the personal privateers in public capacity in the Bar Association had attempted to wipe off the face of the earth years ago. Furthermore, with their knowledge of commercial processes they could enforce their court decisions (all based upon Biblical & constitutional law) with commercial, non-judicial liens on the assets and empires of those public officials who would create damages through contempt, violations of their oaths of office (commercial breach of contract), violations of rights, and more, ad nauseum. These also could be applied against various entities of government, private individuals, etc. We'll explore more about the liens later.

If this information spread, think about the devastating impact it would have on the control and revenue generating capabilities of the lawyers, judges, politicians and other personal empire builders who act in public capacity. It would be their ruin. This was a huge threat to the status quo! Pressure was again building.

DENIED ACCESS TO PUBLIC OFFICE
The 'Seven' began filing their 'peoples One Supreme Court' orders & decisions into the appellate courts of 'The State' and intervening in other cases. They were making filings with the County Clerk & Recorder's offices on civil matters to establish and preserve the record as well as to record the necessary commercial processes.

This lasted only a very short time when Frank and Dale were deliberately refused access to the County Clerk's office. Excuse me!? Refusing the public access to its own public offices is a big no-no. Frank and Dale immediately walked down to the sheriff's office nearby to file a complaint against the errant public servant. Dale was wearing a sidearm as he always does. When they entered the building, they encountered a sign: "No firearms beyond this point'. In compliance with the posted order he took it off, wrapped it in the leather holster belt and offered it to the deputy before they proceeded. As soon as he did they were pounced on by several deputies, thrown to the floor facedown and handcuffed with their arms behind their backs. This is where they remained for several hours. It looked like a setup.

While this was going on, Dale & Frank had John Trochman and another friend waiting patiently in the car, minding their own business out in the parking lot. Several deputies approached the car with shotguns. Without warning one deputy smashed the driver side window with the butt of his shotgun and both were physically dragged out of car without notice, warrant, probable cause, or even reasonable suspicion that a crime was committed.

Just like in Rex's case, as surely it is in many others as well, because these gentlemen were purveyors of the truth and fighting in law with paper through the well-established legal system, they had to be vilified, marginalized and demonized. As per the norm, their law enforcement portfolios had them labeled as "armed and dangerous" members of an 'extremist militia group' with 'white supremacist' beliefs. The vilification had begun.

What followed was typical paranoia fueled by ignorance. The sheriff must have anticipated an armed onslaught by waves of 'militiamen' because he had called in law officers from throughout the county and there were squad cars lined up around the sheriff's office as far as the eye could see.

There were no legitimate charges they could bring which would stick so they brought forward an age old law from the labor union days of the '30's and '40's and charged them with 'criminal syndicalism'. This charge avers that one would be fomenting violence or unrest in a labor dispute/strike.

Since when does the demand and reasonable expectation that our paid public servants be law abiding and respectful of the people, their principals, and such mandates become criminal? And since when does the filing of 'Affidavits of Truth' to which the signatory is personally responsible for, in the public records equate to 'fomenting violence'?

Another long and interesting story made very short: the men were eventually released and the charges dropped when enough pressure was brought to bear. Was this just a show of force designed to intimidate and show just who has the 'control'? It's hard to tell for sure but one thing was definitely established, these guys had everyone's attention, including Rex's!

Rex had Frank Ellena aka 'Max' as a guest on his radio show and they had a very lively and interesting discussion covering several key issues which exposed what was going on in Montana and their legislature among other things. That however, wasn't enough.

The American Law Club and others in Denver needed a more in depth study of their research and its applications. Rex set a date to bring Max into town for a weekend seminar. Once the date was set he got busy making all the arrangements, promotion, and advance ticket sales in order to fly him in and take care of him for a few days. The seminar was a huge success. They covered all costs and most important, learned critical information that would be very significant down the road.

The weekend was a huge success.

Not only had they cemented a good friendship with Max but were on their way to establishing the first common law court Colorado had seen in a long, long time. The attendees and particularly Rex's American Law Club members were devouring the information, digesting the documents and research and discussing how, when and where they could re-initiate 'the republic' on the territory of Colorado.

The ball was rolling.

CHAPTER 13

THE COLORADO COMMON
LAW GRAND JURY

IN JUNE OF 1995, AMERICANS from the several states convened in Wichita, Kansas to review evidence and hear testimony pertaining to:

1) The continual state of emergency and suspension of constitutional processes that our Federal government has been operating under since March 9, 1933, and

2) The amendment to the Act of Congress known as the 'Trading with the Enemy Act' of 1917, which in effect then classified U.S. citizens as an 'enemy' of the U.S. government. See 'CONSTITUTION-FACT or FICTION' by Dr. Eugene Schroder.

After several days of testimony and deliberations, the Grand Jury produced a 'Finding of Facts' and 'Conclusions in Law' which they incorporated into an *Order to Show Cause* why said emergency should not be terminated immediately whereby our country would revert back to the de jure constitutional republic it once was.

This 'show cause order' was signed, sealed and then delivered to Congress, the White House and all necessary parties. It was official and lawful. The fraud (one of them anyway) that the U.S. government had perpetrated on the American People had been discovered and through due process and our 1st Amendment protected right

183

to petition for redress of grievance, our agents were being put on Notice.

It was also discovered that most of the several states had then followed suit to the Federal lead in this area. The states had then passed specific legislation bringing them in under the Federal Emergency Powers which suspended lawful money and subjected the states republican form of government to a corporate democracy. This legislation was blatantly unlawful being wholly unconstitutional. To wit, the national constitution states:

"No State shall enter into any Treaty, Alliance, or Confederation; grant Letter of Marque and Reprisal; coin Money; emit Bills of Credit; make any Thing but gold and silver Coin a Tender in Payment of Debts; pass any Bill of Attainder, ex post facto Law, or Law impairing the Obligation of Contracts, or grant any Title of Nobility."

However, under the emergency, the states have created a labyrinth of interstate agreements and huge bureaucracies just to administer these compacts and have subjugated themselves to Congress in doing so. Thus, our once 'de jure', sovereign states capable of self-determination with political power wholly vested in it from its own people, have become subjugated to the federal power and have become 'compact party states' now subject to the overlaid federal jurisdiction imposed in part by the Buck Act of the 1940's.

Entire books have been written on this subject alone. Suffice it to say, it was necessary to go beyond a national common law grand jury. They had to convene a similar event on the state level in each state.

This was soon organized and set to happen in Cañon City, Colorado on August 19-20th, 1995, the weekend of Rex's 37th birthday. What a fitting celebration!

The people convened at the Cañon Inn Hotel in Cañon City Saturday morning the 19th. It was a 'who's who' assembly of conservatives, Patriots and politicians from both sides of the fence.

Numerous national leaders of the movement came in from out of state as well. Dr. Gene Schroder and his group were the primary organizers. Colorado state senator Charlie Duke and state representative

Tebedo represented the state legislature. Kevin Tebedo of Colorado for Family Values was also involved as were a host of teachers and researchers from the common law court movement, i.e., Dan Meador, Dave Shecter, Darryl and Sally Frecht, and many others. It was to be a splendid and historic event and he didn't want anybody miss it so Rex arranged to do a remote broadcast of his radio show live on location.

The state attorney general (who had federal cases and private liens filed against her from Gary) was very concerned about the event and sent down a scout team, by invitation, to have private meetings with the organizers. Evidently they were anticipating a militia group to be stirring up unrest or some crazy thing. Why are our politicians always the last to figure things out?

THREATS AGAINST THE PEOPLE

During the week preceding the Colorado common law grand jury, one of Rex's Tuesday night American Law Club friends, Andy Anderson, was picked up by Aurora police with no warrant and no probable cause. He was held and interrogated for about eleven hours again with no charges or even reasonable articulable suspicion (R.A.S.) presented to support a detention as the lowest possible threshold for such treatment. This was just another very serious affront to the liberties they are supposed to be protecting, not thrashing. During his detention, police were ransacking his house. Yep, you guessed it... again without a warrant.

Remember how, during the Cold War, they just absolutely shuddered at the mention of Communist police state tactics that were being used by tyrants against their own people in places like Romania and East Germany? It seems 'we' have become 'them'. With that in mind and the backdrop of recent disclosures of invasions into once revered rights of privacy; domestic spying on national citizens by the NSA now becomes the 'new normal'.

The interrogation of Andy was primarily directed at finding out about the activities of our group and others as they pertained to re-establishing the Peoples' common law court, our <u>one supreme Court of the county</u>, with original jurisdiction exclusive to the People. Evidently, they are scared to death that the People are rediscovering their power which of course would naturally diminish theirs! Our crooked public servants well ought to be scared!

Anyway, this interrogation is a story in and of itself but the point is that it ended up with investigators from the Attorney General's office and Aurora police threatening Andy that anybody involved in a common law court would go to jail!

Excuse me!? When did the exercise of the Peoples' unalienable God given rights become a crime? Point in fact of the need for our common law grand jury to make a Finding of Fact and Conclusion in Law as soon as possible!

The "Citizens' Rights Forum" show in Cañon City that day was the best ever. They rolled from one powerhouse guest to the next, in between live reports of the proceedings which were focusing on the validity, the power and the need for the Peoples' common law courts to be resurrected all across the country, which is in fact exactly what was happening.

The guest he spent the most time with was Colorado State Senator Charlie Duke. He asked Charlie for his reaction to the threats made against anyone who participated in a common law court. Senator Duke took it quite personally and you could feel the hair rise on the back of his neck. To paraphrase his words, he responded "If anyone wants to attack or arrest me for not only exercising my rights but also in doing the job that the people have elected and paid me to do, well then bring them on!" He continued on and when he finished there was absolutely no doubt in anyone's mind as to where Charlie Duke stood on the issue. In an age of shady politicians, Senator Charles Duke was a rare statesman! If only others would follow his example.

The hour long show went by and it seemed like five minutes. Rex highly encouraged every one of his listeners to get the tape of that show and share it. It was an historic event.

Rex wrapped up the show and went back in to the hall to participate in the balance of the morning's business. They broke shortly thereafter for lunch and he hopped in the car with a couple of friends to head into town to find a quick lunch somewhere.

KIDNAPPED

When they finished lunch they stood outside the restaurant for a few minutes talking and soaking in some sunshine. They then got in the car and very casually drove out of the parking lot onto the main highway out front that goes through town. Rex offhandedly made the comment that he had sure noticed a lot of police cars in Cañon City as he watched one drive by after seeing several others just prior to that. Rex's friend Chris responded, "Well you know Cañon City is the prison capitol of Colorado." which it is. He didn't think anything more on the issue.

Immediately after that they heard a siren and saw flashing lights behind them. They weren't speeding, nor did they run a red light. They wondered aloud to each other what this was all about. Three more police cars pulled up in a 'V' formation behind them and at least a dozen state patrols, local police and sheriff deputies fanned out on both flanks behind them. Pistols, rifles and shotguns were drawn with all of them taking a bead right on the three. Rex thought to himself, "I guess this wasn't going to be a routine traffic stop!"

Many of the cops were behind the cars using them as protection all with their guns drawn. Rex saw one in the bushes over in front of Burger King to his right. They shouted through the bullhorn, "Put your hands up on the ceiling of the car. DO IT NOW! DO IT NOW! DON'T MOVE! DON'T MOVE! Now driver, put your hands out the window! NOW! NOW! Passengers don't move! Driver! Come out of the car! Hands in the air! SLOW! DO IT NOW!"'

Tim followed the instructions. He was the first one out. When he was out they continued, "Hands out to your side. Walk backwards towards us!" As soon as he approached the first car he was frisked, handcuffed and brought behind the first car on his knees, hands behind his back in the execution position. He was not advised of any rights, shown a warrant, or advised of any charges. He was just a piece of chattel property to be used or abused as they saw fit and was now a prisoner being held with a gun to his head.

Next it was Rex's turn. Here we go! "Front right passenger hands out the window! Slowly get out of the vehicle! Keep your hands out to your side! Slowly, walk backwards towards us!" he was walking through weeds in the ditch and was concerned that if he stumbled on a pop can or something, 'a sudden move', might be cause to be blown away. So he turned his head to see where he was going and saw all the guns aimed right at him with fingers on the triggers! He had at least 30 lethal weapons of all kinds trained on him. He thought to himself, "Wouldn't some of these guys just love to have an excuse to pull and get some 'action' for the day?"

They immediately screamed at him, "Turn around, turn around!" As he approached the forward car with his back toward them and both arms out to his side, the officer he told him "keep your right arm out, put your left arm behind your back!"

As he grabbed Rex's left arm he felt the cuff go 'click' and challenged him, "What are you doing?" He replied, "You're being detained."

Rex said, "Detained, hell! You are restricting my movement and liberty against my will. You are putting me under arrest and I demand to see a warrant. Where's your warrant? I demand to see it immediately!"

The cop ignored him and asked him to move over behind the car. Rex refused until he could show him a warrant. Of course they didn't have one. They didn't advise him of any charges, nor did they advise him of any rights with a Miranda warning. He was cuffed and they ganged up on him and forcibly put him behind the car next to Tim, and forced him down on his knees in the gravel.

While he was there, a plainclothes cop took out a photograph and flashed it in Rex's face and demanded, "Is this you?" Rex quickly responded, "No. This is me over here. That's only a picture of somebody." Which was 100% accurate. The cop didn't see any humor there. Cops are always so straight. Rex wasn't about to identify himself or cooperate in any way unless or until they could do their job properly.

In the meantime, they brought Chris out of the car. He was the last one. They weren't so nice with him as they were Tim and Rex. Once outside the car, he was thrown face down in the standing water of a mud puddle in the ditch. A cop cuffed him and in the process of doing so another one walked up to him, put his gun up against his temple and said, "One move and I'll blow your brains out!" Seriously he did! While one cop cuffed one hand, another took the heel of his boot and dug it into Chris' hand and into the gravel on the ground. Isn't it nice to know that peace loving, money spending tourists and conventioneers are so warmly received by the local officialdom? Ahhh, America!

Rex observed the massive operation going on around him. He noticed city police involved. County sheriff's deputies were involved. The Colorado Bureau of Investigation (CBI) were there, Plainclothesmen were there and several guys in black military suits with no insignia. He thought to himself, he must be 'making it in the world' as somebody thinks that I'm really important! Wow!

For general purposes he deliberately does not usually carry I.D. on him as a matter of principle. He will of course identify himself whenever there's a legitimate or lawful need. In this case such lawful need was not shown and he refused to comply when asked. Despite repeated demands, they would show a valid warrant.

After unauthorized body, property and vehicle searches and some ridiculous questioning, the plainclothes cop looked at Rex and said, "That's him."

Rex was stuffed in the back seat of a police car still demanding to see a warrant, to no avail. Although he did get one deputy to admit, "We don't have a warrant, We don't need one!" Rex replied, "Oh really? It must make your job oh so much easier." The question now is, what exactly is the job that they are doing and for who? This definitely was not your traditional peace officer routine! Tim and Chris were released and Rex was off to jail.

Once in jail they wanted to do the routine booking procedure; information questionnaire, fingerprints, photos, etc. Rex refused to cooperate in any way until they could show him a bona fide warrant and show him lawful procedure. Since they didn't have one they were quickly at a stalemate and the dark side minions started getting quite agitated. During this process Rex just happened to notice that he was wearing a name badge sticker from the event, which nobody seemed to notice. Jeez! he thought to himself 'Damn'! Now what? I have to get rid of this." He was still cuffed.

He asked to go to the toilet. They uncuffed him and pointed him in the right direction and an armed officer in military garb was on Rex's heels and followed him into the toilet. As Rex peed the goon was right behind him. Rex could only surmise his thoughts being, 'You never know what these crazy 'militiamen' will do when they're peeing, right'? He was ready! As he flushed the toilet he stood there and waited until the very last moment, then as the flush was about to take its last swirl, he tore off the name badge sticker, crumpled it up in his left hand which was away from the right side the goon was on and he tossed it into the toilet as it all went down the pipes.

The goon freaked out. He saw him do it and there was nothing he could do. He didn't know what it was that he threw down. He came unglued and was just out of his skin and was all over him: "What was that? You have drugs? Was that coke? What else do you have?" He physically spun him around and started searching for something more he might have, checking Rex's hands and pockets. Just seeing his futility and frustration at letting Rex get one over on him was enough to make the entire episode worthwhile! Ohh such fun!

The plainclothesman later sat down with Rex and tried to reason with him. He seemed like a nice enough guy. He thought he was being reasonable asking Rex to comply with booking procedures, fill out forms, give the usual admissions and confessions. You know. The usual! It'll just make things so much easier.

Rex said "Is it unreasonable for me to demand due process and demonstration of probable cause before being placed within an inch of his life and being thrown into jail without explanation?" This isn't done in America, or so the story goes. Evidently it is these days.

Rex was coaxed and cajoled for over an hour and he held his ground refusing to comply with anything. He was finally told that Denver was supposed to come and get him on Monday (this was Saturday) and if he wasn't booked in they couldn't release him and he'd be stuck. What they conspicuously didn't tell him was that, without a valid warrant or any positive I.D. which would even confirm who he was, they couldn't hold him either! Rex replied, "Oh well. I'll just have to set up housekeeping here I guess. Where's my bunk?"

While he was being prodded at the deputy's desk he made several attempts to look at the N.C.I.C. (National Crime Information Computer) printout sheet the deputy was working off of. He deliberately shielded it every time. The deputy didn't want him seeing it for some reason.

When he finally gave up on gaining Rex's cooperation he jumped up in a fit of exasperation to go over and give instructions to an intake clerk. In his emotional tiff, he absentmindedly left the N.C.I.C. printout which he was so cautiously protecting earlier, sitting on the desk right in front of Rex. Rex quickly learned that, according to law enforcement, he was the "person of interest" allegedly "armed and dangerous", was "a member of an extremist militia group", and a "white supremacist". This was all quite interesting news to him! He wondered to himself, "when did all this happen?"

Isn't it interesting how labels and innuendo quickly attach to anyone who dares to be an independent thinker, especially when you want to hold public officials accountable to the same laws they hold us accountable to? Of course all of this was necessary as a part of the standard 'vilification ritual' that one must endure if you don't agree with officialdom. It made perfect sense.

This country was built on the strength of free spirited individuals who dared to be true to themselves and break from the norms and traditions of their modern contemporaries. Today, if you do not 'conform' to the politically correct set which suffers from 'group think syndrome' you are smeared as a radical extremist and cast in the light of being a 'threat to society'. The sad thing is most 'sheeple' are ignorant of how they are controlled and manipulated by the establishment media and their superficial political rhetoric.

We need more free spirits who are critical thinkers and can see through all the hoaxes that are heaped on us by our progressive social reformers.

"And he heard another voice from heaven saying, "Come out of her my people, lest you share in her sins and receive of her plagues. For her sins have reached to heaven and God has remembered her iniquities." Revelations 18:4-5

Back at the Grand Jury proceedings word spread quickly about the armed assault and kidnapping. Immediately Senator Duke and several other friends stormed down to the jail to demand an explanation and a visit. They were blatantly denied both, but were told to come back at 6:00 p.m. and they'd be allowed a visit. They were furious and the incident certainly put a few sparks in the air when, really, it wasn't needed because the day was already electric enough.

For the next couple of hours Rex was in the 'hole' and they'd periodically check on him asking, "You ready to cooperate?" he'd respond, "You ready to show me a warrant?" They'd turn away in silence for a while longer.

WHISKED AWAY

About three hours into the ordeal he was brought out of his cell into the presence of a young man in green military garb, black boots and a conspicuous bullet proof vest. He had chains, cuffs and shackles and started putting them on Rex. It looked like he was going on a little trip.

Once sufficiently chained and shackled he led Rex out to a large enclosed garage area. In the immediate vicinity were two police cruisers, two unmarked cars and about a half dozen men in military type assault uniforms, black ball caps, black glasses, bullet proof vests and all had

Tech-9 semi-auto guns slung over their shoulders being held in a ready position. I am dead serious! Rex thought to himself that this must be how the American hostages felt in Lebanon when being held by the Islamic Jihad.

But wait a minute, isn't this Colorado!? Hmm.

Without saying much at all they put him in a car with one deputy driving and one 'commando' riding shotgun. They departed stealthily with an escort car behind, and one in front. Both contained four other commandos. After getting through town quietly they hit the highway at about 90 miles an hour with the emergency lights blazing. For a minute he thought about the possibility that they were taking him up to the wooded mountains to shoot him, but there were too many people who knew of Rex's situation. Let's put it this way, this didn't seem like a 'normal' situation.

Rex broke the ice with his captors and started a conversation. They were actually pretty nice guys; a couple young pups whose closest brush with independent thinking was deciding how soon to follow the next order. They wouldn't tell him where they were going. Apparently, that was top secret. But it didn't take long to see that they were headed toward Denver, 90 miles away, now pushing 100 m.p.h. Rex was hoping he had a good driver.

Rex asked, "Why all the security and lights and speed?" They responded, "Precautionary measure in case of ambush." Pause ..... Okaaayy. It was coming together for him now. They had kidnapped him, somebody they never could get a positive I.D. or proper booking on (i.e. legal possession). They used massively excessive force in broad daylight, shutting down the main 4 lane state highway through town for about 40 minutes in the biggest armed assault Colorado had likely seen in years. They did so without a warrant or probable cause on orders from *somebody* in Denver. They had an angry mob back home in Cañon City waiting for them including a State senator breathing down their neck.

Uh huh. O.K. It seems that they were afraid of all of the 'armed and dangerous' friends in the 'extremist militia group' of 'you know who' who might also be 'white supremacists' and who might wage war on the jail or lay in wait to ambush the transport commando team at any point. Aside from having absolutely no basis for any of that crap, it could sound plausible for an official press release and might even help them to look like good law officers becoming heroes of the day!

Apparently somebody had advised these people in Cañon City what a hole they had dug for themselves and he was too hot to handle. They wanted to get rid of him and quickly! These guys weren't waiting until Monday for Denver to get around to come and get him. They were scared to death to have a God loving radio talk show host in their jail who, by now they knew was setting them up big time.

"But wait a minute! Hold On! I just remembered.... I can't leave! I haven't been booked in yet! What about what you said ....about...you know ....administrative procedure...and how I'd be stuck there forever if I didn't cooperate, and all of those things??"

Rex couldn't stop laughing for five minutes straight. And they call the Patriots paranoid? This was definitely the most exciting birthday Rex had ever had, although it wasn't really what he had envisioned for a birthday.

Meanwhile it was getting close to 6:00 p.m. The senator and his posse, now in full force, came back to the jail like clockwork to see him and get some answers. They were previously told visiting would start at 6:00 and Rex would be there. They were on a mission. When they came back at the appointed time...Ooops! Rex was already long gone. Sorry!

Interestingly enough the jailers, being the strong defenders of the truth that they were, didn't want to deal with it. What did they do? They just put up a sign outside on the locked door: "Visiting hours canceled today." Charlie was fuming! He would later write a very strong letter to the local district attorney deploring such despicable behavior and demanding that legal action be taken. This incident, along with many others led to a bill being introduced by Charlie to curtail and check such abhorrent arrest procedures which were becoming routine statewide. (mostly against Rex's friends among others) This bill would have made law enforcement actually follow what used to be known as 'due process'. What a novel concept! They have to pass a law requiring law officers to follow the law! Think about it. And what if they don't follow that law? They pass another law to force them to follow the first two they didn't follow? It's what you call, a 'state of lawlessness'. This is what's scary. Anything goes!

The law enforcement community lobbied hard against Charlie's bill and killed it. After all... think how inconvenient it would be to have to actually get a warrant and follow due process and all that. It's much easier to arrest people on a whim even if they aren't committing a crime!

Back in Denver, Rex's Tech-9 commando team entourage pulled up to the county jail facility. When they pulled up, people started coming out of the building, from cars, from every corner lining up and getting close to get a glimpse of him. Apparently word had gotten out that he was coming and he felt like a rock star pulling up. Everyone wanted a piece of him. Apparently few of these people had ever actually 'seen' a real 'white supremacist' 'armed and dangerous' 'militia leader' before and this was their chance! It was comical. But it was Rex's birthday after all and they did make him feel very special!

Rex was put in solitary confinement with twenty-four hour lock-down under video surveillance and was refused a shower, toothbrush, and phone call for four days. What fun! Remember, this was Saturday. Court didn't resume until Monday and then he'd have to be put on the docket for who knows what and who knows when?

The deputy guards continually refused Rex's repeated demands for a phone call, a shower and/or a toothbrush. One guard actually showed him the log book where they keep track of the daily 'offers' to each inmate for phone and shower. They check off every time they do it. There were numerous entries in the book indicating that he had 'declined' such daily offers. So much for the official record.

After four days of grueling solitary confinement, on the following Tuesday, he finally got in front of the judge, when he soon learned that the reason for all of this (according to them) was that he didn't appear for a hearing he had on Rex's pending case that nobody bothered to tell him about. Nice.

The judge didn't even want to discuss Rex's alleged failure to appear and Rex's bond was revoked. He was incarcerated and they started moving ahead immediately to 'other business' on Rex's case without any discussion whatsoever about Rex's set up. He interrupted: "Excuse me judge, we need to address this issue of non-appearance and revocation of bond."

Rex knew his paperwork and case file inside and out even though he didn't have the pleasure of having it with him. He said, "We need to discuss the facts and then the circumstances on this issue and we will see that there are some 'er, 'corrections' which need to be made for the record. The facts are as follows. . .' he cited the dates he was in court, the papers he received accordingly, the dates he was noticed to appear. He exposed the fact that as a matter of standard procedure Denver courts did not issue a single 'setting form' which outlines all the dates of pre-trial hearings, etc. as they did it pretty much on the fly. This was different from other counties.

"The circumstances are such that on Saturday the 19th, I broadcast a live radio show from Cañon City openly telling the whole world exactly where I was. Now, I'm not the brightest guy in the world but if I knowingly failed to appear and skipped out on my bond and was hiding out to evade authorities, would your assessment of me include that I am stupid enough to do such a thing if I were knowingly avoiding my responsibilities to the law?"

He didn't stop until he was completely finished in order to make it all part of the record. The judge asked the prosecutor to rebut Rex's statement and he couldn't. He had nowhere to go but to agree that there was no *intent* to violate bond conditions which is a crucial factor as it is in any crime. The prosecutor had to set the record straight and release him.

This whole thing stunk of a cheap trick to try once again to get him off the streets with maximum intimidation and harassment. Since Rex was a public figure due to his radio show and following, he apparently needed to be an example for others, in some peoples' eyes. The trouble is, everything they tried was backfiring!

Once again, it didn't work. Rex stuck to his guns and kept his wits about him and he made it through to the other side.

As a side note, he was due to be released at 2:00 PM later that afternoon. He had people there waiting to pick him up and celebrate his release after all the excitement and publicity. The goon squad knew better than to invite a PR event and they waited until 2:00 AM before kicking him out the door. It was the dead of night when everyone was long gone and it would be nearly impossible to find a taxi anywhere.

There you go sir, have a good day!

PART IV
STRATEGIC SUMMIT CONFERENCES

CHAPTER 14

THE GENERALS MEET IN MONTANA

REX HAD SPENT A LOT of time studying the current research on the common law court and its lawful foundation and procedures. The group which had developed this information and implemented it in its most advanced state at the time was Dennis Smith and Tinker Spain and their groups in Oklahoma and Texas respectively.

However, the guts of much of their research had come from the boys in Montana. Rex understood that Dennis had made seven or eight trips up there to get a grasp of the issues which he had subsequently developed. This knowledge, coupled with the information which Max had shared with the Denver group, led Rex to only one conclusion: he needed to tap into this wellspring of knowledge and bring it to fruition in Colorado.

STRATEGY SESSIONS

Leroy Schweitzer, Dan Peterson, Dale Jacobi, Rodney Skurdal, et al, had been conducting small personalized classes for ten to twelve people at a time twice a week up in a beautifully appointed log home nestled in the trees of the Bull Run Mountains near Roundup, Montana. Leaders in the legal reform movement from around the country were quickly learning about the availability of this critical information from these men. Classes were booked solid for at least six weeks in advance.

Rex was able to reserve a session time for several weeks out and arranged to make the trip with a couple of his more astute law club associates.

When the time came in September of 1995, they loaded up the car and headed north on I-25 from Denver. The trip was pleasant as they wound their way up through Wyoming toward Billings and then continued north toward Roundup on a state road, much of which was torn up with construction and was little more than rough. Upon arrival they checked into a local motel, settled in and called the ranch to confirm their arrival and secure final directions for the next day's class.

The following day, as they wound their way down the heavily wooded mountain road they were somewhat tentative as to which ranch was the intended destination. That was, until they came upon a very direct 'Notice to all Trespassers and Government Agents' sign posted at the perimeter entryway. Yep! This was the place! The sign was a 'Notice of Governing Law' in the territory of Justus Township that all who enter shall abide by that law which of course included all constitutional protections and recognized no corporate statutory code.

They were a little early and interrupted Leroy and a woman who was still in a nightgown finishing breakfast. They didn't seem bothered and took it all in stride. Rex was somewhat surprised at their acceptance of what felt to him like an invasion of privacy but they were all very hospitable yet businesslike at the same time. There was work to be done and the day's mission was just beginning. Rex's team were just a few more, of a steady stream of visitors they had been seeing for several months now.

Rex's team came with video and audio equipment, wireless microphones, tape decks, etc. Once the stuff was set up along with the other participants it looked like a veritable network media event.

The entire morning session for both days was devoted to Bible study. Knowledge of God's law in both the old and new testaments was the foundation for all that would follow.

It was made very clear and in absolute terms, that these guys were not at all concerned about offending others' religious sensibilities. Rex appreciated this approach versus being politically correct and attempting to please everyone for fear of offending someone.

Contrary to the popular belief fostered by the media, Jews, non-Christians and other non-whites had attended the classes and were welcomed with open arms. There were even several attorneys who attended, some more than once. Firsthand experience made it very clear that the portrayals by the media that these folks were 'racist', white supremacists, armed and dangerous were contrived and inflammatory merely to manipulate public opinion. In fact, intentionally using these labels is exactly the type of 'hate speech' that the accusers were decrying, but engaging in themselves. The beliefs of the Montana folks were simply what the Bible says they should be, pure and simple. Their only mission was to enforce the law as it was written and originally intended so that the people could have some peace and security the way it was intended. These people were very serious, law abiding, freedom loving Americans who loved God and were living by HIS word and the 'de jure' law of the republic, not the corporate legislative democracy.

While we certainly can't say that all participants had come and gone with a total adherence to all of the beliefs espoused by the Montana Freemen, there was undoubtedly a certain level of enlightenment which was gained by all sides of the teachings, as there always is with positive open hearted human interaction.

They didn't care if you agreed or not. They stood firm on their position and you knew what it was without question regardless of who may or may not like it or be offended. Such directness was refreshing in light of today's climate of tip-toeing around our *multicultural sensitivities*. This was a key element in the moral demise of America in Rex's opinion. "Truth is not politically correct. You have one or the other. You can't have both!

The Bible study at the ranch centered primarily around some of the key maxims of law handed down from the days of Moses and how much of this has been translated into modern day jurisprudence and statutory code. Unfortunately, they also learned how much of the timeless, immutable 'true law', as recognized by historical legal scholars including the founding fathers and subsequent supreme court judges, has been swept under the rug and hidden, or twisted and perverted by the modern day Bar Association influenced legislatures. It was a mess they had to sort through for their own fundamental understanding.

What started out as painstakingly slow legal research by the Montana boys, started gaining momentum like a snowball rolling down a mountain.

As the people who attended the training sessions went back to their homes all around the country, a national network of researchers was commissioned with orders: dig through your own state archives and the used and rare bookstores to search for information pertaining to a short list of key issues. Critical information started trickling in and grew to a steady stream.

For example, one particular court pleading was found by someone in Larimer County Colorado dating back to the mid 1800's. In this case a woman returned to her homestead cabin only to find a man named Scotty who had broken into her home while she was gone and he was squatting on her property. Despite numerous demands on her part he would not leave. Finally after several days, he did vacate the premises.

The woman, who was naturally quite perturbed by the event, wrote out a complaint and summons on one sheet of paper and delivered it to the County Sheriff.

The affidavit of complaint by the damaged party alleged the specific offense and named the offender. Contained in the same handwritten document was a summons for the sheriff to bring the accused along with a jury of freeholders from the county to convene a court to hear and adjudicate the matter at a time and date set certain by the woman.

There were several things that were particularly interesting and revealing in this homemade but official document in law which is a part of the permanent record of the case.

ONE: The woman (citizen) was the one who drew up the very simple document to commence proceedings. No lawyers or other legal professionals were involved.

TWO: She commanded the public servant(s) (sheriff et al) to do his job and accommodate her, which he did. She set the dates and times with other specific instructions to assemble 'her' court.

THREE: She didn't have the court held in some fancy courthouse or county seat building. She convened 'her' court at her own house!

This is a classic example of due process being exercised in common law by an American sovereign as it was intended by our forefathers. Here we see the government actually serving its master upon request and within the scope of its delegated authority with very distinct limitations of power.

Naturally some of the logistics would vary in today's modern world but the principles of fundamental due process and the Sovereign convening 'her court' was a lesson for all.

This real life example of good government interacting properly with its principals, the sovereign Americans, falls right in line with comments made by Supreme Court Justice Matthews in the case. <u>Yick Wo v. Hopkins, 118 U.S. 370</u>:

"Sovereignty itself is, of course, not subject to law, for it is the author and source of law; but in our system, while sovereign powers are delegated to the agencies of government, sovereignty itself remains with the people, by whom and for whom all government exists and acts. And the law is the definition and limitation of power. It is, indeed, quite true that there must always be lodged somewhere, and in some person or body, the authority of final decision, and in many cases of mere administration, the responsibility is purely political, no appeal lying except to the ultimate tribunal of the public judgment, exercised either in the pressure of opinion or by means of the suffrage. But the fundamental rights to life, liberty, and the pursuit of happiness, considered as individual possessions, are secured by those maxims of constitutional law which are the monuments showing the victorious progress of the race in securing to men the blessings of civilization under the reign of just and equal laws, so that, in the famous language of the Massachusetts Bill of Rights, the government of the commonwealth "may be a government of laws, and not of men." For the very idea that one man may be compelled to hold his life, or the means of living, or any material right essential to the enjoyment of life at the mere will of another seems to be intolerable in any country where freedom prevails, as being the essence of slavery itself."

Further, the New York Supreme Court tells us in the case <u>Wynehamer v. People of New York,</u> <u>13 NY 378</u>, which was a case during the prohibition days in the 30's whereby legislation ordered the police powers to seize liquors (private property) and destroy it for the public good, without compensation to the owner. At the time, the legislature considered 'legislation' as sufficient 'due process' thus enabling them to skirt the 4th amendment protections and the NY Supreme court struck this down.

The crucial lines of the opinion declared that the right not to be deprived of life, liberty, or property without due process of law:

"...necessarily imports that the legislature cannot make the mere existence of the rights secured the occasion of depriving a person of any of them, even by the forms which belong to 'due process of law.' For if it does not necessarily import this, then the legislative power is absolute."

In other words, legislative bodies had no authority to 'legislate away' a person's God given rights and this was not 'substantive due process' which was a concept introduced before its time as it was later adopted by the U.S. Supreme some years later. Should the legislative bodies be able to 'legislate' away a person's rights, then it had absolute power and the people would be under threat of absolute tyranny, contrary to the guarantees secured them by the constitution. At the time, the Montana boys were raising this issue with their own state legislature and the secret 're-writing' of the laws which they discovered.

We see today, how peoples' rights are being legislated away every day. Our rights granted by God have been converted into 'privileges' regulated by the state and are conditional to you, but only on the provision that you **volunteer away** your privacy and 'register', pay fees, taxes and other forms of extortion including all forms of statutory compliance requirements. Failure to file a piece of paper could land you in jail or cost you dearly when they seize your bank account or just take the property away from you entirely! Obamacare is the perfect example. Owning guns, automobiles and property are others, and the list goes on.

LOCAL AUTONOMY

These concepts of sovereignty residing in the people who have a right to self-determination are outlined in each state's constitution. In Colorado it is found in Article V section 25 pertaining to special legislation wherein it states:

'No special legislation shall be passed regarding the townships or the counties.'

In other words, the State government has no business running or interfering in the affairs of the local governments of the Sovereign People. Furthermore, each state constitution recognizes right up front, in clear unambiguous language, that ALL political power is vested in the People and when government becomes detrimental to the ends for which it was created by its creators, the People, we have the unalienable right to alter or abolish it.

What the Montana Freemen did was to establish their own township government, 'Justus Township.' This was in fact a body politic of sovereign Americans formed and organized for the benefit of those unenfranchised people who shared common goals and beliefs. Without asking for or receiving any benefits, privileges, programs, or protections from the STATE OF MONTANA, this band of Free Americans owed **nothing** to THE STATE.

Realizing that far too many people are either dependent upon the status quo or are ignorantly deluded by beliefs that our current state of affairs in government actually provides a benefit to our society, the Freemen chose not to alter or abolish the establishment, which would require either much more enlightenment on the part of the public, or simply an armed rebellion, both of which are not feasible. Instead, they merely chose how it was going to apply (or not as in this instance) to them and they exercised their right as Americans to be self-governing in a local capacity.

These are just a few of the many lawful precepts exercised by the Freemen as it relates to the states.

FEDERAL JURISDICTION

Much has been written about the Freeman's beliefs regarding the Federal lack of jurisdiction to prosecute sovereign Americans who are:

A) Unenfranchised non-U.S., state citizens who "owe nothing to federal government", and;

b) Are located on the land in the states and are not on federal territory (i.e., Washington D.C., its enclaves, territories, forts, docks, arsenals, etc.). In fact, the media and the masses scoff at this which they perceive as belligerent lunacy. They simply don't understand law or legal definitions.

Let's look at this issue for a moment and see what the truth is.

Once the class in 'Justus Township' started digging into the issue, they made some interesting discoveries. The following are just a few of the highlights:

First of all, the federal government only has the constitutional authority to prosecute four classes crimes (according to law).

1. Treason;
2. Piracy on the High Seas
3. Counterfeiting of U.S. securities
4. Violations of the Law of Nations.

Anything beyond these four crimes is outside the scope of authority delegated to the Federal government by the states in the national constitution and is therefore, unlawful.

However, let's play devils' advocate and say that the Feds could prosecute any crime they want. When doing so they would bring the defendant in to be tried in The UNITED STATES DISTRICT COURT, right?

The U.S. Supreme Court tells us in Balzac v. Puerto Rico 258 U.S. 298 (1922)

"The UNITED STATES DISTRICT COURT is not a true United States court established under ARTICLE III of the constitution to administer the judicial power of the United States therein conveyed. It is created by virtue of the sovereign congressional faculty granted under ARTICLE IV, Section 3, clause 2 of that instrument, of making all needful rules and regulations respecting the territory belonging to the United States. The resemblance of its jurisdiction to that of true United States courts in offering an opportunity to non-residents of resorting to a tribunal not subject to local influence, does not change its character as a mere "territorial court". (emphasis added)

What are the territories of the U.S.? Washington D.C., Puerto Rico, Guam, Virgin Islands, American Samoa, all forts, docks, magazines, arsenals and needful buildings. That's it. Unless, you committed a "federal" crime on "federal" territory owned by the U.S. government, the U.S. DISTRICT COURTS have no jurisdiction over an unenfranchised American on state soil.

Next the students looked at another Supreme Court decision made on April 26, 1995. This decision addressed the issue of exclusive legislative jurisdiction of Congress (i.e. powers of Federal government) and the subject matter jurisdiction of a Federal District Court.

Justice Clarence Thomas stated in a concurring majority opinion in the case U.S. vs. Lopez 514 U.S. 549 (1995)

"Indeed on this crucial point the majority and Justice Breyer agree in principle. The Federal government has nothing approaching a police power." He went on to discuss, "a regulation of police," wherein he stated U.S. v. Dewitt 76 U.S. 41, marked the first time the court struck down a federal law as exceeding the power conveyed by the commerce clause. In a two page opinion, the court invalidated a nationwide law prohibiting all sales of naphtha and illuminating oils. In so doing the court remarked that the commerce clause "has always been understood in limited terms and as a virtual denial of any power to interfere with the internal trade and business of the separate states."

Stop and think for a minute how many Federal Laws mold your everyday life and which fly right in the face of, and are contrary to, this high court ruling!

"The law in question," Thomas continues, "was plainly a regulation of police which could have constitutional application only where Congress has exclusive authority such as the territories."

Justice Thomas summed up his opinion with the statement:

"If we wish to be true to a constitution that does not cede a police power to the Federal Government . . ."

Wow! They were having their eyes opened and the entire class was riveted to the material. If it weren't for a few hard core smokers who needed their fix outside, they could have worked through all of the breaks.

So with this information and much more, one of the class participants raised the question: "If the Feds, by law, have no police power then what are the IRS, BATF, FBI, BLM, Homeland Security and the rest of the alphabet soup gang doing carrying lethal weapons, breaking into people's homes, seizing property, arresting and killing people for?"

Leroy's response was a deliberate silence and fiery stare that would put fear into the heart of any man. He didn't need to open his mouth. They all knew the answer. The one who posed the question continued, "this means that people are being killed and jailed (i.e. Waco) all over the country by unlawful thugs!" Another pregnant pause.

They then started talking about the requirements of all 'government agencies' to have a charter with by-laws just like a corporation does. The purpose of the charter is of course, to establish and outline the purpose and objectives of the organization, its organizational structure, it's means of accomplishing its purpose (modus operandi), its general rules and its limitations of authority. This charter must be filed in the Federal Register. Upon this filing then;

"Regulations must be implemented in the Code of Federal Regulations (C.F.R.'s) for the federal statutes (U.S. Code) to have any effect." - California Bankers' Assoc. vs. Shultz 416 U.S. 21 (1974).

This case affirms that without implementing regulations, the statutes have no teeth or ability to be enforced.

Leroy turned around and pulled out a small stack of papers which he started passing around.

This document he produced was from the Congressional Research Service (C.R.S.). It was an answer to a request for the C.R.S. to produce documentation pertaining to the required lawful charter of the F.B.I. The polite response contained in the document essentially said that this charter "did not exist"! They couldn't believe their eyes!

In effect, according to the decisions of the U.S. Supreme Court, the F.B.I. would have no lawful authority outside the specific limited territories of the U.S. if it were a legitimate, legal entity. But what they were seeing was that it is not even a legitimate lawful institution to begin with!

So right then they knew what it was not and is not. The question arises, what is it? We understand the nature of the bankruptcy this nation has been under since 1933 that a bankrupt entity has no authority to pass title or judgment on any issue or property except at the bequest of its creditors (IMF, the FED, World Bank etc.). Then the logical conclusion would be that it is a private enforcer created to protect the interests of the international bankers. The American people ('natural resources' creating tax revenue etc.) and the property of the American people are then the subjects' of this private army, among others.

They continued the study along these lines before they went back to the historical roots of the court system and its governing law which was almost exclusively the common law.

COMMON LAW BEGINNINGS

As was appropriate, any study of the history of the judiciary whose purpose it is to protect the rights of man goes back to England and the Magna Carta of 1215.

The Magna Carta, referred to as the 'Great Charter of Freedoms' essentially was the result of a group of Barons who had had enough of the King's crap, drew up a document outlining many of man's perceived rights of the time and included enforcement provisions. This was done while King John was traveling abroad. The document was presented to him upon his return, with an ultimatum; Accept this and sign it or else!

It was from this point that the peoples' common law, based upon biblical principles, began to flourish. It was from these roots that the basic precepts and philosophies of the founding of our great land became the structure of American life.

In class they discussed the roles of the various players in the 'Peoples court' i.e. justice of peace, bailiff, clerk, sheriff, secretary, notary, constable, etc.

This information was quite intriguing. To study the functions and procedure of a lawful court was an interesting contrast to the courts of today. Tremendous research had been done in this area and everything they covered was backed up by the authentic historical documentation which was discovered and pulled together by this scholarly team.

One particular point of interest was that these courts they were studying made perfect logical sense in for whom they operated and by whom they were controlled, the people i.e. plaintiff, defendant and the defendants jury of his peers. No attorneys or so called full time professionals were involved (D.A.'s, judges) except for the sheriff or constable who was there to keep the peace and to make sure that all parties were present. Common sense and fair play were the prevailing legal doctrines. What a bold concept!

THE ABA TIGHTENS ITS GRIP

The group discovered how, until just recently in the mid-60's, so many issues were resolved on a local level by the 'Justice of the Peace' who was a county official hired by the people. He was not an attorney. Remember these guys? They performed a myriad of judicial and administrative functions and the townsfolk who had disputes could go to the Justice of the Peace to get it resolved. The logical question arises. "What ever happened to the Justice of the Peace?"

Well, the J.P. was not usually a member of the Bar Association and was settling many a dispute that never reached the greedy clutches of bar members. The legislatures of most states (controlled by whom? Attorneys!) along with the emergency power county commissioners phased out the position and role of the J.P. The result of this process was to tighten the monopoly grip which the Bar Association members have on 'law' and the purse strings of Americans.

It's amazing to compare the notes, scenarios and circumstances of pre 1933 America (F.D.R. emergency) with those of today. To actually see, through documentation, how rights to due process, our courts, our involvement in the judiciary, our law and our heritage have been subverted, hidden, replaced and interposed upon by our corrupt officials and evil designs. It is simply astounding. These items, along with many others, prepared us for the bombshell that Leroy was about to drop on us.

A KEY DISCOVERY

He now pulled out copies taken from a law book of the early 1900's. In these pages were outlined the duties of the clerk as they related to "our One Supreme Court of the county"!

What? What was this? Many were not familiar with this court title. To make a long story and piles of documentation very short, "our One Supreme Court of the county" is the highest court in the land. It is a court of common law for the sovereign people of the county - the ultimate body politic under full sovereign control of the people. It was the court of first and last resort with original and exclusive jurisdiction to the people, a true ARTICLE III court which was distinctly separate and apart from all of the 'legislative' corporate courts under the corporate government's appellate division which operated from the municipal court all the way up the ladder to the U.S. Supreme Court.

The cumulative evidence that Leroy produced left no doubt or question whatsoever that the Peoples' simple, easy, cost effective and powerful remedies 'at law' available from ' our One Supreme Court' had been subverted and stolen from us by the powers that be.

Amazement and anger welled up within him. Rex was excited and furious at the same time. He wondered to himself how these treasonous and seditious acts could be allowed to happen. The research that these honorable men from Montana were showing us was in part, how our country and our heritage had been stolen from us. There is no other way to put it. It is clearly a deliberate attempt to seize control of the judicial and legislative branches to the detriment of the American People by the American Bar Association which is a division of the International Bar Assoc. (London) who are akin to or a/k/a 'the international bankers' and 'money powers'.

Based upon this research which was in fact the original, immutable 'Law' of this country, 'Justus Township' was formed with its lawful court of justice and the *de jure* republic (not democracy) previously known as the united States of America, was reborn albeit in feeble condition.

POTENTIAL FOR CONFRONTATION

In view of the thievery of our heritage and the perversions of our once protective (not intrusive) law, Leroy went on to explain how Justus town ship began putting local, state and federal officials on NOTICE of these errors and to keep their distance.

Once put on notice, establishment officials were required to do either one of only two things;

a) Be true to their sworn oath of office and do something to defend and uphold the constitutions as written, or

b) Do nothing and now be a knowing, willing and voluntary party to the sedition and treason.

Of course these Montana men had many more causes of action than we have the luxury of getting into here. But suffice it to say, that there were many notices which went out to many officials, all based upon good faith with the expectation that the officials would make efforts to correct these problems in accordance with the law which they are sworn to uphold.

They were wrong. The non-responsive silence was deafening. This was where the confrontations began to develop. Justus township started publishing public notices of their court's declaratory judgments and arrest warrants were issued against errant public officials.

In turn, local and state officials issued their own warrants for these guys for attempting to influence and intimidate public officials. However, they knew the guys in Justus township were serious, were armed and were right. The local officialdom didn't dare come onto the sovereign property. The sheriff was quoted by a neutral associate when asked why he wouldn't enforce his warrants; he replied "it wouldn't be logistically feasible!" Good one!

Conversely, Leroy and his Justus township friends didn't leave the property much either. The so-called standoff actually started about a year earlier than most people have been aware of by newspaper accounts.

FINANCIAL FINESSE

As we learned earlier from Hartford Van Dyke, a damage occurs in commerce when a public servant (trustee/agent) violates his oath and either acts or fails to act as required, in a manner which is contrary to the interests of the People who are the public servants'/government creators, beneficiaries and principals.

This led the group to begin study on how Justus township was planning to enforce their lawful court mandates. The answer was in the Uniform Commercial Code which is embodied in all state statutes except Louisiana. We all have heard the saying that it's "money that makes the world go around" and Justus township was going to hit them where it hurts – in the pocketbook.

In addition to scouring all the usual sources of information on the U.C.C., Justus township had obtained an original book, recently published, entitled "The Official Bankers' Handbook" which was an insider's publication not even available to many bankers.

This was the 'coup de gras'! With it Leroy and his associates had proceeded to decode the last remaining banking secrets that stood in the way of them achieving ultimate success with a heavy weapon.

The commercial U.C.C. documents which were created with this knowledge unequivocally put Justus township in the position of surpassing the IMF and Federal Reserve as the United States number one creditor. Think about that for a minute.

Due to the endless uncovered fraud, violations of public oaths, etc., the ensuing U.C.C. presentments of 'Notice and Grace' which gave all intended respondents an opportunity to do the right thing and provide remedy in good faith, coupled with these same respondents defaulting and thereby rendering 'Judgment Nihil Dicit' (he indicts himself by his silence), put Justus township in a position to lien the guilty parties in accordance with clearly established and long standing commercial principles and procedures.

However, they added a twist and boy was it a kicker! Pay attention here. Justus township was operating under the common law as free sovereign Americans under the de jure (at law) constitutional republic, right?

This was as opposed to operating under the admiralty/maritime statutory law of the de facto bankrupt U.S. Inc. as U.S. citizens/subjects. So in the supporting U.C.C.-4 financial statements underlying the cause, basis, damage and amount of the liens, they demanded satisfaction (payment) of the liens in *substantive money* which would be either gold or silver coin or notes backed by same. This of course is the legal definition of money in each of the states' respective constitutions as well as the federal constitution. There is only one problem. This medium of exchange is not available any more. We now know it was stolen from Americans beginning in the emergency of 1933 and given to foreigners.

So what was to be the solution? Since the U.S. federal government was principally responsible for the primary lien debtor (whoever it may have been for the particular instrument in question) being unable to pay in real money, the Comptroller of the Currency - U.S. Treasury was made a secondary or co-debtor to the lien.

What they had created in their commercial liens, was negotiable commercial paper backed up by the full faith and credit of the United States government. One of the documents was shown to a Swiss banker who remarked that this was, in effect, a bona-fide 'T-Bill'. He said it was worth from 100% to 150% of face value because it was 'virgin paper' and hadn't been leveraged or discounted and marketed again and again like most of the commercial paper available and used as collateral or currency in the world banking system.

They learned that all banks are nothing more than a 'debtor in possession' which means that all we do with banks is to deposit negotiable credit instruments i.e. checks, drafts, notes etc. The banker then is obliged to 'pay credit' on the instrument once he collects on it. So he is a debtor to the deposit as he is in possession of the negotiable instrument which needs to be collected on.

This paper lien was something that could be taken to the bank. They did. Leroy explained how they had taken one of the many liens which they had now perfected down to the Norwest Bank in Butte where they had an established checking account.

They very casually walked up to the teller and handed her a deposit slip with a lien for $550,000. It was one of their smaller ones. Being somewhat unusual the teller summoned a vice-president who invited the men into his office for a brief meeting.

They shortly came out and everyone was smiling, the banker had authorized checks which could be immediately written against the account. Checks were written. Checks were cleared and paid by the bank. The Montana Freemen had successfully established bona fide credit, which is our only medium of exchange in today's economy. Remember, there is no 'substantive money'. This credit was backed up by the assets of the lien debtors (i.e. public officials et al) and the U.S. government.

Stop and think of the importance of this for a minute. This is earth shattering. Using the bankers' laws (U.C.C. etc.) the Freemen had started their own private banking system using the Federal Reserve member banks and were in fact creating credit (money) that was actually backed by solid assets which is more than the Federal Reserve can say about the fiat scrip which they expect the rest of us to use. This was a momentous and historic feat.

Of course we all know that the cabal and their Federal Reserve abhors competition and we also have learned about one of their private enforcement divisions: The F.B.I. and who they really are.

Leroy had the group riveted to their seats as he explained the events. The next event came as little surprise.

The F.B.I. stepped in before long, seized the lien documents from the bank, closed the account and essentially removed it all to the Comptroller's Office at the U.S. Treasury. Undaunted by this unlawful seizure, which was what looked to be a serious and costly blow, Leroy was well founded in his knowledge and calmly shifted gears.

He explained that since the U.S. Treasury was now the 'debtor in possession' it was going to be the new 'bank' that would clear drafts against the assets represented by the seized commercial paper which was still owned by and listed the original lien creditor (damaged party citizen). This could not be changed.

Leroy used his computer to design a legally correct and authentic: "Comptroller Warrant" which is a technical name for a 'draft' or 'check' written against the U.S. Treasury Department. He printed out as many blanks as he needed using a provision in the U.C.C. (3-419) where he was able to lawfully sign his name on behalf of the Treasurer of the U.S. Treasury as an *accommodation party* along with his own name (signature) as registered lien creditor.

The only drawback to this method was that he could not be beneficiary of the warrant/check. So, to prove his success to any attendee of his Justus township law classes who requested it, and to generate cash flow, he would write up to five warrants in any amount. He had trillions of dollars of value in liens, backed by assets of corrupt officials and government bodies to pay off mortgages, credit cards, court judgments or other bank/government debt. He was writing the warrants in an amount equal to double what was owed and telling the people to demand refunds of the difference. The refunds were coming back with the zero balance statements and the skids were greased!

He was right on in his procedure backed up by the full weight of the law as it was written. It could not be ignored! The bankers always have to follow their own rules! Since peoples' rights have been stolen in the name of 'regulating commerce' then it would be by the 'rules of commerce' that he would play by.

From Rex's interaction with various people on this issue, he had in his possession certified copies of original warrants, refund checks and affidavits pertaining to the discharge in full of debt obligations to/from the following entities:

1) Bank of New York Delaware. Newark, DE
2) Household Credit Service Inc., Salinas. California
3) U.S. Post Office, Billings, Montana
4) Mitsubishi Finance Corporation.. San Marcos, CA
5) IRS - U.S. Treasury, San Francisco, CA
6) Dennison State Bank '. Bolton, Kansas
7) Fleet Mortgage Group, Milwaukee, Wisconsin
8) Kaw Valley State Bank & Trust Co., Wamego, Kansas
9) St. Mary's State Bank, St. Mary's, Kansas
10) U.S. Post Office, Phoenix Arizona
11) GM Credit Card.. Salinas, California
12) El Capitan National Bank, Sonora, California
13) MasterCard/Visa National Credit Group, Buffalo, Now York
14) Bank Card Services, Wilmington, Delaware
15) IRS - U.S. Treasury, Kansas City. Kansas

There were many, many more in Rex's possession and hundreds more in existence all over the country. Refund checks were in the hundreds, thousands, and tens of thousands of dollars.

The establishment wants you to believe that this is fraud. To the contrary, it is to the letter of the law. Obviously, the legal staffs of some of the largest corporations, banks, and government agencies in America agreed and complied. These corporations submitted to the law and cooperated fully. What does that mean?

If Leroy's commercial process was a fraud, then all banks are operating in fraud. It can't be legal for on preferred group and not be legal for others in the private sector! It only confirms everything that the Freemen were telling us about regarding the corruption and illegitimacy of the status quo.

The Montana Freemen, with the help of many others concerned about the corruption of our once great land, had found the God given truth and were prepared to use it to benefit all Americans.

One example of this was in the fact that they had $7.5 trillion in cured, registered liens on the natural resources of the STATE OF IDAHO alone. These liens were properly assigned to a trust in the name of 'Idaho Posterity Trust' which was to be used for the sole purpose of benefiting true Americans and the newly resurrected de jure government of the People in Idaho.

These men had a plan and by sharing this knowledge freely with all comers, as they had, it wouldn't be long before the assets and the power in this country were given back to its rightful owners, the People.

Most of us don't realize that the Federal U.S. Government has extended its bounds and now claims ownership in excess of the entire land mass in the country. Add to that, the state owned lands and that which the bankers own due to massive debt and what's left?

These two days at a quiet log home in the Bull Run Mountains of Montana had been a truly liberating revelation. One of Leroy's closing comments to us was, "The battle is over. The victory is ours. All that's left is to clean up the mess they (government officials) left behind." He said, "They don't know what to do and they're running for cover!"

Once again... legally, he was right.

The audiovisual equipment functioned beautifully and the group packed up and headed back to Denver with excellent recordings and copies of the most astounding information they had ever been fortunate enough to have access to.

The materials were duplicated in numbers and widely distributed to the American Law Club gang back in Denver and beyond.

The truth was now spreading across Colorado and the nation like a Kansas grassfire on a windy day!

What was learned in Montana about how the government has been twisted, exemplified what the French writer Frederick Bastiat foretold us in the nineteenth century in his book 'The Law' which is highly recommended as a 'Must Read':

"When plunder becomes a way of life for a group of men living together in society, they create for themselves in the course of time a legal system that authorizes it and a moral code that glorifies it."

If the true Americans, the Freemen, the Patriots, have anything to say about this current state of affairs it would be . . . "Not for long!"

CHAPTER 15

TACTICAL COUNTER MEASURES

FROM THE TIME HE WAS a first time guest on the radio show, Rex became quite familiar and talked regularly with Tom Schauf, C.P.A. If it weren't enough that the boys in Montana had uncovered several nuclear tipped legal bombshells (figuratively speaking) of their own, Tom Schauf had found more legal ammunition and had created a winning strategy of his own to almost single handedly crush the scheme of usury and theft by the Federal Reserve banking system and its legion of protectors.

Through numerous and lengthy phone conversations and personal meetings Rex had become fascinated with the work and discoveries that had become Tom's work product.

First of all, not only does he have the credentials of being a Certified Public Accountant, but he has taught over 2000 C.P.A.s nationally for the C.P.A. required continuing education and has been used as an expert witness in court many times. So he is credentialed and speaks with authority in his area of expertise.

Tom's discovery about the true private nature of the Federal Reserve led him to understand many things about how the Fed and the U.S. government together were deeply involved in activities which are inimical to the interests of all Americans. He brought up to Rex the fact that Benjamin Franklin once said that the key issue of the revolutionary war was in fact banking.

Tom told him that in one of his continuing education seminars he asked the group if any of the C.P.A.'s in attendance were also bank auditors. One student responded affirmatively. Tom asked the auditor to show him the bank's bookkeeping entries that it makes when granting loans. The auditor agreed.

The auditor said, "The entries look legal until you see the second half of the bookkeeping entry." The bank auditor showed him the second half of the entries and asked Tom, "Do you see the fraud?" Tom wasn't catching on right away. He told Tom, "Every bank loan is a fraud." He then showed Tom that when you combine the two bookkeeping entries it proves that the bank did the opposite of what the alleged loan contract stipulates that the bank should do.

Let's look at the actual loan transaction and see how this works.

First of all, the promise of all bank loans is that the bank has all this money on hand and it wants to loan you some of it. If you qualify, the bank will loan you some of its money if you promise to pay it back with a fee (points and/or interest). Just to make sure the bank doesn't lose its money they usually get you to give them the beneficial interest (ownership) in your property (collateral) until the contract is fulfilled. This is how most of us are led to believe the bank loan transaction works. It's a fairytale. Let's analyze it.

THE MECHANICS OF BANK FRAUD

Tom Schauf and his bank auditor friend have revealed the true loan transaction as follows:

First, the bank doesn't care much if you qualify when you can offer tangible property as collateral because they know that mathematically they will foreclose on a certain number of properties without anything having been put up or risked to get it, adding significantly to the bottom line. But they maintain the illusion that credit qualifications are important because this covers what they are really doing.

Secondly, once you (or more accurately your collateral) have been approved, nothing happens until you sign a 'promissory note' and give it to the bank.

Remember a 'note' is one of four forms of negotiable instruments identified in the U.C.C.:

1) Note
2) Check
3) Draft
4) Certificate of Deposit.

Negotiable instruments are used as 'money' being instruments of debt and credit. Remember, 'credit' is the medium of exchange (money) which we use daily in almost every transaction.

Now pay attention to what the bank does in its books to reflect the loan transaction: Your note is deposited as an **asset** to the bank and is credited to the bank's asset base. If you understand double entry book-keeping you know the bank must now enter a *debit entry* to offset its *credit entry* and zero it out. The account which gets *debited* is the bank's checking account demand deposits or DDA (demand deposit account). In bookkeeping terms a debit is a liability. Remember this as it will be important in just a minute.

What the bank did here so far was to deposit your promissory note as 'money' on its books. Then they transferred **your** 'money' into the bank's checking account as if it were their own and did so without your permission. This is fraud and criminal conversion for starters.

It is out of this checking (demand deposit) account that the bank writes **you** the check for the loan. Now let's examine a few things right here.

One: remember just a minute ago when we saw that a debit is a liability? The 'money' deposited into the bank's checking account was a *debit* (liability) right? And the bank just wrote you a check (loan) from that account right? Well if a debit is a liability and the check was written from that debit account, then what the bank actually loaned you was a liability and not an asset! Weren't you led to believe that 'money' is an asset and that's what you wanted to borrow? What does the loan contract say, that you are being loaned an asset? or a liability? Are you starting to get the picture? Let's look further now.

The next thing to recognize is the fact that the bank deposited your note as 'money' on its books. They transferred that 'money' to another account and gave it back to you in the form of a bank check, didn't they?

Now you say, "Wait a minute. I thought I was borrowing the *bank's* money not *my own!*" You're right! That was what you thought, but they tricked you. Not only did they trick you with deceptive and misleading advertising: "Money to Loan", but they are making fees (points and interest) off of loaning you your own money and forcing you to risk your own collateral for the privilege!

ADMISSIONS FROM THE FED

The Federal Reserve tells us point blank how this works in their own publication entitled, "<u>Modern Money Mechanics</u>", which was free for the asking from the Chicago Federal Reserve Bank public information officer and may still be available online.

They are not ashamed at all about their banking practices as is exhibited by the following excerpts from that publication;

"What Makes Money Valuable? In the United States neither paper currency nor deposits checking, savings, etc. have value as commodities. Intrinsically, a dollar bill is just a piece of paper, deposits merely book entries. Coins do have some intrinsic value as metal but generally far less than their face value.

What then makes these instruments - checks, paper money, and coins acceptable at face value in payment of all debts and for other monetary uses Mainly it's the confidence people have that they will be able to exchange such money for other financial assets and for real goods and services wherever they choose to do so.'

What do you think about that? Was it what you would expect the Federal Reserve to tell you? It gets better as they continue in the same publication.

"Who Creates Money? Bankers discovered that they could make loans merely by giving their promise to pay (liability in the form of a check from a debit 'DDA' account) or bank notes (Federal Reserve Note) to borrowers. In this way, banks began to create money. More notes could be issued than the gold and coin on hand because only a portion of the notes outstanding would be presented for payment at any one time. Enough metallic money had to be kept on hand, of course, to redeem whatever volume of notes was presented for payment (prior to 1933 anyway).

Transaction deposits are the modern counterpart of bank notes. It was a small step from printing notes to making book entries crediting deposits of borrowers (your note), which in turn the borrowers could spend by writing checks, thereby printing their own money.

There you have it! The Fed admits that YOU created your own money by depositing your note with the bank. So they don't really have any "money to loan" as they advertise.

Stop and take a breath. Let's think about this for a minute. By the way, the parentheses above are insertions by this author.

What did the Federal Reserve tell us above?

ONE: Bankers make loans by giving their promise to you (liability).

This promise to pay never gets paid does it? The banker gives you a check which can only be cashed in Federal Reserve Notes. A Note is nothing more than a promise to pay. So the bankers' promise to pay is only redeemable in the Fed's promises to pay. They know now that a Federal Reserve Note is not redeemable in anything of value by any bank. So all you got from the banker was a promise to pay which never gets paid: a liability that gets passed on but is never settled.

You put up your property, a tangible asset of value as collateral. You signed a contract to pay the banker back in assets, the hard earned fruit of your labor, and all he gave you was a liability. He never had any money to loan you in the first place. He loaned you money that you created, your own money! And now, in the case of a 30 year mortgage you are going to pay the bankers three times the amount you loaned to yourself!? What was the bankers' risk? Nothing. What did the banker do to earn 30 years of your labor? Nothing. What did the banker do to earn the right to steal your house from your family if you get laid off after paying him for twenty years and can't make a few payments? Nothing.

TWO: "Banks create money; credit and liabilities."

Didn't the people, the principals and creators of government, delegate our power to create money (substance) to Congress (our agent)? Didn't we (the People) put in the constitution that it was unlawful for any state to emit bills of credit? Wasn't it unlawful for Congress to delegate their limited authority to coin money of substance? We delegated this power to them and them alone, not to private bankers, most of whom are not even Americans?!

THREE: "Only a portion of those notes outstanding would be presented for payment at any one time."

This is false and misleading. The bankers now are dealing in Federal Reserve Notes which are NON-REDEEMABLE period! Take one into any bank anywhere and ask them to redeem your $10 bill. See what happens. Put yourself in the bankers' shoes. It's a pretty nice racket, huh? You get liens on everyone's property, homes, cars, RV's, incomes, labor, etc., and you not only don't have to put up a dime of your own but you know your lousy bank notes will never be called for actual payment in substance either. You've got the best of both worlds! Regular people go to jail for Ponzi schemes like this!

FOUR: "It was a small step from printing notes to making book entries."

Money is nothing more than book entries made by the banker after he locks in your collateral and promise to pay. He knows that since he only created the principal amount of the loan in new 'money' and the money to pay the interest on all of his loans is never created; then by pure mathematics some people are guaranteed to fail on his loans and he will get his collateral, your property, your substance... Free and clear through foreclosure.

Since the borrower is, in effect printing (figuratively) and borrowing his own money, the banker is nothing more than a paper shuffler who will collect so much collateral without risking one thin dime of his own. Question: If you created the money via your promissory note, couldn't you discharge your liability with another note, which is the current medium of exchange that exists today? This has been done!

Using this information as a basis for his work, Tom told him that his auditor friend was very concerned about this information getting out to the public for fear that if the American people understood all of this, in his words, "they would demand that all the bankers, lawyers and bank auditors be sent to jail." Tom said, 'Exactly!'

He explained that it is the same set of bookkeeping entries that would occur as if a burglar stole your property and returned the stolen property back to the victim calling it a loan. Then the victim must repay the principal and interest to the thief who stole the property in the first place!

The auditor told Tom that obviously the bank doesn't want people to know about both halves of the transaction. This is the oldest bank trick in the world and it keeps its victims, the American people, in debt and forever paying interest and property (through foreclosures) to the bankers who never loaned one red cent of legal tender, or other depositor's money, to obtain the promissory notes.

Do a search on the net for 'Bank of England admits that loan comes first'

Have you noticed that not too long ago many banks were willing to loan you up to 100% of the value of your home in equity loans? The loan to value ratio has traditionally only been 70% to 80'% hasn't it? They really want you to stay in hock up to your eyeballs. When we saw this in the 90's we knew they were going to pull the rug out from under all the suckers whom they pulled into the fraud. It's called 'Easy Money'! Others called it 'The Real Estate Bubble'.

How many credit card applications have you received or seen all over town in little displays in stores? Are you starting to see how the credit trap works from a little different perspective now? Now in 2009 in the throes of the financial crisis which started in 2008 how much property do the banks own?

In getting to know Tom Schauf personally Rex recognized early on that he was obviously a man with strong Christian beliefs who was committed to helping his fellow Americans release themselves from the bondage of this debt virus, these false weights and measures of the Federal Reserve monetary system of the United States.

His call to action was direct from the Bible: Deuteronomy 25:15. You must have accurate and honest weights and measures so that you may live long in the land the LORD your God is giving you.

With the basis of information that his auditor friend showed him, Tom went to work. He met with one of the partners of a big Chicago C.P.A. firm which specialized in auditing banks.

He started asking questions and the firm partner became very defensive. The partner denied that bank loans were a fraud and said they loaned cash. Just as Tom teaches in his bank fraud package, the bankers, as this partner did, kept trying to redefine terms and regularly used lies to cover up the truth.

And just as Tom teaches people to expose the truth by simply asking questions, he asked the partner about twenty questions. This guy never really understood banking until Tom exposed it for him through his clever questioning. Once this was done, the partner could do nothing but admit to Tom that all bank loans are fraud. The partner now admitted that he understood banking in a way like he never did before. The problem now was that he was in a position with a major accounting firm that audited the books for many major banks, and he was now aware of huge fraud being perpetrated on the American people and business community.

He could go to jail as a co-conspirator if he didn't do something. If he did do something, think about the impact it would have on his business and his reputation in the industry! He has a real problem!

Tom Goes to the People

Tom has used his training as a C.P.A., a teacher, and as an expert courtroom witness to put together an informational package of audio tapes and books geared to help your counsel bring an action into court and do the following;

1) Frame the issues.
2) Expose the weaknesses of the banks.
3) Teach how the other side will lie and how to expose the lies in court.
4) Use the banks' own financial reports/information/books, which say they call it a loan when in fact there is no 'loan'.
5) The bank reports admit that the bank never loaned you other depositors' money or legal tender to obtain your promissory note and collateral.

Rex found his work to be extensive, on point and thorough enough to provide as much overkill as one would like.

For example: Tom has put together over 120 questions for the banker or auditor to answer on the witness stand. They are all intricately interwoven.

If the banker answers one he has to answer them all. He can't say he didn't know. The answers all show up in the books or bank literature. It is a trap he cannot escape.

When the banker answers the questions, if he lies on one, he's exposed by another one because he gave another answer on a third one. So either one of two things happens, either the banker admits to bank fraud on the stand, or he proves himself to be a liar and perjures himself on the stand. Either way he goes to jail! Either way, plaintiff wins! Not a good position to be in.

Tom's program was put together to teach anyone to understand the bank's bookkeeping entries regardless of how little accounting you've had. The manual is about 150 pages showing court cases, bookkeeping entries, law, details of banking, about 30 pages of questions for the banker or auditor that they won't want to discuss how to expose their lies, the theories of the suit and more.

Upon reviewing the package he was fascinated that the science of it all had nothing to do with the usual arguments of lawful money, the facts that banks lend credit unlawfully, etc. It is a killer shark attack based purely on the contract, the books and the felonies; Pure and Simple. Any and all bankers would fall if this were applied properly.

After talking to so many businessmen, farmers, ranchers and families over the years who have come to him in desperation and were about ready to lose the family inheritance and livelihood because the banker was forcing them to default through his refusal to renegotiate or accept a reasonable workout plan on the loan... finally Rex could offer these victims of circumstances and/or greed a weapon which they could wield to defend themselves, their property and their family's future.

This is very sensitive information and it is a bombshell indeed. Tom does not brag about victories. Usually settlements are reached out of court to avoid this becoming a public precedent. As a condition for these settlements the plaintiff is required to keep his mouth shut, as you might imagine.

One case which was known to be particularly notable was won in court. Not only is the case file unavailable, but nobody in the courthouse will admit that the judge who presided over the case was ever on the bench to begin with! He disappeared physically and from everyone's memories as well! This is not surprising at all. They are poking the tiger (Fed) in the eye again and again with a long sharp stick on this one.

If it weren't for the fact that Tom has already been on several broad based radio shows like Rex's and that his package had already been widely distributed, Rex would have expected him to be dead by now. But he was smart and got it out quickly to many people which probably saved his neck.

However, the fact that Tom promoted his program openly to the public and on a regular basis, surely garnered some demerits with the cabal. He was well aware of this when he began his war on fraud and thought "to hell with them. Let the truth prevail and let the chips fall where they may. We do not fight for the approval of man, but for the grace of God!"

If used by enough people, this program alone could possibly win the country back as the parasitic vultures of the Federal Reserve banking system watch their house of cards burn before their very eyes with many of their brethren trapped on the inside. In view of the broken families, suicides, divorces, poverty and enslavement of the masses caused by these demons, Rex could envision many more smiles than tears in watching these S.0.B.'s burn in their own self excavated pit of immorality.

So people then naturally ask, now that we're tearing down the old system what do we have to replace it? A good question deserves a good answer.

We go back to the basics that were originally intended for the country as follows:

1. Abolish the Federal Reserve and the I.R.S. entirely. They are absolutely unnecessary in each and every respect.
2. Abolish the Federal Reserve Act of 1913 which opened the door to the whole mess.
3. Force Congress to take back the responsibility that they had unlawfully given away in the first place, that of coining and minting our own money, U.S. Notes, and constitutionally defined dollars.
4. Now we can spend the money into circulation for the cost of printing ($27 per thousand notes) instead of paying taxes to cover the face amount of principal and interest (potentially over $1 million per thousand notes). This eliminates the need for income taxes. Government can and should exist on excise taxes and imposts alone.
5. Repudiate all government obligations to the Federal Reserve which will cancel, in all probability, more than 50% of the national debt.
6. Without the huge drain from our incomes that taxes once took, Americans can now save and invest which provides a huge

surplus of capital for cheap loans to create investment, employment, help to businesses, rebuild a private educational system that is affordable, etc.

Most of us are not economists or social planners but the benefits seem obvious. Tom Schauf was on to something here and Rex with the A.L.C. was right behind him 100%. Rex's only regret was that his personal adversaries created so many distractions for him that he couldn't do more with Tom's program. However, through the radio show and a few personal contacts, he did help him establish a beachhead in Colorado and in other parts of the country and for that contribution he was glad.

For words of timeless wisdom on this issue we should look back to Thomas Jefferson in 1816:

"We believe that banking institutions are more dangerous to our liberties than standing armies. Already they have raised up a moneyed aristocracy that has set the Government at defiance. The issuing power should be taken from the banks and restored to the people to whom it properly belongs."

Could Mr. Jefferson have described our modern day society any better?

"The real truth of the matter is, as you and I know, that a financial element in the large centers has owned the government of the U.S. since the days of Andrew Jackson." -- Franklin D. Roosevelt in a letter written Nov. 21, 1933 to Colonel E. Mandell House

PART V

BATTLE CRY - THE ENEMY ENGAGED

CHAPTER 16

WASHCO ATTACKS

BACK ON THE LOCAL BATTLEFIELD, the lines had been drawn. As discussed previously, WashCo had arrested Rex in the courtroom during one of Gary's hearings for 'criminal impersonation' whereby he was apparently 'impersonating himself' by using his own name. They set bond high enough where they figured he wouldn't get out for awhile if at all. While hit and run defendants and murderers were getting bonds set at $5000 and $10,000, Rex's was set at $50,000.

Rex's counterpunch was broadcasting two live radio shows from inside their jail on their phone exposing their fraud by interviewing some of their incarcerated victims. Furthermore he later did get the bond amount reduced (to $30,000) and did get out after all, but not without a pending court date for two class six felonies hanging over his head.

Rex's expose and attacks against the fraud of WashCo via his radio show continued and intensified with the help of Gary Woodland and James Black who were still being held there and were regular guests on the show. The ridiculous nature of the charges against him was indicative of the intellectual and moral void that existed in the D.A.'s office, the Sheriff Department, and the courts over there. It made for some cheap humor and some sad wake up calls for Rex's listening audience.

Aside from winning the case, Rex's goal was to cost them as much time, frustration, money and embarrassment as he could possibly generate and to use this experience to educate and empower the public in the process. He looked forward to exposing their vindictive, oppressive, unlawful persecution for what it was. Despite his inexperience in the courtroom he was confident, albeit a little nervous, that he could do just that.

Rex's attack on the case started with a "Notice of Military Flag and Lack of Jurisdiction". This 'Notice' advised the court of the military (admiralty/maritime jurisdiction) yellow fringed flag hung in the courtroom which implied that this territory was a prize of conquest by the Federal Government which was exercising extra-territorial jurisdiction outside of its constitutionally imposed limits of the 10 mile square Washington D.C. and its possessions. Some people say this is nonsense. No. It's the law. Look it up in the footnotes of the appropriate section of older U.S. Code books in Title 5.

Furthermore, being in Admiralty/Maritime jurisdiction there must be, in fact and in law, a contract which provides a nexus for the court to assume jurisdiction over the matter since they were exercising equity law which is based on contract. In other words, if the parties do not have a contract which is in dispute, and both parties do not agree to submit to the court's jurisdiction, then the court has no jurisdiction to hear the matter. It's plain and simple.

Rex's 'Notice' included all the necessary and pertinent law and even included a quote on the flag from army regulations which supported his position. With all the supporting information needed to make a winning argument, knowing that they had no contract in dispute nor did they have his agreement to submit to the court's jurisdiction (since this 'Notice' is in fact an objection) he demanded that in the absence of an expressed written agreement whereby he have knowingly, willingly, and voluntarily submitted to this court or that he was military personnel that this court dismiss the case or in the alternative replace the military flag with a proper civil banner of the united States of America as defined in the U.S. Code title 4 section 1. (Bear in mind that much of the information found on the internet is quite limited compared to the original Sessions Laws and codification of the statutes.)

This 'Notice', if submitted to a lawful court, should have been acted upon unilaterally. However, this District court in WashCo would hold it until the motions hearing hoping for Rex to make a mistake and grant jurisdiction by filing a 'motion' or by making a voluntary appearance in court thus waiving his right to object.

He recognized this but being on a tight leash on the terms of the bond with assets put up by friends, he'd go in and argue the facts and the law, and beat them over the head with their own stick which would be even more satisfying.

There's an old saying, "When they have you over a barrel on the facts argue procedure. When they have you on procedure argue the facts. When they have you on facts and procedure argue jurisdiction."

Well... he could brush up on his procedure because he knew they screwed up on that plus he was confident in the facts and the law, so he didn't push the jurisdiction issue but he did want to set the record properly for appeal if needed. So Rex's 'Notice' went in and he objected when they predictably failed to rule on it. It was just ignored.

It is important to understand that any case falls apart at the first defect... So we start at the very beginning.

First off, felony charges were brought forward by what is called the 'information'. This was done as a product of the work of our good friend Patty Putin of the WashCo Sheriff Department without the aid of any damaged or injured party or any complaining witnesses or parties to the cause of action. This is in direct violation of Rex's constitutionally secured rights not to be accused of an infamous crime other than by a grand jury indictment. There was no complaining party, nor any grand jury indictment on the 'felony' charges.

We are seeing masses of people in this country imprisoned for victimless 'crimes against the state' without the constitutionally mandated Grand Jury investigation/indictment. Lenin and Khrushchev would be proud.

This one instance alone is a perfect example of how the people of this nation are directly affected by a government which has developed policies and practices in excess of its constitutionally delegated authority.

The next place to look for defects was in the Affidavit in support of the Arrest Warrant. This was Patty's work as well and what a piece of work it was! To start with... it did not even meet the requirements of being a proper affidavit.

A proper affidavit is sworn to under penalties of perjury (risk) where the affiant swears to the following- a) that you have firsthand personal knowledge of the 'facts contained therein. It's not *hearsay* where 'he said she said' etc. b) that the information being sworn to is true, complete, accurate and not misleading, and c) that the affiant is of legal age and sound mind and is competent to testify to these facts.

Putin's so called affidavit contained none of the above prerequisites. She only wrote that she was "duly sworn upon oath". Rex had to ask himself, "what oath? where is it?"

Is it the oath to Satan whereby she swears against God to tell the half-truth, the un-truth and nothing close to the real truth? With no penalties if she gets caught in her lies, so help her god? What oath? This was wholly inadequate.

An old maxim of law states that "Where one incurs *no risk* he holds *no authority*."

We see this in effect every day. For example, we see the political candidate risk his time, money, good name and character to intensive public scrutiny during his campaign and subsequent office. When successful, his risk has earned him the authority of that office if elected.

The soldier who risks his life to take the enemy's foxhole on the hill, when successful takes the foxhole and holds that authority against all who would come against him.

The weasel that writes an unsigned anonymous letter of complaint to his boss, councilman or representative, holds no authority and his letter gets tossed out with no consideration. This is a simple but eternal and universal concept. 'No risk' equals 'no authority'. Patty Putin did not subject herself to the risks of the penalties of perjury in her affidavit and thus it was void on that basis alone.

However, there was a reason for this fact to occur. The statements of the affidavit were full of half-truths, untruths, slander, guilt by association, innuendo and other numerous attempts to fabricate a flavor, color and texture to this alleged case which did not exist in reality.

Aha! This explained the oath (or lack thereof) and the no-risk, no fault approach.

Rex put in a 'Demand for Dismissal' based on the grounds that the Affidavit in support of the arrest warrant carried no authority, and he proceeded to outline the facts and the law in support of his argument. This was a fundamental flaw upon which everything else rests. Again, this issue was not dealt with forthrightly by the court and was deferred until the motions hearing.

The preliminary hearing was soon approaching where it would be determined if there was sufficient probable cause to move ahead to trial or not. The preliminary hearing is like a mini-trial before the judge of county court. Since the probable cause for arrest must be established by the affidavit in support of the original arrest warrant, this would be the focus of Rex's attack and defense in the preliminary hearing. Without sufficient probable cause, there would be no trial.

Patty Putin would take the stand to support her affidavit by her testimony and this was Rex's opportunity to expose her trickery, lies and deception which he did the best he could. However he was shut down by the judge more often than not who was apparently trying the case on behalf of the prosecution.

To Rex's amazement none of these defects in law or procedure nor the factual inconsistencies and half-truths/untruths seemed to have any impact on the judge whatsoever. County judge Jackson seemed to be on automatic pilot to accomplish what must be done, 'find sufficient probable cause to turn the case over to district court for trial'. And so, upon completion of the hearing, it was done, regardless of the defects, the facts or the law.

This wasn't a court. It was a prosecution machine for the DA! The machine continued grinding on. The next phase of the process was the arraignment where they wanted Rex to enter a plea. He refused to enter a plea (agree) to an unlawful sham proceeding and the arraignment was twice reset to new dates which amounted to about a forty five day delay. Finally, district court judge Gaspar Franz Perriman entered a plea of not guilty for him, over Rex's objection.

Rex asked Perriman if he could show him a power of attorney whereby he gave him authority to act on his behalf. And in doing so wasn't he 'practicing law from the bench' which violates his mandate to be an unbiased, impartial referee? He stonewalled Rex and refused to answer the question. Everyone in the courtroom knew the answer.

Rex then asked if "not guilty" was a 'judicial determination by the court' hoping that if Perriman slipped and said 'yes' Rex's response would be something to the effect of: "Well then if this court has under its judicial power determined on the record that I am in fact not guilty, there is nothing left to resolve and we'll consider this matter closed. Thank you and good day!" Perriman didn't fall for the trap.

Rex would soon learn that the judge would flat ignore virtually any issue or question which was raised challenging the authority or jurisdiction of the court, the validity of the prosecution was virtually untouchable regardless of their flagrant deviations from acceptable procedure, law or ethics.

For example, rule 5 requires the prosecution to provide the accused with complete copies of all charging documents immediately upon filing. Well, Rex had been arrested, spent several weeks in their jail, had been to an advisement hearing, a preliminary hearing and two previous arraignments, all without copies of the required paperwork. During the third attempted arraignment he demanded dismissal for the prosecutors' failure to comply with rule 5. Here he was, after all this time and technically he had not even been formally advised of the nature of the charges against him. How's that for due process? In our system you are not expected to have to defend yourself from 'secret' charges!

As soon as he made the demand, the prosecutor was obviously shaken. She nervously flipped through her file and pulled out her copy of the charging documents. She then jumped up and handed him her copy while she lingered at his side making sure the judge saw her give him the papers. She was still in violation of the rule as she wasn't 'timely' in her delivery.

Rex continued to argue his case and the judge never ruled on his demand for dismissal. This poses a problem for judge Perriman as Colorado Revised Statutes (C.R.S.) provides that should a judge fail to make a ruling on a motion within ninety days of the motion, he forfeits his salary for a full three months. When he failed to rule Rex quietly let it slide. He'll be in for a nice surprise!

So with the involuntary plea of 'not guilty' made on his behalf a date was set for a motions hearing, other pretrial deadlines and trial.

The first thing Rex did was to check and see if Perriman's position as judge was duly occupied or vacant. Article XII of the Colorado constitution, as in all states, requires all state officers to have a duly filed oath of office on public record upon taking office. Failure to comply renders that position vacant and that person has no authority and is in fact impersonating a public official.

Wouldn't that be interesting? A case whereby he was accused of 'impersonation' which upon further investigation, uncovers an imposter on the bench impersonating a judge!

He went down to the Secretary of State's office and they did have an oath on file for Perriman so he got a certified copy. As he learned from studying the commercial liens, this oath is his official contract with him (Mr. John Q. Public), to uphold, protect and defend Rex's constitutionally secured, God given rights to liberty and due process, etc. He would later use the certified copy of his oath as an attachment to a 'Notice of Contract' which he drew up simply to remind him of these facts and he submitted it to the court for the record.

During both the preliminary hearing and the arraignment Rex tried intently at getting judge Perriman to inform him as to the nature of the charges (civil or criminal) and the nature of the jurisdiction in which this matter was being heard. This is a basic right of due process. Criminal cases can only be heard in either common law or admiralty jurisdiction. Courts of civil, maritime or equity jurisdiction are not criminal courts. These different Jurisdictions have different sets of rules and he had a right to know so he could apply the appropriate rules. It's basic due process.

Now, we know that the court can't operate under common law because if they did they would have to produce an 'injured party' or 'corpus delicti' a complaining witness or proof of damage. If they were held to these standards they wouldn't have hardly any 'customers'. Think about all that 'business' they would lose if they couldn't prosecute all these heinous perpetrators of victimless 'crimes against the state'!

Of course we're not naive enough to think that the judge would come out and openly admit that he was captain of an admiralty ship even though his gold fringed flag was very explicit about this fact. We know this sounds ridiculous and incredulous to you if you don't have the legal background and understanding of this issue. But the legal precedent and written word is clearly set and is undeniable. In law, words mean everything! Look up 'the flag' section in the U.S. Code (Federal Statutes) and follow the footnotes.

However, Rex fully expected some deceitfully clever response such as, "We're in statutory jurisdiction" which he has seen judges say before. Had this been the case he would have held his feet to the fire and asked him to identify for him where in the constitution, which he has sworn by oath to support and defend... does it mention 'statutory jurisdiction?' It doesn't and it's not in there because there is no such thing in the real world. It's only a fiction.

Despite Rex's overture and invitation for the judge to act in good faith by informing Rex of the *'nature'* of the charges and the nature of the jurisdiction of the court, whereby he could then understand the rules of procedure of the court, Perriman dodged the issue entirely. Rex's alternative was to put the prosecutor on the stand under oath and have her tell him. He was denied that request as well... over Rex's objection.

Judging by this behavior, one is left only to conclude that this court must be operating in some secret jurisdiction that only the American Bar Association (to which both the judge and prosecutor are members) knows about. And by keeping this secret to themselves, they are exhibiting extreme bias and prejudice by forcing Rex to play their game with high stakes money and Rex's life and liberty at risk while they refuse to inform him of which set of rules they are using. This amounts to slavery being administered by a Star Chamber, which brings up a whole host of other problems for officials who are sworn to uphold their oaths of office.

If the truth were known, one of two things would happen:

a) If they admitted admiralty/jurisdiction they would have to prove that he was either in the armed forces or that they had a contract which provided a nexus for the court to assume jurisdiction. Of course they had neither and would have to dismiss.

b) If they admitted common law jurisdiction they would have to produce a damaged party 'corpus delicti'. They couldn't, and again would have to dismiss.

Either way, he wins. Now we know why the judge refused to address the issue. His ship is more like a tank on automatic pilot. Obstacles were ignored and consequently crushed.

That was fine with Rex, as he was well aware of several Federal court decisions which stated unequivocally that once jurisdiction is challenged, it must be proven. Failure to do so is reversible error. He had set the record properly for appeal, if needed. This was Rex's backup position, should he need it. This bias was witnessed by several court observers Rex had in the public gallery.

In addition, Rex had discovered that judge Perriman was the judge who administered the oath of the District Attorney who was prosecuting him. While this was not necessarily a conflict of interest or automatic bias, the fact that one *might* have a potential vested political interest in the wellbeing of the other gave the *appearance* of a possible bias or conflict which is all that is necessary to recuse the judge and force him to step down from the bench on this particular case.

He drafted a motion for recusal of the judge and attached the required affidavits from two disinterested parties who were also Rex's court observers. He used the 'potential' bias of the vested political interest and the refusal to inform him as to the nature of the charges and jurisdiction and the fact that he was also hearing the politically HOT case of Rex's friend Gary Woodland, as grounds for the appearance of at a minimum, potential prejudice. The facts were clearly sufficient and the form of Rex's motion was dead-on accurate and correct.

Case law clearly states that the facts contained therein are presumed to be true and the judge has no jurisdiction to determine the accuracy or content of the facts. If facts are merely stated or alleged, they are unimpeachable by the reviewing judge for the purposes of recusal. He can only deny the motion based upon insufficiency in its form i.e. no facts stated as grounds or no supporting affidavits etc. Rex was sure he had him nailed. He only hoped that he could get an honest judge as a replacement. Sure. He'd better buy a lotto ticket too!

This was submitted prior to arraignment and he did get him to rule on it at the final attempted arraignment which he felt was progress anyway. He declared, "Motion denied due to insufficient facts!"

At this point Rex realized that he might be able to at least make some money laying bets on how much reversible error he could get this clown to lay on the record for him. He figured that he had better start keeping track because at this rate he could start quite a collection of errors and they hadn't even gotten to the motions hearing yet!

He continued mining Patty Putin's Affidavit for nuggets and like a prospector who hits a vein, gold kept surfacing. Upon further analysis he found that her wording and explanation of the alleged crime committed (impersonating himself) matched that of another subsection of the statutes of which he wasn't even charged! In other words her affidavit was so sloppy that it did not even support the specific statutory violation that was alleged in the charging documents. He was charged with crime (b) stemming from an alleged affidavit which established probable cause for crime (a).

This obviously leads us to a false arrest which is not supported by affidavit whatsoever: a blatant violation of due process and constitutional limitations. This was turning into 'Keystone Cops'!

These facts brought him to whip up another Demand for Dismissal based upon the fact that the complaint/information failed to charge an offense supported by oath or affirmation. He hadn't had so many nice gifts since Rex's childhood Christmas at grandma's house.

In all, he had submitted a total of twelve notices & motions, most of which exposed glaring and fatal defects in the prosecution's case whereby, in a true court of law the case would have been killed many times over. Unfortunately he was in a kangaroo court of power and politics and neither law nor ethics were the least bit relevant here. There was an agenda to serve and justice wasn't a part of it, obviously.

At the motions hearing the prosecution tendered one motion to obtain handwriting samples. It was granted. All twelve of Rex's solid and well-grounded demands and motions were flat denied and Perriman didn't even allow an oral argument. Some of Rex's Notices didn't even require a ruling or action and all were denied anyway.

For example the 'Notice of Contract' with the judge's oath attached was nothing but a reminder, for the record, requiring no action or ruling. By denying it he was denying his own oath of office! How's that for blatant abuse of power? This seemed to confirm Rex's suspicions that the Chief Justice Perriman was probably a higher up in the Masonic Temple who has sworn the 'Kol Nidre'.

THE KOL NIDRE

The Kol Nidre is a Jewish prayer named from its opening words, "All vows'. It is based on the declaration of the Talmud:

"He who wishes that his vows and oaths shall have no value, stand up at the beginning of the year and say: 'All vows which I shall make during the year shall be of no value.'"

The oath of Kol Nidre Vol. 8, pg. 539 of the Jewish Encyclopedia is stated as follows:

"All vows, obligations, oaths, anthems, whether called konan, konas, or by any other name, which we may be bound, from this Day of Atonement unto the next... we do repent. May they be deemed absolved, forgiven, annulled and void and made of no effect; they shall not bind us nor have any power over us. The vows shall not be reckoned vows; the obligations will not be obligatory, nor are the oaths."

All judges and elected officials are bound by an oath and vow to support the united States Constitution which guarantees your unalienable rights according to Article VI: (2) of same. All attorneys, as officers of the court, are also sworn with a vow to support said Constitution according to the same Article.

On page 183 of the Masonic Handbook it says:

"Whenever you see any of our signs made by a brother Mason, and especially the hailing sign of distress, you must always be sure to obey them, even at the risk of your life. If you're on a jury, and the defendant is a Mason, and makes the grand hailing sign you must obey it- you must disagree with your brother jurors, if necessary, but you must be sure not to bring the Mason guilty for that would bring disgrace upon our order. You must conceal all crimes of your brother Masons, except murder and treason, and these only at your own option, and should you be summoned as a witness against a brother Mason, be always sure to shield him. Prevaricate, don't tell the truth in this case, keep his secrets, and forget the important points. It may be perjury to do this, it is true, but you're keeping your obligations."

Masons have infiltrated most all aspects of societal strongholds: law, politics, banking, media etc. These networks of influence are pervasive and books have been written by former leaders who have disenfranchised themselves. Check your local Christian bookstore.

So it was that the machine kept grinding in low gear toward a trial date. Rex already had several strikes against him in the pre-game warmups.

One: He had no attorney and was handling his own case without a rep from the lawyers' monopoly (ABA- American Bar Association). So he was not giving tribute ($$) to the club. One could say that the system takes this as an insulting slap in the face and does not earn political points for him at all.

Two: He had publicly challenged the authority of the court in ways they are not used to (effectively) which go right 'to the root' (look up the word 'radical' in a Webster's dictionary).

Three: Rex's pleadings exposed the fraud of the prosecution's case along with their sloppiness and lack of professionalism. He was making fools of them.

Four: Rex was a relatively high profile 'smart alec' who wasn't afraid to come at them head on with the uncensored truth via his radio show or any other means.

Five: Because of the radio show and the American Law Club it was perceived that he had 'followers' and thus an example must be made of him to give second thought to any of these 'followers' who might get ideas about pursuing the truth and challenging authority as well.

For these reasons, Rex was dangerous and must be dealt with harshly.

Both sides had set the battlefield and had taken their positions. Time would tell.

The battle of trial was fast approaching.

CHAPTER 17

TRIAL

THE DAY HAD ARRIVED. He awoke just before dawn and the sky was a clear dark blue with orange slivers on the eastern horizon as if to announce the coming of its master, the sun.

As he put on his double breasted business suit and fastened his tie Rex felt like a Roman warrior girding for battle as he approached the day of reckoning with confident solemnity.

He had a large briefcase which he filled with law books and files. It must have weighed thirty pounds. He didn't mind, knowing that this was his weaponry and ammunition with which to slay the adversaries.

As he completed the crosstown trek to the county seat in WashCo and parked his car, he thought about reviewing some notes when he realized how futile it would be. He had several months of preliminary positioning with the court and if he wasn't prepared by now, he never would be. The time for practice was over. Rex's frame of mind was identical to that of his old pre-game football days: he was suited up, locked, cocked and ready to rock!

He walked in to the new "Hall of Justice", otherwise known by locals as the 'Taj Mahal' for its grandiose, self-exalting edifice, replete with its Masonic symbolism built into the modern architecture. Despite the fact that he could feel the evil spirits swirling about him in every direction, as he did every time he approached this building, he felt good. He wasn't nervous but anxious. He was ready to get out onto that 'field of play' and hit somebody hard! He passed through security, went up the elevators and approached the 'arena'.

Rex had a team of supporters and court watchers there waiting for him and this support bolstered his resolve. He entered the courtroom and the judge was tending to some other matters so he went back out into the hallway to spend some time with his people. Several friends were there to attend as court observers and be witness to any shenanigans that were most likely to occur.

Kevin McGuire, a close friend, had agreed to sit with him at the defendant's table and assist him through the trial. His help and moral support, along with that of his dear friends who came as observers, was invaluable and motivational.

The team had pretty much claimed the area outside the entrance to the courtroom. Ms. Susan Warriner the deputy D.A. who was prosecuting the case and her entourage approached the entrance from down the hallway. As she approached she conspicuously looked straight down at the floor and passed Rex with no eye contact or acknowledgement whatsoever. From the beginning Rex had always been gracious and forthcoming with her prior to this and gave her no reason to be hostile or intimidated. Her body language told him that she knew she was an intellectual prostitute and was ashamed to have to be prosecuting this case. Good! Frame of mind is everything!

DAY ONE

It was time for battle. All the players entered the arena and took their positions. The case was called, both parties entered their appearances including Kevin. Immediately Ms. Warriner challenged Kevin's presence at Rex's table since he 'wasn't an attorney'. Apparently it didn't matter that she had three assistants with her at her table including County Sheriff deputy Patty Putin who was one of her listed witnesses and who was driving the investigation and prosecution of the case behind the scenes.

Not only did Kevin stay over Susan's objection, but Rex got the judge to make Putin leave the prosecutors table. 5 yard penalty and loss of down!

In football, Rex always wanted to kick off to start the game so his defense could get on the field and nail the opponent's offense for a loss and get some spit and blood spilled just to *set the tone* of the game. This, he did.

The prosecution was now on notice that there would be no 'steamrolling' today.

The *'voir dire'* (jury selection) was the first part of the process and would probably take most of the morning to accomplish. Rex considered this to be the most critical part of the whole trial: finding people who care, are critical thinkers who will fight for what they believe in and are leaders not followers. This is a daunting task considering the limited time frame and the general level of education of the public. You never know what you're going to get from the jury pool.

The bailiff went to bring in the first batch of prospective jurors. When she did, the courtroom was filled up with close to fifty people. They filled up the jury box with twelve. The judge asked some blanket questions to weed out jurors who have an obvious bias or prejudice then both parties started taking turns questioning them one by one. They started weeding them out.

As soon as one was dismissed from the jury box, another from the gallery would take their place.

Rex wanted to sell the theme that he was going to use in the trial early on so he tailored his questions to the jurors accordingly. It all revolved around 'intent', which is the critical element of any crime. He tested the sophistication and critical thinking of each prospective juror with questions about their job history, personality, self-image, etc.

Their understanding of the prosecutor's burden to prove guilt *'beyond a reasonable doubt'* was also critical and he queried their understanding of this concept.

He could swear that a couple of them didn't even know where they were they were so far out in left field, or at least that persona was their game plan to be dismissed from jury duty. They were quickly dismissed.

Anyone who had friends or family in law enforcement or government was dismissed.

The prosecutor dismissed anyone who had friends or family convicted of any crime. A big biker with long hair, beard and black leather was put in the box. Rex thought, "great', here's a rebel brother!" The prosecutor deep-sixed him in less than thirty seconds. He was gone.

Rex queried jurors as to their spiritual and religious beliefs to see who might be a brother and sister in Christ. Susan objected and the judge shut him down. So much for finding a jury of peers!

Rex asked a woman of Japanese heritage if she knew what Article II section 10 of the state constitution said, thinking that most immigrants or first generation descendants know the constitution better than most Americans.

Article II section 10 of the Colorado constitution, among other things, says that the jury has the duty to determine the *law and the facts*. In other words a defendant might be guilty according to the facts but if the jury thinks it's a stupid law they can vote their conscience and acquit the defendant regardless. This is called 'jury nullification' and is the last protection that the citizens have against tyrannical laws.

Unfortunately our enlightened modern courtrooms don't operate that way anymore. The judge drives the point that *he* determines the law and that the jury only determines the facts and if the defendant is guilty of the facts, the jury **must** convict according to the law that the judge gives. The prosecutor reinforces this point with a long dissertation that the duty of the jury is such that they must follow the law and that "the place to change the law is at the ballot box and not in the jury box."

This is absolutely and completely contrary to the purposes and intent of our forefathers who instituted the jury system as a last line of defense (next to the 2nd Amendment right to bear arms) against tyrannical laws.

It's up to the jury to decide what's fair and just. If they see that the prosecution is unethical, unprofessional or unacceptable in any way, or if a law is unjust even though facts point to the guilt of the accused in the context of a screwy law, a jury must convict the government by letting the accused off the hook. This is the true purpose of a jury and jury nullification.

Susan objected to Rex's queries and judge Perriman prevented him from asking further about their knowledge of the constitution.

"Okay. We won't continue to ask," he thought to himself, smiling internally. Undaunted, he went from the podium over to his table and grabbed a copy of the state constitution. He asked the lady to read Article II section 10 out loud and then tell him what that means to her. As he approached the jury box Susan objected again and the Judge shut him down again.

Apparently, this court was not going to let the jury be informed of their true constitutional duty and power. This was consistent with judge Perriman denying his own written oath to uphold and defend the constitution which he did during the motions hearing. Of course. This was no place to discuss 'lawful duty'. Nonetheless, Rex made his point quite clear throughout the process.

Not only had he planted the seed with the jury on this critical point, but he had begun to illustrate to the jurors, the transgressions of the law that this court was beginning to demonstrate, as would most surely be their modus operandi throughout.

It never ceases to amaze how modern day 'sheeple' fail to see how these allegedly "outdated, old fashioned" documents (the state and federal constitutions) are the vaults of protection for their liberties and freedom from oppression.

If we move away from this constitution, as we obviously were doing here, we inevitably and unerringly move toward oppression. It's that simple. Rex tried informing the jury of their constitutional duty keeping in mind what Thomas Jefferson told us:

"Enlighten the people generally, and tyranny and oppressions of body and mind will vanish like evil spirits at the dawn of day."

Apparently Perriman had been freed from the chains of his oath, like so many other enlightened public servants today. How convenient for the politically correct N.W.O. agenda!

Once it looked like we had a panel of jurors... Rex wanted a commitment. One of the last and most pivotal points he hit on in the *voir dire* was to get a firm verbal agreement from each and every one of the jurors. He wanted a commitment that each individual would not buckle under peer pressure in deliberations if they felt the slightest doubt in the prosecution's case. The ability to stand alone in their personal convictions, he told them, could mean the difference in a man's liberty or incarceration. "The integrity of the truth and the integrity of the system could possibly rest on just one person's shoulders, and that person could be you" he said, "this requires a great deal of integrity, steadfastness and responsibility for each and every one of you."

He painted the picture that the jury could be hung and they could be stuck in the jury room for days arguing. He informed them that it could be emotional. It could be personal. He said, "You might be the only one convinced that the prosecutor has not met her burden of proof beyond a reasonable doubt. You might be the only one not convinced and all the other jurors want to get home to their families and finish this. He said, "All the pressure could be brought to bear upon you and you alone. Will you make the commitment to me, right here, right now, that you will not cave in under any circumstances to vote your conscience and stay true to your convictions for the sake of the purity of justice and our jury system?" One by one he got twelve individual and personal commitments out loud, on the record from each juror.

The panel was set. Let's play ball!

OPENING ARGUMENTS

The 'persecutor' started with her opening arguments.

She wanted to come across to the jury as being fair by explaining in detail her duty to prove her case beyond a reasonable doubt and exhorted them to acquit Rex if she failed to meet her burden of proof.

Then she went on to say that she intended to show that he felt he was above the law, that he used the name Rex William to avoid the law.

In fact she would show that he deliberately used a 'false name' to unlawfully gain a benefit in avoiding two arrest warrants which were issued against him. She promised to show these arrest warrants and much more evidence which would clearly indicate that he used a false and fictitious name to unlawfully gain the benefit of avoiding these warrants. Listening to her it was an open and shut case. Simple.

Rex's opening pertained to the fact that many if not most of the facts brought forward by the prosecution would not be contested. They would surely bring a volume of facts and he tried to diffuse this before it started.

However, to come to a verdict of 'guilty' the prosecution would have to prove Rex's **intent** beyond a reasonable doubt. While he didn't have any responsibility to prove anything, he would provide evidence of his intent and that his intent would be shown to be entirely contrary to the picture that the prosecutor would like to paint.

By the time the opening arguments were complete it was time for lunch. They would break and reconvene in 90 minutes.

Bring in the Evidence

The Prosecutor was ready to call her first witness. She called WashCo's Sheriff Deputy Don Esters. Esters was the M.J.T.F. (Multi-jurisdictional Task Force) 'hero' who assisted Pat Putin in the raids on the 'Woodland gang'. He was a primary figure to investigate and prosecute concerned citizens like us who wanted to hold public officials accountable. He was also the one who was in the visitors' parking lot at the jail, checking Rex's car out for reasons to pull him over after his famed court appearance with Gary when he got the court order for unlimited visiting privileges.

After establishing his credentials and experience for the record and the jury, Ms. Warriner asked, "When did you first encounter Mr. Freeman?"

He replied, "I first noticed Mr. Freeman in a court hearing for Mr. Gary Woodland. He was assisting Mr. Woodland at the defendant's table. At the time he identified himself as Mr. Rex William. He said he wasn't a lawyer but was acting as assistance in counsel. This was very unusual especially in view of the fact that he got the judge to issue a court order allowing him attorney visiting privileges with Mr. Woodland. We became curious about him at that time."

Ms. Warriner: "Was there anything else that gave you grounds to begin an investigation?"

Mr. Esters: "Yes, my area of expertise involves investigating extreme radical groups and we know that he had a "Sovereign Authority Travel" card which was issued by N.A.F.C. (North American Freedom Council) which is a known right wing extremist group.

Ms. Warriner: "How did you know this card was issued by N.A.F.C.?"

Mr. Esters: "It had a logo or some markings on the bottom of the card."

This was great! They're only on the first witness and already he had a pack of lies and innuendo to attack. Warriner's questioning continued for a short while before she said, "No further questions of this witness."'

It was Rex's turn to cross examine the witness. He stood up at his table, gathered his notes and slowly and deliberately walked over to the podium. He greeted Mr. Esters politely who returned the greeting. Rex paused again reviewing his notes and took a drink of water. He then took a deep breath during the silence. There seemed to be a great deal of anticipation and all eyes were on him.

Rex's nerves subsided and he could feel his confidence build as he now felt as though he had full control of the courtroom. This brought a broad smile to Rex's face which he couldn't suppress. He thought to himself, "Let's go!"

He started, " Mr. Esters, you said you investigate extremist radical groups.

Is that right?"

Esters: "Yes."

He continued, "Mr. Esters, in your professional opinion, would you consider it to be radical or extremist to study law... provide information to people on the supreme law of our land and to educate people on their rights and what they can do to protect and defend those rights? Is that considered an extremist activity subject to investigation generally speaking?"

Judging by the look on his face he could tell that he saw the box approaching that he would soon be in.

Mr. Esters: "No."

"Mr. Esters, you said earlier that the N.A.F.C. was printed on my I.D. card. That would be the North American Freedom Council, is that correct?"

Mr. Esters: "Yes"

"You were sure not to say the full name, but you used the acronym which sounds like either a government bureaucracy or an extremist, radical group, is that what you meant to do?"

He had already made the reference so he had to stay true to his earlier testimony. Rex was getting him to dig himself in a little deeper.

Mr. Esters: "Yes, their activities are considered radical and anti-government and that's the kind of thing we keep an eye on."

Now Rex would begin layering the bricks rapid fire seeking only yes or no answers; "Mr. Esters, do they sell memberships?" "Yes," he said.

"A lot of companies do that is that radical?" "No."

"'Mr. Esters, do they sell information and books?" "Yes."'

"A lot of companies do that. Is that radical?" "Not really," he said.

"Mr. Esters have you seen anything of theirs not pertaining to the law, civil rights, history, commercial law, constitutional law or anything contrary to people's personal and property rights?"' "No," he said. Then realizing what was happening he blurted out, "It's their interpretation and the crazy things they do with it that's extreme, they're anti-government!'"

Rex paused to let the energy of this frantic plea linger in the air a moment, just like teargas, so that everyone could clearly feel his sense of desperation.

Then, calmly Rex asked him, "Mr. Esters, our forefathers wrote and signed the Declaration of Independence and subsequently our constitution. They were considered radical extremists who were anti-government at the time, weren't they?" His response was not necessary as this question, while directed at Esters, was meant for the jury.

Like the boxer who has his opponent on the ropes, Rex kept up the attack while shifting gears looking for the knockout punch. He felt as though it was coming.

"Mr. Esters, you said earlier that when you first knew of me in this courthouse, you went down to investigate my car to try and determine more about me after the court hearing is that correct?"

Mr. Esters: "Yes."

"You also said you decided to investigate further after you saw my I.D. was from North American Freedom Council, correct?"'

Mr. Esters: ""Yes,"' he said again.

"Mr. Esters are people required to show an I.D. to enter the courtroom?"

Mr. Esters: "No."

"On that day when I first got your attention, did I have any reason whatsoever to show you my I.D. in the courtroom?"

He had to tell the truth.

Mr. Esters: "No."

"Then how did you know enough about my I.D. in the courtroom to start investigating me immediately afterwards when you hadn't even seen it at that time?"

Mr. Esters: "Well..." He tried explaining, "It wasn't seen actually until you checked in down at the jail for a visit."

Now he was obviously getting tangled up. Rex loaded the chamber with one last bullet.

"Mr. Esters, you said earlier that the primary reason you started investigating me was due to the fact that my I.D. card had insignia or lettering pertaining to the N.A.F.C. correct?"

Esters: "Yes."

"Mr. Esters," he said as he approached the witness stand and handed him his sovereign authority to travel I.D. card, "is this the I.D. card you saw?

He looked it over and confirmed that it was.

Knowing that there was no insignia for N.A.F.C. as he alleged, he instructed him, "Please show the jury where on that card is the N.A.F.C. insignia or logo."

Once he realized it wasn't on there he mumbled something inaudible and had to admit the markings didn't exist. Rex got him to confirm clearly for the record that there were no markings as he has just said. He then tried to explain that he really wasn't the one who saw it initially but he was told by his associate Patty Putin who told him about it.

"So Mr. Esters, you're sitting here on the witness stand under oath giving us hearsay information which is not even correct. Is that right?"

Rex figured he'd had his fun and would leave this witness on the stand with the dagger plunged very deep. He said, "Judge, no further questions of this witness," He turned, made a quick glance over to Warriner at the prosecutors table as if to say 'bring it on!' The credibility of this witness was impeached!

He then deliberately looked over at the jury with some raised eyebrows and a direct look as if to say, "Pay attention! There'll be more!" He sat down again.

The next witness Ms. Warriner called was special investigator for the Colorado Bureau of Investigation, Gary Clayman.

Clayman previously went undercover to infiltrate the groups as a 'plant' in the investigation against Woodland and others. He was instrumental in trying to build cases with various attempts at persecution against the 'legal reformers'.

While Rex was in jail previously, Clayman had come by with Patty Putin to interview him. One of the things they talked about was Rex's self-produced sovereign authority to travel I.D. card. He explained that when he made it there was a lack of space to type in Rex's full family name. He had done his legal research which had indicated that any name or portion thereof would have been fine to use, given that it was correct and there was no fraudulent intent.

On the stand Clayman and Putin tried to ridicule and discredit Rex's reasoning and instead, portray him as a *scammer* and a *fraud* who thought he was above the law. This was the key point for which Clayman was called as a witness.

During Rex's cross examination he asked Clayman how many letters were in Rex's last name. "Seven..." he said after thinking a moment. Rex walked over and handed him the I.D. He said... using the address line below Rex's name on the I.D. as a guide, (it went 6 spaces beyond where Rex's name left off) count off seven spaces and tell me if there is room for the seventh space or not."

He paused while following Rex's instructions, then looked up and said, "No, there is not enough room." This blew a hole in the intent of his earlier testimony and solidified Rex's point. Another prosecution witness destroyed. He told the judge he was finished with this witness. The day drew to a close and the judge called for recess until 9:00 A.M. the next day.

DAY TWO

Ms. Warriner's next hope to try and destroy Rex's credibility was in Orlando Valdez who was an investigator for the U.S. Department of Health & Human Services (social security). She put him on the stand for his testimony to the fact that Rex had not sought an official name change with the social security administration. The presumption was that anyone who had wanted to preserve their social security benefits and use a different name would have to notify them. Of course in order for Mr. Valdez to give Susan the testimony she wanted he would have had to research Rex's file. This would be to Rex's benefit.

Warriner went through a static list of prepared questions very efficiently. When she was through, she had established from Valdez' testimony that Rex had not changed his name and any Social Security benefits would be intact for Rex William Freeman. The implication was that he had no intention of legally changing his name and still maintained his full legal name in order to maintain his social security benefits. The inference was that he was pulling some kind of scam. They thought they were being pretty smart!

Then it was Rex's turn.

It was Rex's cross: "Mr. Valdez, in order to give us that testimony just now you must have researched my file. Is that correct?" "Yes I did," he said.

Rex continued, "Did you find anything else in my file?" "Yes," he said, and he opened up nicely: "there was a fair amount of documentation which had evidently been sent in by you."

Rex continued; "Would you please tell us what you can about that documentation?"

"Well," he said, "there was an affidavit of revocation and rescission pertaining to your SS-4 form which is the original application for a social security number. Then there was a lengthy 'Asseveration' paper which basically stated that you wanted nothing to do with the Social Security Administration. I don't remember all the details."

Rex queried further. "Mr. Valdez, based upon your professional experience, would those be the type of documents that someone would file who wanted to preserve his benefits and association with the Social Security Administration?"

"No. I don't think so," he said.

"Mr. Valdez, are you aware of any lawful, regulatory, or logical reason why someone who had made it very clear, by virtue of creating and submitting such documentation to withdraw from Social Security that would compel him to inform social security of anything from that point forward?"

He responded, "No I'm not. It wouldn't seem to make much sense." Without saying so directly, he admitted that Social Security is purely voluntary (which it is) and, as was becoming a pattern, the truth destroyed the illusions Ms. Warriner was trying to create for the jury. So far so good. Mr. Valdez, the prosecution's witness, was very helpful to Rex!

Susan's next shots would come from an administrative manager from King Soopers, a local grocery chain where Rex had a check cashing account set up years ago. Susan established that he had the account set up and had cashed checks in the name Rex W. Freeman.

Susan was trying to show that Rex was seeking to do business in one name while using his shortened name for fraudulent purposes. However, he had stopped doing business with Federal Reserve member banks (i.e. checks) some time ago.

When Rex got the grocery store service manager to admit that the account hadn't been used for quite some time, the prosecutor's designs once again melted into a puddle.

They came up to lunch break and Rex joined his group of friends who came as observers for lunch downstairs in the cafeteria. They were all very upbeat about how things seemed to be going. They couldn't believe some of the sleazy tricks the prosecutor was using to paint him to the jury as a whacked out extremist who was trying to scam the world. They all enjoyed the lunch and had a few laughs. Rex was encouraged by everyone and went back up to the courtroom refreshed and ready for more gladiator activity in the arena.

Once the players were in place, the judge entered, and then the jury and they picked up where they left off.

Susan called Sgt. Miller of the WashCo sheriff department as her next witness. He was presented to the court as a handwriting expert. Rex immediately realized that the prosecutor would try to throw some razzle dazzle 'high tech 'evidence' at the jury and try to impress them with this expert. It seemed ridiculous to him that this would even be an issue since he had never denied that his family name was in fact 'Freeman'. She was clearly going to use the handwriting expert to 'expose' to the jury with great fanfare that Rex's signatures on various documents using Rex's full name and Rex's shorter given name, were in fact both written by 'him', God forbid!

Thinking quickly Rex stood up as soon as Susan started her questioning. Rex interrupted, "Judge, these issues are not in dispute. I am willing to stipulate that whatever signatures they have of Rex William Freeman are written by the same person as "Rex William". This is not an issue and with such stipulation in view of keeping these proceedings expedient there will be no need for Sgt. Miller's testimony on this.

After confirming Susan's intentions, the judge agreed and dismissed Miller from the stand. She wanted to make a big drama and Rex just stole her 'thunder'. So much for that idea. Next witness.

The prosecution next brought up Ron Hurtado of the Colorado Department of Motor Vehicles. Warriner used Hurtado to establish the Colorado point system used for revoking a drivers license. They then went to establish that a conviction on two tickets they issued to Rex in WashCo and Denver County would have put him over the limit of points for the year thus jeopardizing Rex's drivers license. This would have established one important 'element of the crime' which was the *potential benefit* for him using a 'false & fictitious' name.

They also established how the DMV computers worked to match names with date of birth and addresses with records on file and how, knowing this, he could have foiled detection during the two traffic stops in WashCo. She had laid out the roadmap for the jurors and had done her job. She was quite content with what she gained from this witness.

Then Rex's cross examination came up. He started calmly attacking one issue at a time. First was the business about the computers. He asked Hurtado how much training employees at DMV get to understand the computer system. Hurtado said it was a fair amount. Rex then asked, "… if it was reasonable to expect the average guy on the street with no experience or exposure to DMV methods, to understand how their computer system works?"

He admitted, "No. It was not." Rex just established reasonable doubt. Then Rex asked if he had any reason or knowledge whatsoever to believe that Rex knew how the computer system worked. Of course he said, "No." One issue handled. Reasonable doubt fortified.

Rex then went to remove the impression that he received a 'potential benefit of saving his 'license' from having 'too many points' which the prosecutor had effectively established in the minds of the jury.

Rex would use the same approach here as he did with Valdez from social security. He asked Hurtado if, during his research of Rex's DMV records, he noticed anything else in the file? He said, "Yes I did. There were several documents. One was an 'Asseveration and Notice of Rights to Travel' which you submitted and it contained many legal citations and basically revoked your original application for drivers license for fraud by the DMV. There was another "Affidavit and Revocation of Power of Attorney" and there was something else I don't remember what it was." he said.

Rex continued, "Mr. Hurtado based upon your understanding of what you saw in those documents would you say that those would be documents filed by someone who wanted to keep their drivers license? "No", he said quite plainly.

Rex continued, "To the contrary, would your professional opinion lead you to believe that the intent and net effect of those documents was to legally cancel my drivers license and render it null and void by my own volition? He replied, "Yes that would be my understanding." Rex had him confirm the date of those documents which was February of 1994 a full eight months prior to the points assessed by the tickets that he was allegedly trying to avoid.

He asked one final question, Mr. Hurtado... in your professional opinion could you see any reason whatsoever for someone to try and save points on his license when he went to great effort at least eight months prior, to get rid of his license?" "No," he replied, "that wouldn't make much sense."

"Thank you..." Rex concluded, "No further questions."

Rex again looked over at Warriner. She was completely bush-whacked and she was trying to hide her embarrassment by keeping her face buried down in her papers. The prosecution couldn't seem to gain any ground on him no matter what she tried to pull out of her hat. It was like the video game 'Pacman'. Rex was eating up everything she could throw at him. He could feel the tension and frustration building over at her table. At the same time he felt confident and in complete command of the courtroom, ready to take on all comers. The psyche war and momentum was definitely on Rex's side.

As his defense was now hitting on all cylinders he was closely monitoring the reactions of the jurors. He noticed at least a couple that were paying very close attention to him and occasionally seemed to smile when he would glance over at them. This was an encouraging sign.

This wrapped up the second day of trial. He went home feeling loose like an unwound rubber band. He was well in the driver seat if he could just maintain his command of the prosecution's witnesses and stay one step ahead. Later that night he crammed for his own testimony and when his notes were better organized, he went to bed and slept well.

The next day began with anticipation. The first witness called by the prosecution was a Denver Police officer who issued Rex a traffic ticket about 2 years prior. It just so happened that he pulled him over the very first day that Rex had started using his 'Sovereign Authority to Travel' I.D.

As is Rex's usual procedure when pulled over, he only rolled the window down a couple of inches as a security precaution. Rex's I.D. did not carry his 'date of birth' as that carries commercial and legal implications which he did not want being attached to him.

As a result of these circumstances, after he had given the officer his I.D. during the traffic stop, he asked him Rex's birth date and he verbally give him the correct information. Unfortunately, the officer wrote it down incorrectly.

Susan attacked that issue trying to make him out a liar who was trying to get out of the ticket. Lo and behold... to Rex's utter delight, when the officer took the stand he noticed that he had not just one but two hearing aids! It was plain as day. Boy was this going to be fun!

On the stand the officer established his version of things which was that Rex gave him a 'false' birthdate and Susan's intent was to expose him as a scammer.

When Rex had his crack at him he set the stage trying not to tip his hand too early. Rex had the officer help him establish several key facts that were needed:

a) that the officer had pulled him over on a very busy street with
b) very heavy traffic
c) it was during rush hour and that
d) Rex's verbal responses to his questions weren't real clear due to the fact that the window was only down slightly leaving only a small gap for us to communicate through and a lot of background noise.

Once he had set the stage, Rex popped the question: "Officer do you wear a hearing aid?" Of course he had to say "Yes".

Rex asked him again: "Do you wear only one hearing aid?" He had to reply with the truth as it was obvious to everyone who noticed or would look, "No. I wear two hearing aids, one in each ear."

Rex queried further, "Officer with all that traffic noise in the background and the window only slightly open, is it within the realm of possibility or could even the slightest possibility exist, that you might have possibly made a mistake and that you heard me wrong when I told you my birth date through the window?" He said emphatically, "No."

Without hesitating Rex then responded, "So what you're telling me is that under those extremely adverse noise conditions which you told us about, and with the two hearing aids which you use, one in each ear, you're telling us that it's not even possible that a mistake could have occurred. So then, if I may ask, is it standard operating procedure that the Denver Police Department never, ever makes a mistake? Or is that condition exclusive only to you?"

He didn't know what to say. He didn't need to. Rex drove the point home like a dagger in a melon. "No further questions your honor." The jury got the point. It's called 'reasonable doubt'. Next witness.

Susan then brought up an accounting manager from the city of Denver in regard to the disposition of the fine that was imposed upon Rex due to the traffic ticket issued by the Denver officer who just stepped off the stand. It was a well-orchestrated attempt to weave a web to trap him.

It is important here to understand what occurred in regards to this traffic ticket. At the time, Rex needed practice conducting jury trials as he had never conducted one before, so he took the city to the wall on the traffic case. He put together a sound argument about the right to travel without a license based solely on court precedents and established law. None of Rex's argument was allowed to be used and the judge ruled against him.

After the fine was imposed he was called into the judge's chambers where the judge told him that he was intrigued by Rex's arguments and while he had no authority to give any leeway in 'his' lowly municipal court he genuinely seemed interested and suggested that he appeal and get a ruling on the issues in a higher court where it would be more important because he would like to see what happened. This was some unexpected support and encouragement. The judge actually did him a great favor by doing what he did! Not only did he get what he came for, experience, but he also got an open door to move it to the next level and make an important point which could then be a matter of record.

More to the point on what he did with the fine imposed with the ticket: he tendered a C.M.O. (Certified Money Order) as discussed previously. It was a proper 'U.C.C. negotiable instrument/promissory note/credit/medium of currency/money of account' to discharge the liability of the fine. The instrument was redeemable through a private party (bank by legal definition but not a federal reserve bank). Attached to the instrument were specific instructions to follow for redemption of the credit. They were very simple and clear.

The prosecution put the city accounting manager on the stand for the purpose of establishing that the fine was never properly paid which resulted in a bench warrant being issued for him. This bench warrant would have shown cause for him to use a false identity in the hopes of avoiding the arrest which was an element the prosecution needed to prove.

Susan introduced an exhibit which she claimed was the arrest warrant. As soon as she showed it to Rex he couldn't believe his eyes. What

she was showing him was nothing more than some fancy word processing. He immediately objected saying, "Judge this is nothing more than
nice wallpaper. It's not a warrant. It doesn't even contain a signature
or reasonable facsimile thereof from anyone let alone a judge!" It was
on fancy sky blue heavy stationery stock, it had graphics of the scales
of justice, a nice border around it. These things you never see on everyday court paperwork. The fabricator of this fraud was obviously trying
to appeal to the tastes of the jury with this concoction whipped up in
somebody's office.

Amazingly, the judge allowed it to be entered. Rex was in a state of
disbelief. Signs of collusion between the prosecutor and the bench were
beginning to shout in a very loud voice. Of course Rex's objection was
raised for the record and promptly denied.

So at this point it would appear that Ms. Warriner was finally making
progress. It was up to Rex to undo it.

During Warriner's direct examination, the city accountant admitted
that he did not even attempt to redeem the instrument in accordance
with the instructions because, "it was too much trouble" to place it in
an envelope and mail it for redemption to see what might happen, yet
he also admitted at the same time that he 'was' willing go down to the
parking lot, get in his car, drive across town, park his car and meet with
his banker in a private meeting to discuss it with him!

O.K. bureaucrats are so much fun to play with! They are simply not
used to thinking and when forced to, they have a very hard time at it!

He also admitted that once his banker decided he couldn't take it because it was not drawn against a Federal Reserve member bank, the city
accountant technically *refused the tender of payment in full* and returned it
to Rex in the mail with a demand letter for payment of the fine.

This was all being put on the record during the prosecution's direct
examination. It was like he was going out of his way to accommodate
Rex yet he was the prosecution's witness. The poor bureaucratic automa-
ton just didn't know any better. He was clueless, as most are in matters
of law.

By the time the witness was ready for Rex all he had to do was to confirm and solidify the testimony he had already given and ask him one question: "After you returned the tender of payment in full did you receive any more correspondence?"

He responded, "Yes... it was a thank you letter for returning the instrument and thus discharging the debt by law, some U.C.C. references or something." Rex found the voluntary nature of his beautiful responses quite entertaining. Knowing the answer in advance he had to drive the point home for the benefit of the jury.

"Were you aware that Colorado Revised Statutes 4-3-603 states that when a tender of payment in full is refused that the obligation is discharged?"

His anticipated response was "No, I'm an accountant not a lawyer."

Rex wanted to go further but couldn't. The areas he wanted to get into weren't within the scope of his earlier testimony. He would save it for his own testimony later on.

The prosecution was winding down. She didn't have much left in her arsenal but she would keep up her attack as best she could. She was down to the issuing officers of the two tickets he beat for driving without a license. She started with Deputy Huner from WashCo who was now famous from the tape of the stop which Rex replayed on his radio show.

She tried to make a big deal over the fact that Rex only rolled the window down slightly as though this were evidence of a crime of some sort. Then she went on to establish that he gave Deputy Huner the name of Rex William and did other 'unusual things'. Rex thought to himself, "Yeah so what? Tell us something new! I do a lot of unusual things". Her examination of this witness really offered nothing new other than more opportunity for Rex.

Rex's cross was fairly short. He established that Deputy Huner and he both exhibited mutual respect for each other and even shared a couple of laughs during the stop. Most importantly, Huner had to admit that the ticket was later dismissed due to the 'defects' in its issuance. Interesting.

Amazingly enough, the prosecution had earlier used a taped segment of Rex's show, out of context of course... and they entered the tape of the broadcast as an exhibit. Well, in doing so they entered a complete tape of the whole show which would work to Rex's benefit.

When the jury would hear the whole tape it would clearly show that he knew what he was doing when he verbally led the deputy into a technical trap and that with this foreknowledge he would have had no reason to hide his identity as Rex's tactics would void any ticket anyway. Thus, there no possible intent to hide his true identity, which is what Susan was trying to show.

The last witness for the prosecution was State Patrol Officer Gary Rhoads who also issued a ticket for driving without a license. Let's give a little background first before we continue.

Rex did his research on officer Rhoads as he does on all public servants who confront him. He discovered that he did not have his written oath of office on file as required by 'Article XII of the state constitution. This presented a problem for him as the constitution clearly states that failure to comply with this requirement renders his position vacant. This means that he has no authority and if he attempts to exercise authority under that "vacant" position he was in fact *'impersonating a public official'*! This is the case with many 'so called officials today.

When Rex discovered this in the County Clerk and Recorder's office he demanded a certified statement that this oath was not on file or anywhere in their records. After much discussion and checking they refused. Anticipating this little problem Rex had the statute book with him and showed the clerk the statute which required them to provide him with this. He suggested that she "...probably wouldn't want to knowingly deprive me access to public records contrary to state law, would you?"

She came back, "Can we borrow your book?" She took it and scurried back to her boss' office. She emerged shortly with a hesitant smile and began preparing the certified statement. This was a 'no bullshit' day for Rex as he was getting tired of dealing with incompetent minions!

He used this certified statement to prepare a demand for the District Attorney to begin a 'quo warranto' action. This is a challenge of title/authority and could result in removal from office if successful.

*"**Quo warranto** (<u>Medieval Latin</u> for "by what warrant?") is a <u>prerogative</u> <u>writ</u> requiring the person to whom it is directed to show what authority he has for exercising some right or power (or "<u>franchise</u>") he claims to hold."* - - Wikipedia

The demand for the D.A. to start a quo warranto went in just prior to the trial date for the ticket Rhoads issued which leads us to the county courtroom where this ticket matter was to be heard during the time they were after him in the other courtroom for 'criminal impersonation'.

Because of the Quo Warranto he used different tactics on this ticket. He went to court on it and was eagerly awaiting the opportunity to get Rhoads on the stand. He had the County Clerk's certified statement in tow and had his line of questioning down to a 't'. This was going to be quite a show and several friends had come to observe the festivities.

All parties were in the courtroom apparently ready to proceed. The county attorney, trooper Rhoads and Rex were awaiting the judge to call the case. When called, the county attorney entered his appearance.

It was Rex's turn to enter his appearance. The other case was all about which name he used, the complete name or Rex's given name and he knew that they were looking for him to put something on the record that they could use in the other case. He was certain that no matter which name he entered for the record, it would be a trap that would come against him one way or another. It was a very sticky wicket!

Rex entered his appearance as "the party referenced in the citation" without declaring his name on the record. The county prosecutor pushed the judge to have him enter his name into the record and the judge obliged by putting the screws to Rex to enter his name formally for the record.

Out of the blue, the words of Jesus came to mind when he was brought in front of Pontius Pilate to answer charges where he was being accused of claiming to be 'King of the Jews'. Jesus said: "If you say I am, then I am. I am whoever you say I am." These were intensely clever words providing his adversaries neither an admission nor a denial.

Rex used the exact same approach and the response from the judge was a miracle in itself. The judge raised his eyebrows and looked over at the county attorney. The expression on his face was as if to say 'so what do you say to that counsel?' When no response was forthcoming, he prompted again, 'Counsel?'

The county attorney was dumbfounded and had no substantive reply. This was not the way things were supposed to go! He immediately requested that the case be continued so he could regroup and try again.

It seemed quite odd. Everyone was here. It was a simple traffic ticket. What's the issue? The judge looked confused because all parties were present and ready to go. He asked for grounds for a continuance to which the county attorney explained that there were 'other pending matters' which required him to put off this case.

Rex objected vociferously saying "No way! This is the time and place set certain for this proceeding, I'm ready to go; the prosecution's witness is here. Let's go to trial right now!"

Rex had his own bag of tricks and he wanted to play!

So, when was the last time you saw a defendant chomping at the bit to go to trial and the county attorney begging for a continuance so he could figure out how to proceed?

The judge was bewildered as the county attorney kept up his argument for continuance. Rex interrupted and said "Judge, I've done my duty by responding to this summons, I'm not coming back again. If they're not prepared to proceed with all parties present, willing and able, then I respectfully demand dismissal for *want of prosecution*. The judge shrugged his shoulders and agreed and said. "Case dismissed!"

Rex just had a case against him dismissed and all he could think of was, "Damn!" He was all set to defrock this guy impersonating a public official and wanted so bad to get Rhoads on the stand. He was never so disappointed in getting a case against him thrown out!

On the other hand, the persecutors were sure that they had laid a trap that would put him in a corner and hang him. But somehow, this renegade freedom freak had slipped the noose again!

So... back in the district courtroom on Rex's impersonation case, it was not yet a matter of public record that officer Rhoads had no authority to issue him a ticket. This was likely one of the reasons that the county backed off on prosecuting the ticket. By this time, Rex was well known in the office of the Secretary of State and the WashCo Clerk and Recorder's office. Word must have gotten back about the encounter there and on the documents he was extracting from the public records, and perhaps they saw it coming.

Or, it could have been that their sole intent was to get Rex to enter a name, any name, onto the record and use that to really nail him in the impersonation case which would cause him much more damage than a little traffic ticket.

Back in District Court, the prosecution's direct examination of deputy Rhoads was redundant by now and since she didn't get into the issues he was waiting for Rex couldn't address it on his cross examination. It would have to wait, but not for long.

The long list of witnesses Susan presented was as long as your arm. After listening to the 'volume' of information and theories she presented, you'd think Rex was the worst guy since Ted Bundy went on his mass murdering spree. But Rex was clearly holding his own and by this time he felt as though he had survived the prosecution's gauntlet of attacks virtually unscathed.

Now Susan was out of ammunition (witnesses). Rex had his full arsenal of weaponry still ready in the wings. He was ready to pull it out and let it loose.

The prosecution rested her case. It was fairly obvious that she was emotionally worn down. It must have been quite unsettling for her team that a complete, 'unschooled' novice in the courtroom like this self-styled renegade could have so successfully deflected their attacks and destroy their witnesses one after another. The professional exhaustive investigation... the long list of expert witnesses, all the corroborating documentation and the web of traps which they had set, all the actors from the various state agencies weren't enough to overcome the truth. This ended the second day of trial.

DAY THREE

It was time for the defense to take center stage. As witnesses, he started with several friends and associates who knew him well from the law club: John Syvertson Rex's old roommate; John Bartholomew whom he started to work with when he first moved out to Denver; Joe Hill who was active in our Civil Rights Task Force and a couple others.

Rex clearly established that it was well known that his given name was 'Rex William' and that's how everybody knew him in his circle. Thus, it was not a 'false and fictitious' name. They established the open door policy at the American Law Club weekly public meetings and with that, had any officer arrived to enforce a warrant against him, that anyone in the audience could have pointed him out easily in addition to the fact that Rex always introduced himself at the beginning of each meeting. Rex's public presence and easy access were indisputable. Never had any public official ever presented themselves at the open public meetings they held. It appears that the cabal prefers to operate in the shadows and we can see why.

Rex established that this, of course, never happened even though there were numerous opportunities which the police would have had. He was getting across to the jury the fact that he operates in an open and forthright manner. This important fact was entirely contrary to the image the prosecution wanted to portray.

He had decided that he would take the stand and testify on his own behalf to set the record on some key issues. So now it was time for Rex's testimony. He called myself to the stand with his powder packed cannons of exhibits and testimony ready to fire.

He informed the judge that, for clarity of the record, he would conduct his testimony in a question and answer format to keep the record concise in addressing specific points clearly. It is not normal for a witness to be asking himself questions on the stand, without the aid of an attorney addressing him in a dialogue from outside the witness box.

In doing so, for maximum theatrical effect, he took on two personas. 'Mr. William' was the witness and 'Mr. Freeman' was asking the questions from the position of what would normally be the attorney. It would go something like this: "Mr. William isn't it a fact that you ...", and he would respond to the question; "Well, yes Mr. Freeman, in fact . . ." The effect was that the questioning was very clear for the record and it became so repetitive he even had the judge addressing him as 'Mr. William' which was the allegedly false and fictitious name! Then when Perriman would realize what was happening he would correct himself. It was hilarious!

With Rex's identity clearly established by his witnesses showing that William is not a false or fictitious name, this fact was well established. He then began to work on the 'intent' issue. The prosecutor had tried to show that by using a false name Rex was trying to; a.) avoid arrest warrants and b.) save his drivers license from too many points and suspension due to the additional citations issued by Huner and Rhoads. The testimony was very methodical and to the point.

First, he went through his notes of the prosecution's witnesses' testimony and heaped additional information upon what he had already done in his cross examination of the prosecution's witnesses. He recalled each of the prosecution's witnesses one by one.

Rex was about to confirm his point about not needing to inform Health & Human Services/Social Security about anything such as a 'change of name'. This would have implied that he wanted to keep his benefits. He then brought out copies of the *revocation and rescission papers* which he had previously formally submitted to social security, some time ago. In addition to the verbal discussion already accomplished previously, he wanted the documents entered into the record for the jury to see and examine for themselves. They were done in good faith, with clean hands and full disclosure with appropriate citations of the law and legislative code. The objective was to clearly show that he wanted nothing to do with Social Security, long before any of these court issues ever arose. He was overtly severing any expressed or implied contract or application for benefits with the S.S.A.

For every benefit received from government it incurs a return liability which is a contractual nexus. This brings the feds into your life when they otherwise wouldn't be. You end up exchanging your 'God given rights' for 'regulated privileges' that come with penalty clauses attached. Rex wanted nothing to do with this. He wanted nothing from government other than good roads, national defense, a stable currency and an honest justice system to keep the playing field level for all. That's it.

In regard to the warrant from Denver for 'failure to pay a fine' he asked himself out loud on the witness stand, "Mr. William, weren't you concerned about a bench warrant being issued for not paying that fine on the Denver ticket?" he replied to himself, "Mr. Freeman I was not the least bit concerned because the law clearly states at 4-3-603 that when a tender of payment in full is refused that the obligation is discharged. It was very clear that the Denver city accountant had discharged that obligation as an operation of law."

"Well... Mr. William, according to the prosecution there is an outstanding warrant on that ticket. Are you at all concerned that you could be arrested as you try to leave the building today?" he replied, "Mr. Freeman I would hope that I would be arrested because now every state actor in this courtroom is fully aware that the alleged warrant in question is unlawful and if they knowingly allowed me to be arrested on a bogus warrant they would be liable for *misprision of felony, conspiracy* to deny me of my rights, *false arrest, false imprisonment* and that's just on the state level. On the federal level we have crimes under Title 18 sections 241 and 242 of the US Code leading to a denial of rights under 'color of law' and more." he said, "That could be quite a lucrative endeavor for me in the end!

As a matter of court record in front of all the witnesses in the courtroom, Rex was thinking that this was sufficient notice. What do you think?

He then brought out all of his rescission documents pertaining to the voluntary, willful and intentional self-revocation of his 'drivers license' and thoroughly covered the law, the Federal and Supreme court case decisions which back up the entire 'right to travel' issue. These all relate directly to the so called 'license' they wanted to use against him. The idea was - why would he be trying to keep points off of a license that he had previously terminated and surrendered voluntarily of his own free will?

He continued getting into all of his other sovereignty paperwork which clearly established his desire to separate himself from any and all contracts and privileges with 'the state'. These documents were all public record having been filed some time back with the Denver County Clerk and Recorder's office. The County Clerk's stamp for filing, complete with dates and time of filing authenticated the establishment of his intent. It could not have been more clear!

Next on the defense list was to establish a conflict of law. The research he had done before deciding to put 'Rex William' on his I.D. was fairly extensive, concise and right on point to his issues.

He compiled quotes and citations from numerous court decisions into a document entitled 'Constructive Notice by Affidavit'. This document clearly established that case law establishes that he can use any fictitious name he wants to so long there is no fraudulent intent. Yet they want to persecute him for using his own given name, not even a fictitious one, even though a fictitious one is permissible by law if used properly.

This is a 'conflict of law' which goes to nullify the law they were trying to get him on. How can a citizen be expected to follow the law when it contradicts itself? He can't. Nor can criminal intent be established when one side of the law says its O.K.

Rex's testimony and exhibits were exhaustive and overwhelming. He was on the stand for over three hours having a great conversation with himself. He was doing what he normally does with the law club. He was giving a seminar. The only real difference was that this seminar was to the jury who had the power to put him in jail. The entire time he maintained eye contact with them and personalized his approach throughout.

If you recall Rex's personal history, he was a 'thespian' in high school with some experience in acting which helped him here. He routinely used some very pregnant and timely pauses. There were times when he had the entire courtroom anticipating his next reply and the silence, anticipation and energy in the courtroom at times was almost unbearable. You could almost sense people holding their breath waiting for the next, critical statement or rebuttal as he was making revelations in the law that none of these people had ever heard of. He used a variable and animated tone in his voice to try and keep it interesting. Rex felt that he kept the jurors on the edge of their seats much of the time. They were with him the whole way. It was beautiful.

At times during the 'seminar', he would periodically look over at the prosecution's table. They looked weary and worried which only served to motivate Rex to keep the pedal to the floor and don't let up!

At long last he was ready to drop his bombshell on the prosecution's case and blow it to smithereens. He took out a copy of his letter of 'Refusal for Cause' which he had previously sent to all parties pertaining to the traffic ticket written by deputy Huner which was made famous by the radio show.

A 'refusal for cause' is the proper procedure in the Uniform Commercial Code when you are given a commercial 'presentment' which is defective in some way. The Refusal for Cause letter is submitted to the party who issued the presentment (ticket) and the defects are identified in good faith and the issuer now has a chance to correct those defects and make the presentment again, this time correctly. It is basically a good faith notice of defect with opportunity to correct.

In this document, which was Rex's immediate response to the court regarding the issuance of the ticket, he identified himself as Rex William a/k/a Rex William Freeman.

The prosecution wanted the jury to believe he was hiding his true identity to get out of the ticket and save his license.

This exhibit proved he was acting in good faith with full disclosure all along.

This was the final spike in the coffin and he drove it straight in with a sledgehammer. As soon as the ringing of the hammer head hitting the nail had stopped reverberating in the courtroom, he looked over and saw Warriner bury her face in her hands at her table.

Rex's testimony had finally concluded. He felt that he had really accomplished the overkill that he desired. It was the prosecution's opportunity now to cross examine him.

It was pretty obvious to all, that throughout Rex's seminar 'er 'testimony' that he was enjoying himself immensely in giving the jury a fairly complete treatment on a variety of 'freedom' issues which were very sensitive to the 'powers that be'. The cabal was trying to shut him up and put him away, yet here he was giving a freedom seminar, on record to the entire courtroom!

Warriner started out her cross examination. In view of Rex's 'strong' attitude, she had been trying through the whole trial to paint him as a wild eyed lunatic who had no respect for authority or the law. She now tried to goad him into gloating before the jury with an inflammatory opening question: "Mr. Freeman, you're really having your day in the sun aren't you?"

He knew exactly what she was trying to do. He didn't want to come across the wrong way to the jury, so he was demure. "What do you mean?" he responded coyly. She tried to bait him "You really think this is all a bunch of fun and games don't you?"

Rex wasn't biting. He gave another pregnant pause and you could hear a pin drop in the courtroom as everyone was awaiting his response. He leaned forward in the chair and softly replied, "If what you mean is that I revel in the truth, then you are absolutely correct!" Her tactic backfired. He got her again! He tried very hard to hide an 'ear to ear grin' which he felt inside.

She made some feeble attempts to challenge him but he was shooting each one down. She was losing and she knew it. Then she pulled out a surprise.

Rex had previously testified once, some time ago, as a common citizen in front of the Denver city council in regards to some stupid gun

legislation they wanted to pass. Ms. Warriner started quoting Rex's testimony from that hearing. Wow! These guys had really done their homework! They must have really felt he was an important person to nail if
they were going to all this trouble. He was honored.

She continued to quote him from that old hearing: "if it was up
to me I'd like someone to drop this proposed bill from the ceiling so
I could shoot it down with my SKS semi-automatic rifle." Aren't those
your words Mr. Freeman?

He thought to himself after hearing this that she's really lost it. All
she has is innuendo and is doing nothing more than trying to engage
him on inflammatory issues where she might be able paint him to the
jury as a dangerous radical. He thought to himself 'no thanks'.

He couldn't hold it in and he laughed out loud with a sigh and a
shrug shaking his head. He turned to the judge and objected saying
"Judge I object, not only is this ridiculously off point but it is inflammatory and irrelevant to everything going on here today." The judge
agreed and sustained the objection.

She turned and sat down. She had nothing left in her arsenal. She,
the D.A.s office, the M.J.T.F., Esters, Clayman and the entire weight of the
Colorado Masonic, N.W.O. power establishment were utterly defeated and
now humiliated by one upstart, self-taught freedom fighter due to their
own desperate, overzealous stupidity. "No further questions," she said.

Rex stepped down from the witness stand, approached the podium
and said to the judge in the microphone, "The defense rests."

In closing arguments the prosecutor shifted gears. Her 'hard evidence' was blown all to hell but she still wanted to convince the jury that
those bogus warrants were real. However her main thrust was now, "Mr.
Freeman thinks he's above the law. How could we have an orderly society
if we let him and others like him flaunt the law like he does? He doesn't
respect the law one bit!" She was using the force of Rex's legal arguments which he used, to do unconventional things, against him which
was a good move. She was now appealing to the conventional ignorance
of the jurors which was the only thing for her to do.

She made her final plea for the jury to come back with a guilty verdict and then sat down. "Good riddance", he thought.

Rex had not really prepared for his closing argument but he said a short prayer and remembered a scripture (to paraphrase): *'in times of need do not fear for what to say for the Holy Spirit will fill your heart and put the words in your mouth.'*

So it was Rex's turn and he paused to collect himself and allowed the Holy Spirit to fill his heart. He had no fear, only determination, strength and passion.

Rex started his closing argument and reviewed what the prosecutor tried to prove. He reviewed the points the prosecutor 'wanted' to make. Then he reviewed each piece of rebuttal testimony and corresponding exhibits that would at least raise a 'reasonable doubt'. He pointed out that this was not a trial over whether someone should have a drivers license, it was not about whether someone should participate in social security or not. Nor was it about participating in the system we have today. The issue was purely restricted to the charges and evidence you have before you as it relates to those charges. You will see from this evidence that it clearly shows that the intent is to remove myself as distant as I can get from government granted privileges, contracts and licenses. The prosecutor has asked you to use your common sense again and again. Does common sense tell you that I would criminally conceal my identity to protect and preserve a drivers license that I had previously surrendered of my own volition?

He told the jury, "I agree with the prosecutor. Use your common sense! You may not agree with my politics. You may not agree with my stance on the legal issues involved but you *must* make a decision based upon the facts as they relate to intent without clouding the issues. Do we have a situation here where a guy tried to conceal his identity by giving his full name in print on court documents as demonstrated by the exhibits or do we have a case of malicious prosecution against someone who has embarrassed the local establishment status quo? Someone will be convicted here today. You will either convict me with criminal intent as it relates to the charges, or you will convict the prosecution for wasting taxpayers' dollars and your precious time on frivolous, malicious and capricious persecutions such as this one.

The power of the Holy Spirit filled him to such a degree that the words coming out of him were doing so with such force and conviction as he has never felt before. It was a strong, passionate and logical closing argument to conclude a strong defense. He felt like a mountain climber who had endured great pain and suffering but had finally reached his goal - the summit! He completely used up his allotted twenty minutes.

The jury retired to the jury room after being given their instructions by the judge. They deliberated for several hours before the end of the business day came up. They went home without a decision on that Thursday night.

DAY FOUR

The next day started out with a long cup of coffee waiting for the jury to come back from deliberations. During the day Friday, he was called up into the judge's chambers a couple of times to help clarify questions that the jury had. Being that he had no representation, he was sitting with the judge and the prosecutor discussing procedural issues. He found it interesting in the fact that this would normally be done a bit off the cuff with counsel from both sides having some privacy from the 'defendant' to discuss such things. Yet, here he was, right in there with them working out some of the details to come in proceedings.

The jury continued deliberating, and deliberating and deliberating.

Toward the end of the day the judge sent in a message that a decision should be made that day. He didn't want this matter overflowing into the court docket he had arranged for Monday.

The minutes ticked by ever so slowly. It was clear the jury was having trouble on this case and there was some internal struggle going on trying to get consensus. Finally around 4:30 Friday afternoon he was called into the courtroom. Rex's friends were with him and they all had anxious but hopeful anticipation.

When the jury was brought into the courtroom one of the first jurors in was a young woman whom he had shared several smiles with during the proceedings that week. She was intellectually engaged in every aspect of the trial from the very beginning. As she entered the room the first thing she did was to look over at him and smile. He took that as a good sign.

The judge asked the foreman of the jury if they had reached a decision. The foreman then informed the judge, "We have not reached a decision and we feel that we have reached an impasse that will not be changed. All are firm in their positions.

Rex thought to himself that his efforts to get a commitment from each of the jurors to stand firm and be true to their beliefs no matter what, in the *voir dire* had paid off. One or more of the jurors held out for him against some serious pressure.

The judge thanked the jury and declared a mistrial. Rex was a bit amazed on one hand that in view of the overwhelming evidence relating to his clear intent that it wasn't an open and shut case for them in Rex's favor.

On the other hand, he remembered an old saying that 'a jury of slaves will never let a freeman go!' Clearly, some in the jury didn't like Rex's politics and wanted to convict him purely for his political and unconventional 'Freeman' ideologies and application of the law. It's easy to understand how this clouded their judgement in view of the obvious.

In the face of the long string of expert witnesses and the exhaustive concerted effort to oppress him, he was very pleased with the strength, the wisdom and the flair that the good Lord gave him to get through this ordeal. While it wasn't total acquittal, he did consider it a solid victory to have been able to single handedly repel this very serious effort to put him away. In the process he was able to inform and sway some typical government educated citizens in the jury who he's sure were exposed to some unusual arguments for the very first time.

Now that Rex's oppressors saw with their own eyes what one man, armed with little more than the truth and a passion, could do to their 'tyrant friendly' legal machine, he figured that there would be no way in hell that they would even consider subjecting themselves to another similar humiliation by putting on this week long circus again at taxpayers' expense.

They had sorely underestimated him and they paid the price with this public embarrassment in failing to get a conviction. Rex was still on the loose! Think about the radio shows to come!

The judge made a special request of Rex. He asked for Rex's exhibits and the judge said that "because you aren't an attorney we don't have jurisdiction over you (he got that right)." Because of that he felt it would be better to keep the defense exhibits in the custody of the court until the prosecution had determined if they were going to try the case again and he asked if that would be alright with him.

At this point in time Rex was so relieved and happy he didn't think twice about it. He was already in celebration mode! If he had thought about it at all it would have seemed strange that the judge didn't trust him with his own exhibits!?

Two weeks later, Rex was informed that the prosecution wanted to try the case again! He couldn't believe it. Man, did they want him bad!! The following month they began this whole charade all over again.

This time there were a few new twists and they would leave nothing to chance. WashCo was not going to stop at anything to get their coveted conviction. If they couldn't get it fair and square, they would go to their bag of tricks.

Here are just a few that they used:

1) Using a different approach this time around, Rex introduced his own expert graphologist to rebut the testimony of Sgt. Miller on Rex's handwriting. Rex's expert witness was denied an opportunity for testimony. The prosecution's was unhindered without any chance for rebuttal from a competent professional with the same training. Nice.

2) A *'motion in limine'* (motion to exclude prejudicial or tainted evidence) was granted the prosecution whereby the court ordered

that he not use the words, or make reference to any of Rex's activities with Rex's law club 'The American Law Club' or Rex's radio show 'The Citizens' Rights Forum'. Apparently, to mention these would only be 'prejudicial' against the government case (certainly not Rex's). However when Warriner used these terms in a castigating way and demonizing him out of context, Rex's objections were overruled. The court order evidently only applied to him in Rex's defense, not to her in her prosecution. Interesting. So much for the level playing field.

3) The court also ordered that they not mention the first trial in front of the jury for this, the second trial. That was understood. However, when the prosecutor blatantly violated this order by reading directly from the transcript of the previous case, Rex's forceful objections were immediately overruled and she was allowed to continue. But when Rex followed her lead and made only a slightly veiled reference, the judge cleared the courtroom and held him in contempt. What drama!

4) Rex was denied the entry of some of his most important exhibits that were admitted in the first trial. They didn't want another seminar in front of the jury.

5) Rex's most crucial and exculpatory exhibit, the Refusal for Cause Letter as sent to the court; showing that he did divulge his full complete name was 'mysteriously' missing, or should he say stolen! Rex felt like such a stupid and naive idiot for thinking that ethics and fair play should be expected. This was the direct result of agreeing to leave his exhibits with the court. He should have seen that one coming. Lesson learned. Sometimes inexperience sucks. This was one of those times.

6) The judge was observed numerous times sending hand and facial signals to Susan, as to when to object. He was blatantly assisting the prosecution. At one point he blurted out loud "Ms. Warriner if you object, I'll sustain!" Rex couldn't believe it! The judge was overtly helping the prosecutor by initiating objections

that she was missing! What happened to the impartiality of the bench? He immediately challenged the judge that if he would like to prosecute the case from the bench, that he should immediately recuse himself. Rex asked him to show him where his name is listed on any briefings as counsel to the plaintiff. Absolutely unbelievable!

There was more but let it suffice to say that this was no more than a kangaroo court or more accurately, a 'Star Chamber' with a pre-determined outcome. He wasn't given a 'snow balls chance...' to put on a defense of any kind. Apparently they had determined that the damage that they could suffer by allowing him to win fairly in court and continuing to be free to teach law to common people was far more egregious than the damage they might incur from a blatant departure from well-established law and legal procedure in the courtroom. They chose their course and Rex's fate was sealed.

The result was inevitable, despite Rex's objections and despite the fact that they were clearly railroading him to a predetermined outcome. Any good jury would see this and *convict the court* with a 'not guilty' verdict for the defendant.

Rex's second jury was comprised of purely government educated slaves as he was completely shut down on his *voir dire* jury selection techniques as well. This was ultimately the key to Rex's previous victory and they knew it. He was not allowed to ask certain critical questions in direct violation of his right to free speech. The verdict was expected. This time when the jury entered the court room with their decision, not one juror dared to look at him. It was clear. The verdict: 'Guilty' on both felony counts of 'criminal impersonation' (of himself). Sentencing was set for October, almost two months away. The grinder had finally produced the desired sausage and he was the dead meat!

CHAPTER 18

REMEDY & EXILE

So now Rex was convicted and awaiting sentencing by the District Court of Washington County in THE STATE OF COLORADO. Certainly such victimless 'crimes against the state' cannot go unpunished! He was still out on bail and moving about freely.

By this time, the collective study and research of the historical roots to the judicial system and how that related to the sovereignty of the people vis-à-vis the duties of the public servants in response to that, had laid sufficient foundation for great things. Fortunately for Rex, the timing was ripe to reset our 'one supreme court of the county' in common law. Their knowledge and training was sufficient enough to become operational through Rex's group in Denver. This was not a minute too soon for him. He organized the group to assimilate the necessary details and they officially created the first court of its kind in Colorado since before the national bankruptcy with H.J.R. 192 in 1933. It was an historic event.

The first priority was to outline the court rules with clearly defined responsibilities and boundaries of the players. This was no simple task as merging the organic principles of natural law as outlined in the Mosaic code with ingrained modern day thought proved to be quite a task. However, the common goal was the focus and they were able to finally reach agreement. Unity was imperative.

The people published a 'Declaration of Creation' for the court in the Legal Notices of the local paper. They did so for three weeks to give a 'Public Notice' to the world that this forum now existed as a judicial body. In furtherance of this aim they combined the list of court rules with a 'Declaration of Creation'. They made copies of these and delivered them to all legislators, key state executives, and all judges of the 'State of Colorado' as a courtesy presentment with a demand that if anyone contests the lawful nature of peoples right to self-governance they should let it be known now, or forever hold their peace. This way if any potential adversaries did not contest and show lawful cause to keep them from proceeding right away, they certainly could not later complain or legitimately cause problems down the road. Silence is consent when one has the opportunity and the duty to object!

The stage had been set. There were no objections and the common law courts with original jurisdiction exclusive to the people had been resurrected in Colorado. Now it was time to get down to business.

The first step which he needed to accomplish was to complete a 'Quiet Title' action on the 'property' (person) known as Rex William-Freeman. This process is commenced as an *ex parte* action (one side only) and its purpose is to determine who has perfect title and jurisdiction to the 'property' in question (him). This probably sounds crazy. But once you understand the true nature of the legal tyranny that has corrupted and convoluted the American system, you understand how the people have become nothing more than chattel property of the government without any rights, but only revocable privileges and liabilities.

Here's a common sense illustration of that point: How many times have you found yourself saying, "How can they do that?" Every day the transgressions of what is right and moral by government agents leave people scratching their heads saying "that doesn't seem right" and it's not. You know in your gut, with no legal training, what's right and what's not. It is this corruption of the legal system which has relegated people to being serfs in their own country. It equates to a bloodless 'coup d'etat' and takeover of the country and what it once stood for. Now back to the story...

Prima facie evidence is now to be presented to 'Rex's court' in Rex's 'Quiet Title' ex parte hearing. The documents were previously drawn up by him and then presented and reviewed by the justices of the peoples' one Supreme Court. When everything is in order, they approve and sign the documents to give them legal authority. All parties who would have any potential interest then in challenging Rex's claim (to ownership of himself) are notified either by direct service of paperwork and/or public notice by publication in the paper. Once again we see the doctrine of 'Notice and Grace' in action. 'Notice' of facts is given and a general period is allowed for response or rebuttal from anyone who would contest the prima facie claims.

Rex's paperwork consisted of five documents:

1. A 'Letter Rogatory', (letter from one court to the other [people's court in the republic to the corporate state])
2. Declaration to Quiet Title,
3. Judicial Notice
4. Finding of Facts (by the justices of the one supreme court) and,
5. Writ of Prohibition.

The *Letter Rogatory* was a short and simple letter from the clerk of Rex's court to the clerk of the District Court wherein their previous case involving him was referenced. It advised the other clerk of a pending action in another jurisdiction on this matter. It identifies the attached paperwork which satisfactorily established proper jurisdiction and venue for the case in question and requested that this paperwork be filed in accordance with the rules and it provided a return address for any further needs or questions.

The *Declaration to Quiet Title* simply established that he has chosen to proceed in his own right, obligation and power to choose applicable law within the proper territorial application in which he was born (not the one they wanted to put him in which was contrary to Rex's nature and God given rights).

This included the principles of 'law' and 'equity', the law merchant, law of contracts and many other aspects of true law as opposed to the legislative emergency war power statutes that the District Court operates under. It goes on to say that he chose to live up to the obligations and enjoy the birthrights of having been born in one of the several territorial states of the several states of the 'u'nited <u>States of America</u> (the republic). However he is not a subject of the 'United States' corporate body as defined by statute (District of Columbia et al.) nor is he subject to its jurisdiction as it has, by law, no jurisdictional authority outside of the District of Columbia and its possessions, enclaves and federal territories as enumerated by law unless a party volunteers into that jurisdiction voluntarily by way of contract or requesting benefits whereby there would be a return liability.

Furthermore, there was no contract in existence whereby he had knowingly, willingly and intentionally refused any common law rights in order to become a federally 'privileged' person. This document was then signed by him and a duly commissioned and privately bonded Notary for the People.

In Rex's case this document was prepared for him, with advance preparation, by the people in special session after the statewide common law grand jury was held in Cañon City. This was done very shortly after he was kidnaped and was sitting in jail during that little escapade he had on his birthday in Cañon City.

Judicial Notice is essentially a memorandum of law pertaining to the removal of the case from the corporate state District Court into Rex's court based upon the facts and the law on Jurisdiction and Venue. This was to remove the case in which they had obviously railroaded him, and would move it into a jurisdiction of the common law which would require the prosecution to produce an actual damaged party who filed a complaint in order for the complaint to proceed. This was obviously favorable to him because there never was such a 'person' and with no injured party to make a complaint there can be no 'crime' to prosecute.

The Finding of Facts is just as the name indicates. The facts were presented before Rex's court and found to be complete and correct which established the basis to proceed on the whole matter in Rex's venue. It basically states that he was born of free parents who were the natural born free People in the county of Cook in Illinois state and that he was not a Federal Emergency citizen of the U.S. nor a 'resident' of the corporate 'STATE OF COLORADO' etc.

If this is all new to you, you must understand that 'THE STATE OF COLORADO' is not the same legal entity as 'Colorado state'. They are two distinctly different animals in law. These are all legal and corporate terms having specific meanings and implications which may or may not apply to a free person who is born upon the land who is not engaged in a regulated commercial activity or contract governed by the corporate legislative statutes, depending on his legal status.

To the uninformed, this all may appear as superficial rhetoric (gibberish) based on semantics or wishful legal theory. However there is a very substantial basis in law and legal precedent 'to provide an unimpeachable foundation of truth and fact to support each and every one of these statements. Unfortunately this book is not the forum to get into all the details and background. The true student can only get a flavor of these issues here. To sink one's teeth into the meat of these issues will require more in depth study.

The last document submitted in Rex's case was a *Writ of Prohibition* which was an order from Rex's court to the District Court to cease and desist all activities in this case against the Freeman character with a Christian name in upper and lower case letters known as Rex William: Freeman who is in fact not the fictional entity (trust) which they have identified in their paperwork as REX W. FREEMAN. Corporate fictions are identified by all capital letters and acronyms i.e. initials. The courts and government agencies use this type of false identification for a very specific reason. Check your mail and documents from any government agency. Your name is in all capital letters. So you say, "it's just a matter of: form, style, custom?" No. There is a reason for everything they do.

It's all part of the deception and trickery being imposed on the American People. To fully understand this issue one needs to study the issue of 'misnomer' which is covered quite well in the "non statutory abatement" study package. Google it.

Attached to Rex's Quiet Title paperwork as exhibits were;

a.) Copy of a court order from the Federal District court in the 10th district Denver wherein circuit judges Anderson, Baldock and Broody made a ruling in the case Warren E. Ensminger v. The Farm Credit Bank of Wichita No. 94-6415, April 7, 1995. This case was a dispute over the lower state court trying to impose its jurisdiction over Ensminger's property after he had established *Quiet Title* using the common law process described earlier under the purview of the Peoples' one Supreme Court of the county in common law.

This federal court ruling was significant. In short, the court used Ensminger's own wording to state that the banking entities which were using the courts to try and impose their will over Ensminger's property were of the 'United States' not the united States of America. They recognized the Seventh Amendment to the constitution for the united States of America which states that once a matter is heard under common law it is not reviewable in any other court in the land except by the rules of common law.

Since Ensminger's *Quiet Title* was adjudicated in a people's common law Court no other so called 'government court' could review it according to the Amendment because none of the government courts operate under the common law it was already *res judicata* or a thing already decided (done deal).

This federal court also recognized the division between the courts appellate 'Government Courts' and the 'Peoples' court of original jurisdiction which is exclusive to the People and its orders were recognized and placed into evidence for purposes of the Federal court.

Many people today don't want to recognize the validity and substance of the People's common law courts. This, once again is due mainly to ignorance of the facts or fear that the status quo will somehow be altered in a negative way. Nothing could be further from the truth.

b) Also attached to Rex's exhibit to the Quiet Title paperwork was a copy of the Civil Rules of Procedure - rule 60 which states: "This rule does not limit the power of a court to entertain an independent action to relieve a party from a judgment... order, or proceedings or to grant relief ..."

Since Rex's Quiet Title was in fact an independent action executed in our One Supreme Court of the county, independent from the District Court which was trying to persecute him under the compelled performance statutes of admiralty, this was a reminder that according to court rules recognized by the District Court, that they had the power and full legal authority to honor Rex's Writ of Prohibition. It was in their rules!

The Quiet Title paperwork was complete and courtesy copies were served upon a Denver judge, the Denver D.A., a Denver D.A.'s investigator (another case working against him) ' the WashCo District Court ' the Colorado Attorney General's Office, and Janet Reno the U.S. Attorney General at the time. Publication was also done in local papers. The purpose of publication in these papers was an invitation to the public for open rebuttal or contestment, should there be any.

No response or rebuttal of any sort was ever received from anyone. Therefore, Rex's claim to being of a 'Freeman character', self-governing and subject only to the sovereignty, rights and penalties of God's law and his sovereignty became res judicata according to well established law.

Since Rex's scheduled sentencing was for Monday October 23rd, 1995, he needed to work fast on the balance of the court work which needed to be done.

Many other people in the area also had urgent pending matters which needed to be heard, as you might imagine. They set a convening of the court for Saturday October 1st. They were able to secure a suitable venue for the event. It was to be conducted in the Dacono city hall chambers. Dacono is a small rural township north of Denver in Weld County. It was well suited for a court set up. Now, they needed to ensure the peace during the proceeding and needed to enlist the support of the Sheriff's office. The sheriff in Weld County was friendly to the group as was, obviously the president of the city council of Dacono.

A delegation from the A.L.C. had already paved the way, as several of them had previously arranged a meeting with Sheriff Jordan of Weld County. The purpose of the meeting was to advise him of the formation of the common law court so he would have advance notice and wouldn't be caught by surprise having to act or react to false rumors. They tried to condense the education on the subject and share what they could with him so that he would understand where they were coming from and what his role would be in the big picture. Once again, they were operating in Good Faith, with Clean Hands and Full Disclosure!

Sheriff Jordan was very receptive to hear them out and he was in agreement with many of their positions. They wanted a direct line of communication with the highest law enforcement official in the county and they got his ear and support!

In fact, he was so impressed with the approach and the substance of the activities, that he arranged a second meeting which would include he and two other sheriffs from neighboring counties. Once this process completed they felt that they had made a very solid step in the right direction.

Next, court organizers had published the 'Notice of Hearing' in the legal notices and invited the public to attend. Unfortunately not many people read the legal notices but they did have the local Patriot persecutor Don Esters of the WashCo M.J.T.F. show up (of course) with his sidekick Gary Clayman from the Colorado Bureau of Investigation (CBI) who was there along with another deputy District Attorney from Weld County. Good! Enlightenment is impossible without exposure!

Rex started the meeting out by getting everyone organized and clear on the intent and purposes for the day. He made some announcements including a public welcome to Esters to make sure everyone knew who he was. He pointed him out with an introduction and asked him to stand up. He declined to stand but did raise his hand and waved to everyone.

They started out hearing 'quiet title' actions and the first party began by setting his court, or in other words, appointing the people he needed to serve in public capacity for his court.

Things went quite smooth. The peoples' knowledge and study of procedures etc. was reflected in the efficiency of the court that morning. It was direct, to the point and very professional. In fact, so much so that the Weld County Deputy D.A. in attendance, made the comment to his boss, the Weld County District Attorney, that he was so impressed that he would like to have any matter he may have in the future, held in this court! This news came directly from Sheriff Jordan who was part of the conversation after the proceedings.

During the morning recess, Esters and Clayman approached Rex. They had a little chit chat and then Esters asked him, "So will you be showing up for your sentencing hearing in Washington County?" he replied, 'I'll be making an appearance, you can count on that!" Understanding the 'meaning of words' Esters continued to try and pin him down: "So does that mean you'll be present?" Rex responded again, "I'll be fulfilling whatever my legal requirements may be at the time." Of course it was Rex's full intention by the actions of 'Rex's court' with original jurisdiction of the people that the case he was referring to would be removed from the 'state court' by that time and they would no longer have jurisdiction over the issue. Rex said, "By now you certainly understand that, right?" Esters didn't seem satisfied with Rex's reply and said 'O.K. we'll see then."

Of course you can make an 'appearance' by way of legal briefs submitted by attorney or messenger, as the case may be and Esters picked up on what he was saying.

Esters was looking to see if Rex would 'skip bond' and not appear in WashCo for the sentencing hearing. If he could get a 'heads up' on that in advance, he could start investigating and tracking him 'before the fact'.

They went back in and wrapped up the morning session in handling a number of additional cases and then broke for lunch. Things had gone smoothly and without a hitch, so far.

Rex had gone out to lunch with a couple of friends and when they came back, the Dacono city hall looked like a teaming anthill. But instead of ants the place was crawling with guys in unmarked black military style jumpsuits with black boots and sunglasses, which was highly unusual and offensive to law abiding citizens. The citizens were standing around trying to analyze the situation while the black suited thugs were in parking lot writing down license plate numbers and videotaping people, clearly using every type of intimidation tactic available.

Rex and a couple of others immediately walked up and challenged one of them and demanded to see his identification. They would not identify themselves by name nor would they even identify who they worked for or were supposedly representing. There was no insignia on their uniforms which is required of public servants who are always re-quired to identify themselves. These guys refused. They could only sur-mise that the goons were a private security contingent for some group sent to strong arm and intimidate the peoples' court participants. Some of the citizens got in the faces of a couple of them and nearly had several physical confrontations.

The Sheriff's deputy on the scene tried to intervene and he was as confused as the rest of the group as to who these 'Gestapo clones' were.

About that time the Dacono Chief of Police showed up. Two of the groups staunchest proponents, who had made the arrangements in Dacono, Jan and Jim Meisinger also lived in Dacono, were immediately all over the chief. While he didn't want to admit it for quite some time they ultimately learned that these goons were his local police.

As it turned out, and not until after about 30 minutes of confusion and confrontation had reigned, the local chief of police evidently had his feelings hurt because nobody on city council informed him as to the use of the building that day. This was his reasoning for calling out his goons. In his temper tantrum he told the sheriff's deputy that the Sheriff's department had no jurisdiction in Dacono, and to shut up! They found that quite interesting!? They all knew better. The Sheriff is the highest legal authority in the county, all political and judicial figures included.

This Dacono police chief was acting like a spoiled kid trying to keep himself relevant when nobody wanted to play with him!

It wasn't until a couple of other city council members were called over to settle a dispute over 'who' was told 'what', that they got everyone to settle down. In the process they caught one of the black suited Gestapo police in a blatant lie. He was new to the force and from out of town so nobody in the group knows him. He made quite a splash for the local townsfolk.

The next question was, "why do all of these officers have absolutely no insignia on their black uniforms to indicate who they are and who they work for? Don't police, firemen and other similar public servants wear patches to identify their function and jurisdiction i.e. Dacono Police?"

The answer they got was that Dacono "didn't have the money to buy the patches!" Uh huh, right! Then why did the police refuse to identify themselves when asked? No answer. This was not American, it was pure tyranny! Something didn't smell good here.

Despite the rhetoric and explanations from the local police it was clear to Rex that this was a blatant attempt at premeditated intimidation and interference in the Peoples' right to self-governance. While he couldn't prove it, Rex's hunch was that our friend Don Esters, was behind the whole affair. Interestingly enough, Esters left the scene during lunch break and was not present for the festivities which could be a clue.

Things finally settled down and they resumed proceedings inside. Rex had previously tendered other paperwork from his court to the District Court in WashCo and needed to wrap up the last details dealing with these documents previously submitted to Judge Perriman. Here is what he was pondering;

1) Write of Habeas Corpus faciendum & recipiendum with a Writ of Certiorari in aid of Habeas Corpus.

These are writs to bring forward 'the body' (he and Rex's records) before a court of competent jurisdiction. It would remove the records (case file) and bring them to the judge of Rex's one supreme court of the county.

The writ of certiorari was to bring the case up to the higher court (the peoples'). He was satisfied in the documents which clearly showed the separation of venue in common law with that of the imposed admiralty jurisdiction of the District Court. Such separation thus strips the District Court of any authority over him in the matter at hand. This document is packed with legal memorandum and references to the laws and rules of the courts of the appellate jurisdiction including the U.S. Supreme court. This habeas corpus includes a commanding order to the District Court to either immediately show, in view of the facts presented, by what lawful authority it relies upon to hold Rex's case and proceed against him or, in the alternative... immediately release him and Rex's case to the court of Rex's venue.

2) Writ of Prohibition and supersedes as bond with bona fide tender.

This was a more detailed writ than the first one which demanded that the court in WashCo *'cease and desist'*. It was submitted with a Comptroller Warrant (check) drawn against the U.S. Treasury and backed by the assets of the U.S. government as a result of accumulated commercial liabilities incurred and secured by non-judicial commercial liens (remember the Montana boys?). The amount was for $1 million. It was written by Leroy Schweitzer himself and was written against the debt created by one of his many commercial liens. The warrant (check) was deposited with the District Court pursuant to court rules. This was a bona fide bond to give authority to the common law court action.

Remember the maxim we discussed earlier: 'No risk - No authority? They established their authority with this bond. In order for WashCo to follow him into Rex's court they would now have to match Rex's bond to play ball. He didn't envision the WashCo Comptroller writing a check for $1 million without all hell breaking loose.

3) Notice of Error - Notice of removal for cause.

As the name indicates this document notices the District Court of its error in exercising extraterritorial jurisdiction and informs them that the case is being removed from them for lawful cause and explains what that cause is in a memorandum of law.

4) Writ of Replevin

This was a four page document demanding the return of unlawfully held property including, but not limited to; all information / complaint, docket sheet, court minute orders, judgments, decrees, investigation material, public documents, etc. Of course this also was lengthy with its memorandum of law.

5) Writ of Mandamus

*"A **writ of mandamus** or **mandamus** (which means "We command" in <u>Latin</u>), or sometimes mandate, is the name of one of the <u>prerogative writs</u> in the <u>common law</u>, and is "issued by a superior court to compel a lower court or a government officer to perform mandatory or purely ministerial duties correctly"* - - Wikipedia

This was issued in order to perform and enforce the Writ of Replevin in (4).

Copies of these documents were sent to the District courts Of Washington County and Denver. They were also sent to three state and federal agencies including- IRS, FBI, White House, U.S. Supreme Court, Social Security, Justice Department and Governor.

This was done primarily to put them on a courtesy notice and to establish the record with the 'prima facie' case.

"In common parlance the term 'prima facie' is used to describe the apparent nature of something upon initial observation. In legal practice the term generally is used to describe two things: the presentation of sufficient evidence by a civil claimant to support the legal claim (a prima facie case), or a piece of evidence itself (prima facie evidence)." - Farlex Dictionary

Prima facie facts or assertions will stand as fact unless or until properly refuted and rebutted with substance.

Rex's documentation clearly set the record with the law and the facts of this clearly enumerated position. It was intended to do one of two things: A) either correct the problem by following correct legal procedure and deferring to the higher court, or B) by dishonoring the process and its supporting paperwork, the actors would thereby continue to try and cover up the illegal operations of the *de facto* Emergency Powers corporate government. By doing so the actors would put themselves in a position to clearly violate their own oath of office and incur some potentially very serious commercial liabilities for treason and sedition by giving aid and comfort to the judicial money power that was foreign to the interests and government of the people to whom they claimed to represent!

Notice was given that the people are finally cognizant of the fraud and they were marching to correct it!

The business he needed to conclude in Rex's court that day in Dacono was the final hearing on Rex's quiet title action. After serving a 'Notice to Appear' by direct service to judge Perriman and the actors in the D.A.'s case in the District Court, and also by general publication, to any interested or potentially interested parties, nobody appeared to contest Rex's action in any way. Apparently Esters came to gather names and information and little more. By this time he had already left. Default was then entered and the justices signed off on a "Final Judgment and Decree" on Rex's Quiet Title which stated that he was in fact and in law of 'Freeman Character' with no contractual or 'privileged' entanglements or impediments with the state or federal central governments. The case was now 'res judicata' and not reviewable by any other court in the land. This was a significant and satisfying accomplishment for Rex.

As a matter of record and of law, he was now officially a 'Freeman'! The first to be settled in a 'Quiet Title' action over his own person by the newly resurrected one Supreme Court of the county. This was historic.

It was great day in Dacono. Not only did they have some excitement but there was a level of commitment displayed by those who participated. This demonstrated many hours of study in addition to the day they spent 'taking care of business' and reminded him of why he was proud to be an American. Hard work, risk and sacrifice yielded a very productive day.

Many people want to pigeonhole 'Freemen' 'Sovereign Americans' and 'the so called 'Patriots' as being anarchists who believe they are somehow above the law. This is a blatant distortion and lie put out by the establishment who fear the truth and are deliberately trying to polarize public opinion against their creators, as these people try to reassert their proper position in authority over government. All they want is 'law and order' which they don't get from the establishment money powers that have turned everything upside down.

They hold themselves to a higher standard of law than even that which the war power legislative statutes hold people accountable to.

Many things are presented today as being 'legal' which means 'correct in form and appearance'. But 'legal' is not necessarily 'lawful'. There are statutes on the books representing legislation which is far beyond the scope or authority of the legislature that imposed their will upon the people, and while this is 'legal' in form, it is NOT 'lawful' in its substance.

True law does not change with administrations, parties or policies. The law of gravity has never changed regardless of politics! The U.S. Constitution has not changed regardless of the party in power, without 3/5 of the states to change it. The Ten Commandments have never changed no matter what church you go to! Now then, do you want to talk about what is considered 'legal' according to man's legislation as they have tried to apply to the 'law' to our own living conditions and regulations? This is another matter entirely.

Many things can be 'legal' yet not moral or ethical according to immutable 'law'. Several examples come immediately to mind, but let's not devolve into politics here.

From a worldly perspective on man's civil law, many of our detractors have somehow gotten it in their heads that all of our civil and criminal statutes apply to 'all people' at 'all times'. This was the point which assistant D.A. Susan Warriner was trying to make against Rex in the courtroom' that he somehow felt that he was 'above' the law! She was obviously appealing to the jury's ignorance as, being a lawyer, she knew very well the tricks and traps of words and legal definitions, jurisdiction and matters related to the proper application of the 'law'. This is where ignorance leads to perdition and a solid study of the intricacies of man's deceptive statutes bears fruit.

We have: laws, statutes, codes, regulations and ordinances. Can you tell the difference from one to the other? It might be a trick question!

Let's address that issue quickly with a simple and obvious series of questions.

1. Does probate law apply to the estates of living people? No.
2. Does Motor Vehicle law apply to people who don't 'drive'? No.
3. Does juvenile law apply to the management of competent adults? No.
4. Does the income tax law apply to people who have no income? No.
5. Does immigration law apply to natural born citizens? No.

So then, if the state wanted to impose its revenue codes in the above mentioned sections of legislation, to him, a person to whom those statutes don't apply, would you say that he felt somehow very irresponsible, unpatriotic and reckless because he was 'above the law'? Of course not!

He'd only be protecting his personal rights and property against unlawful seizure from a misapplication of the legislative code which applies only to the citizens for whom those statutes were intended, and NOT Him!

A book could be written on exceptions to the law. These are very obvious ones but could lead an active law student on a very long, winding and eye opening trail that would boggle the mind of the average boob tube junkie!

Let it suffice to say that should you encounter a self-proclaimed Freeman -American Sovereign you should ask him some questions about law with an open mind. You might save yourself the embarrassment of rushing to judgment and putting a derogatory label on him or her which tells us more about YOU than it does HIM!

Now, with paperwork complete Rex arranged for friend in the Civil Rights Task Force (C.R.T.F.) to make an appearance on Rex's behalf at the sentencing hearing in WashCo the following Monday. Rex would make a 'Special Appearance by Affidavit' which outlined nearly 30 occurrences of rights violations in his alleged trials by 'the state'. These included perjury, violations of oath, theft of Rex's property (defense exhibits), unlawful arrest under color of law, and a lot more. The affidavit was effectively a detailed criminal complaint.

The jurisdiction of the District court was effectively nullified by Rex's court's paperwork previously described. Should he have appeared back in District court he would have been voluntarily granting them jurisdiction again and negating the extensive work done by his own court. Thus, he could not appear here anymore without nullifying this work and authority. The case had been lawfully 'removed' from Judge Perriman and his state revenue machine.

Prior to handing over Rex's 'Special Appearance by Affidavit' to the C.R.T.F. to serve upon the court for him, he recorded it as a public document with the Denver County Recorder so that it could not mysteriously 'disappear'. This affidavit of truth was not to be scuttled and is now... as it will always remain, public information!

In addition to this affidavit, a 'letter was prepared by C.R.T.F. head-quarters in California on its letterhead which was to serve as notice to judge Perriman and the District court. The letter informed him that he was to be placed in a witness protection program while charges of treason, sedition, barratry, conspiracy to deprive constitutionally secured rights under color of law, perjury of oath, and other high crimes were investigated and cases prepared!

Rex's intent was not to use the corrupt state courts for his remedy but to raise the indictments in commerce using the Uniform Commercial Code and let old Perriman indict himself in the court of public opinion, just as Rex had learned from Hartford Van Dyke and subsequently how LeRoy Schweitzer in Montana had effectively used the process along with the rules of the U.S. Treasury.

Perriman was served the documents while sitting on the bench in his courtroom. Upon presentation of the documents by the C.R.T.F. representative when the case was called, Perriman was somewhat confused and had to ask the D.A. in court what 'barratry' meant (using the courts to persecute for personal gain). This was the same judge whom Rex had observed in proceedings on another matter reminding the defendant, "I'm the professional here!" Yet he had to ask the defendant what is a 'Federal Reserve Note'!?

Once Rex's people had concluded their intended business in the courtroom at the sentencing hearing and presented the 'documents' to the court, judge Perriman promptly issued an arrest warrant for Rex, instructed the prosecutor to take Rex's paperwork to the "proper authorities' and he set Rex's bail.

Since this was in all probability the very first common law court paperwork seen by any court of appellate jurisdiction in the STATE OF COLORADO, Rex fully expected this court to dishonor its lawful duty and ignore the writs and orders of Rex's court. Unfortunately, there were no surprises there.

A plan was already in progress as Rex was on his way to take a sabbatical in the Rocky Mountains for a while and move onward from there.

There was no mistake on either side. It was declared war and open season. Rex was intent on enforcing the law. His detractors were interested in enforcing 'control' using the legislative statutory code and its police power over the people. This duel on the battlefield of truth would leave only one victor. The loser would end up being a humble servant to the other in one manner or another.

Rex felt that he had the advantage. He could do his work from anywhere. Rex's presentments, publications and other business in commerce and truth could be launched for long range attacks from unknown locations. He was fully operational in his chosen battlefield. The enemy was impotent against him unless they could lay their hands on him with use of force. This was a prerequisite for them to inflict any damage or even fight back. Rex's defense against attack was an extensive and supportive network of patriots who operated 'everywhere'.

Just prior to these escalating legal challenges he had made some business contacts who owned many hundreds of millions of dollars' worth of precious metals in a concentrated ore form. They were trying to convert some of this into cash for the purposes of reestablishing the de jure American Republic.

However, since the banking community owns the de facto United States socialist democracy, Rex's group was having trouble getting any bankers to play ball. Once the politics were known, pressure was brought to bear on those bankers who were willing and able to negotiate and everything would then come to a halt. We've seen this before haven't we!

About the same time that this contact was made, other associates of Rex's were dealing with some offshore financial sources. Having put out some feelers through some key channels, they were confident that they now had the funding source that the precious metals friends needed to put the deal together.

They had just started working on brokering this deal when he had to take the 'low road' and have Rex's associates complete the deal on his behalf. Rex had to bow out with his new circumstances. The plan was to complete a transaction that would provide him the funds necessary to acquire a foreign passport along with diplomatic attaché' status from another country. He would take a vacation on a beautiful beach somewhere, make his connections and conclude some business, Then he would come back to work in the states with full diplomatic immunity. This was the easy part. Remember, this was pre 911 and money could buy just about anything back then with the right connections. Concluding the precious metals deal to obtain the funding was the only hitch.

After a couple of weeks of what seemed like progress... things seemed to be in a temporary holding pattern. He wasn't able to contribute any more to the deal than what he had already done. So rather than keep himself at risk, being a 'Freeman' from the point of view of the high court, but a 'fugitive' in the eyes of the corporate court, he headed for a mountain retreat to start working on his 'commercial endeavors' as they pertained to certain public servants he had come to know very well.

The cabin that he stayed at was perfect. It was located at the base of jutting mountains, heated mostly by a wood burning fireplace and was just above the soothing sounds of a babbling brook with the wind whistling through the tall pines and aspen trees all around. He couldn't have imagined a nicer place to settle in and relax intermittently with the work that needed to be done.

He would typically spend several hours a day doing some research from materials he had brought with him. This would then be applied to the U.C.C.-4 Bill, Private Security Agreements which he was preparing for some of the state actors who were impersonating public servants and who had incurred significant liability for breaches of contract in regard to their dealings with both himself and Gary Woodland.

The balance of Rex's days were spent helping out with a few chores around the cabin and then enjoying an absolutely magnificent autumn out hiking and exploring the beautiful Rocky Mountains. This was undoubtedly one of the most peaceful and enjoyable times of his life.

The first 'True Bill' he began working on was for chief judge Perriman who had committed crimes the likes of which he had never observed in Rex's life experience. It was drawn up in the form of a confession sheet as though Perriman drew it up himself. Once completed, the damages totaled fifty million dollars in *substantive* money (not 'funny' Federal Reserve money). Rex wasn't interested in *'promises to pay'. He* wanted actual payment.

The cover letter for the U.C.C.-4 basically outlined, in good faith, the three options Perriman had upon receipt;

1) Agree, sign and return the paperwork, or
2) Challenge and disagree within 10 days with a point for point rebuttal by affidavit sworn to and notarized under penalties of perjury, or
3) Do nothing: dishonor and default whereby silence would be deemed tacit confession with knowledgeable consent and *judgment nihil dicit* would enter at which point he could use the accommodation signature clauses in the U.C.C. to sign on Perriman's behalf as guarantor/surety/accommodation signature. Along with the cover letter he included a W-9 taxpayer qualification form for him to fill out and return for tax purposes.

This was all put together and mailed certified: return receipt requested to Perriman and copied to several other related parties who needed to have 'Notice'.

To maintain Rex's cover he continued to use a mail drop address in the city and he had different people pick up his mail and forward it to another blind drop box elsewhere, where it was picked up and forwarded again in different ways. Outgoing mail was always sent from other zip codes apart from where he was.

The parcel was delivered to Perriman with signature and the clock for the ten day grace period started ticking. As expected, the deadline for response came and went without a whimper. The next step was for him to publish a "Notice of Default in the legal notices of the newspaper. Rex proceeded, in accordance with the doctrine of good faith with notice and grace and informed the world as to Perriman's default, on $50.000.000 private security agreement and that any party in interest, who would contest a default judgment being entered against him, should immediately come forward and show cause as to why judgment should not be entered forthwith.

This notice ran for three weeks and there was, of course, no response. Although in Rex's mind's eye he could hear screaming and the gnashing of teeth in the entire legal community when this notice appeared! He had just placed a legitimate claim for fifty million dollars against the Chief Justice of WashCo, the Masonic center of the N.W.O. in the region!

During this period he had worked on other private security agreements. Ester's and Putin's each totaled to some pretty serious sums. Rex's special project was to work on behalf of the people of Colorado state in regard to Gary Woodland's situation.

During the oppressive attacks against Gary they had collected numerous signatures in support of a *Constructive Notice & Demand* which was later submitted to then Governor Reimer and the Attorney General Gale Nordstrom who later served on President Clinton's cabinet. This *Constructive Notice* essentially informed the top executive state officials of the transgressions of law and ethics by law enforcement officials against Gary. We the People considered these blatant abuses of power against Gary to be overt acts against the rights and protections of all of the People of Colorado and of the peace in general. They demanded an investigation and an immediate response to their concerns as to how this would be addressed. Failure to respond to the People of Colorado would be construed as acquiescence and consent to these frightful and treasonous acts and they would take such collusion as a deliberate act of mixed war against the people.

The constructive Notice & Demand was personally served upon the governor and the A.G.s offices. They dishonored them and never responded in any way. As a peaceful remedy in commerce Rex began preparing a thoroughly documented and factual *true bill* for both Governor

Riemer and Attorney General Nordstrom in both their personal and corporate capacities. Each presentment was worth two billion dollars apiece and once perfected would be assigned over to the Colorado Posterity Trust which was to be created for the general benefit and welfare of the honest hardworking, law abiding people of Colorado. This would be a tool to help recreate the honest republican form of *de jure* government that the people deserved. It would relegate a large chunk of the assets of the de facto socialist democracy's power structure over to the will and true needs of the people.

It would also send a strong message to other public pretenders as to where their true allegiance should be. This could be a watershed event in exposing the true nature of the adversarial public fiduciaries and reclaiming an honest government that truly works for the people. Of course, this wasn't without risk. The old adage came to mind: "If not now, when? If not me, who?" Rex continued working off and on in between his wonderful hiking trips.

He had almost completed most of his Quiet Title and case removal paperwork with the peoples One Supreme Court when an opportunity arose for him to hitch a ride to go north for a second trip to see his friends at the 'Justus township' in Montana. Within a couple of days he was on his way.

The Montana 'Freemen' had moved from their beautiful log home in the wooded Bull Run Mountains near Roundup to an expansive ranch on the plains near Jordan, Montana.

Once Rex's team arrived at the new ranch and got started on the sessions, Leroy had recounted a story about the move. You have to remember the circumstances: by now, the boys of Justus township had exposed massive fraud and corruption in the statehouse, challenged authority according to law and incurred the wrath of politicians and law enforcement at every level in Montana.

They had already cracked the bankers' code with their Comptroller Warrants which were being accepted all over the country and had turned the banking world upside down. They had exposed corruption and sedition in the state legislature when they discovered how the laws were being secretly replaced and rewritten. They had 'seceded' from the corporate state with their common law township and much more. There were arrest warrants flying in every direction for these guys.

But with their knowledge and legal 'ammunition' nobody on the corporate side had the guts to enforce the warrants which were issued by judges who were insulated in their cozy courtrooms encircled by armed guards and deputies.

As the Montana Seven were on their way out of town and they made their move, they drove right by the Roundup city police station and they all waved as they passed by. Not a finger was lifted by authorities to impede their passage. Apparently nobody wanted to enforce any of the outstanding warrants that had been issued some time ago for attempting to 'influence and intimidate' public officials. Interesting.

The word on the street was that once the sheriff deputies from the county of the Freemen's new home in Garfield County Montana heard about their new neighbors coming into town, several deputies just up and quit their jobs! They must have heard well what these guys were capable of doing without firing a shot. Not wanting to get caught in the middle of anything, they evidently decided it was better just to seek other employment than to put themselves in harm's way.

Back at the ranch, as they walked into the newly remodeled classroom which was a converted garage, it was hard not to notice a big T.V. news camera sitting high up on a shelf with a large red tag which was marked 'Grand Jury evidence.'

The media would like the world to believe that this expensive equipment was blatantly stolen by hoods and thieves. The truth of the matter was that ABC News came out onto the property without invitation, to do a news story on the Freemen. The Freemen, knowing how the media operates, declined to be interviewed and asked the news crew to please get off of the property. The news crew was told they'd be trespassing if they did it again.

The crew did not retreat. Instead they started setting up their cameras, still on the Freemen's private property. The township Justices then came out to remove the trespassers from the property after they had willfully violated orders to leave. As evidence of trespass the Freemen seized a beta cam. The ABC news crew was told 'they could have it back if they posted a bond and came into a common law court to defend charges of trespass. Of course ABC declined. The crew went into town to file a complaint for theft with the sheriff. The sheriff was heard to say, "Can't you see we have fourteen other things to do? We can't do that now."

He wouldn't get involved! Apparently the Freemen had his respect.

These three additional days of learning and consulting with the masters were very fruitful. By coincidence, Rex's friend Frank Pepper, founder of the C.R.T.F. in California, who had previously made trips to Denver to work with the A.L.C., was in attendance as were a couple of acquaintances from Southeast Colorado whom they also knew. Upon seeing one another, they shared some fun stories. There had been many more new success stories of financial institutions and government agencies, courts, etc., accepting Leroy's Comptroller Warrants which he was issuing against his U.C.C. liens. People were also getting refunds for the difference between the amounts actually owed and the overpayments in the warrants. Affidavits and photocopies of these successes were coming in from all over the country.

Rex was particularly interested in studying the 'Official Bankers Handbook' which was a rare insider's compilation of U.C.C. secrets as they applied to banking principles. This was the critical link to converting the liens to cash. It is the key to ultimate success with the liens.

Overall, it was an enjoyable and very productive session. To cap it off they took the scenic route home through the Badlands, Spearfish South Dakota and the Mt. Rushmore area. Rex had never seen Mount Rushmore so when they stopped, it was quite impressive. On the way out of the area they went through Buffalo Gap National Park which is aptly named as the buffalo roamed freely and they almost ran into one which was strolling along side of the road. This trip was a nice diversion to an already beautiful autumn of leisure in the splendor of nature's beauty.

The life of a fugitive was not so bad!

CHAPTER 19

CAPTURED

THE TRIP UP NORTH WAS wonderful. Not only did Rex expand on his knowledge and confidence in what he was learning, but it was a beautiful time of year in the warm autumn with the change of seasons and it was as relaxing as it was educational.

But now he had more business to take care of and he used a location in Longmont, just north of Denver, as his staging area for stealthy forays into the city.

This night he was going back into Denver to pick up some cash generated from a friend who helped him sell a few personal items. Rex also went to his legal office on 17th street in downtown Denver to meet with Lou, Rex's fellow C.R.T.F. friend. Lou was the one who appeared for him in WashCo District Court for the scheduled sentencing hearing and he delivered Rex's affidavit to the judge along with the letter from C.R.T.F. with the 'Notice of Crimes' after the case had been removed by the one supreme court of the county. This took some guts for Lou to do that. Rex needed to pick up some important documents and research material in order to continue his work on the commercial processes he was working on so he had quietly arranged this meeting using some back channels.

All seemed fine as he was moving around the city as discretely as possible knowing that there was a bounty on his head. He concluded his business without any events and was comfortable that he was not being observed or followed, having taken several precautions along those lines.

He returned back to his friend John's place in Longmont for the evening where he was staying overnight. He organized his things and turned in for the night with a sleeping bag and mattress on John's living room floor. All was good and going according to plan without hindrance. Sleep came easy.

He was abruptly awakened around 3:00 AM by intense shouting all around him. All he could see was flashlight beams and heard numerous men shouting at the top of their lungs: "Don't move. Put your hands out. Don't move. Don't move!" He was in handcuffs almost before he was even awake. With the cuffs on, the shouting subsided some and the gang started their searching.

He told the goons: "Hey, if I knew you guys were coming, I'd have left the light on with some cookies and milk out for you!" These M.J.T.F. S.W.A.T. guys were all wigged out on power and adrenaline and they were taken aback by Rex's lack of panic and calm.

Of course they create as much noise and confusion as they can, in part, to intimidate and disorient you. Rex was neither intimidated nor disoriented, just pissed. This was a major kink in the plan.

By now, the lights in the house were turned on and he could see that the place was crawling with unmarked, helmeted black suits. Rex thought to himself, "Again?" All of them were wearing helmets which looked very similar to those he saw the Nazis wear in World War II movies. That seemed entirely appropriate.

He heard a voice from a dark corner say, "That's him." Rex was brought to his feet with his hands cuffed behind his back and as he was being led out into the snow in his bare feet and underwear. Certainly, by this time, it would come as no surprise that he did notice two familiar faces emerging from the shadows of another room. You guessed it, Don Esters from WashCo and Gary Clayman from the C.B.I. (Colorado Bureau of Investigation). Esters had a bloodlust look of satisfaction in his eyes.

Rex was then led out to a waiting Longmont Police squad car. He didn't say a thing after that. His main concern at the time was to resume his sleep which was very rudely interrupted. As he entered the secure confines of the Longmont Police station garage area, he was led into the building in his fashionable underwear, bare feet and cuffs.

In recognition of the extreme circumstances and BIG Event, one of the receiving policemen made the comment as Rex was being led passed him way in: "Man you sure must have pissed somebody off!" His comment alluded to the fact that such a large S.W.A.T. team force to be deployed in the stealth of early morning darkness was quite an operation which doesn't happen much in little Longmont, if ever.

Rex felt a broad smile come to his face and said laughingly, "Yes, I did. Thank you for noticing!" He shook his head with a wry smile. Once again he was flattered that such resources would be used to suppress a beginning law student. This reminded him of a saying Bo Gritz used to say on his radio show: *"You don't catch the flak until you're right over your target."* Rex's work was at least validated at this point. He was catching his share of flak.

The U.C.C. volleys of 'truth in commerce' and the 'court of public opinion' must have been hitting the enemy hard and had them furiously scrambling. We can only imagine that the $50 million perfected commercial lien on Chief Justice Perriman, which was filed as a public document with the County Recorder's office and published in the legal notices, may have had some effect on all this. What do you think?

They were fighting back with a vengeance and obviously there was no limit to the resources they would use to accomplish their ends. Despite Rex's new circumstances he had some personal satisfaction knowing this. He asked to be put in his cell to catch up on some sleep before they would transport him again in the morning.

It wasn't long before he was transferred from Longmont city jail to Boulder County jail in Boulder. Just as Longmont was, Boulder police too were without a valid warrant to present him with and by now you know he'd been asking for it from the beginning. What a pity. All that

S.W.A.T. team fanfare and major logistical investigative and ground operations and nobody had any proper paperwork with them. Welcome to the 'New Amerika'!

So, as hard as they tried to trick or intimidate him he wouldn't submit to the booking process. He refused to cooperate and give up his photo or prints until they could follow proper legal procedure. This was not generally pleasant for Rex because until you're booked in you are in a common area holding cell in most cases and have no privacy or comforts of the 'general population'.

In both cases, at Longmont and at Boulder, they put intense pressure on Rex to submit to the booking process or he was going to be 'stuck' in the holding cell 'forever', and they couldn't move him to his ultimate destination, they would have him believe. However, as Rex held steadfast to his position of not volunteering into their jurisdiction by his submission, the story always seemed to change. What they had expressed as being so crucially important to them just a few minutes prior now didn't seem so important after all and in the end, it seemed like they couldn't get rid of him fast enough. It's funny how that works! Lies. All lies.

When you submit to booking, you submit to jurisdiction and by law, they can only keep you in a holding cell for a limited time without booking you or releasing you. Again, that's by law. But as we know, the law is largely irrelevant these days if it doesn't serve government purposes.

So after a short nap in an unusually quiet cellblock in Boulder, he was rousted again and put in a cruiser for the short trip which, now for him, was home sweet home back in WashCo.

Upon, arrival he was quickly whisked up to judge Perriman's courtroom where a date was set to complete the sentencing on his impersonation case. It was to be December 6th about two weeks away.

During this time he settled in and got to know a number of the guys in his cell pod. The general story here with the guys seemed to be holding true to Rex's previous jail experiences whereby, about one third to one half of the guys were there for 'victimless' crimes against the state and/or the D.A.'s abusive exploitation of the system in search of 'sales' numbers (convictions). Most people don't understand that the D.A.'s and prosecutors around the country have little interest in justice aside from some extreme high profile public cases. These offices are like sales offices. There must be a sales leader board up on a wall somewhere which tallies convictions and the deputy D.A. with the most 'numbers' at the end of the month gets his 'persecutor of the month' award or some such thing which is good for career advancement.

Actually, the courts, the attorneys, counsellors, rehab programs, halfway houses, parole officers and the like are one huge business. Rex learned that many of the judges own interests in the privately run halfway houses and related counselling and rehab businesses. Plus, now many if not most prisons in some states are private businesses run for profit. Once you understand how both the public and private coffers are filled with these 'captive' customers, you will better understand how the system works.

Further to this theme, local deputy D.A.'s with high conviction rates (whatever the cost in human terms) move up the ladder in their careers and they can make a name for themselves if they have any political ambitions. You can begin to see how it all fits together and the overriding interest has little if anything to do with the job the people have entrusted them with, that old fashioned concept of 'justice'.

Rex met one young guy in jail with him, who was about as harmless as a dove. He was jailed because he returned home one day to learn that his wife was next door in bed with the neighbor. He went over and found the door open. He went in, pulled his wife out of bed by her ankles and forced her to come home. For this he had just received eight years in prison for breaking and entering, trespass, burglary and various assault charges. How's that for some good 'business'? He'll make a great customer!

Rex also learned that his 'celly' was at home with his girlfriend when they got into an argument. Without laying a hand on her, she called police and lied about an assault that never happened and couldn't be documented with any injuries. He was arrested and hauled to jail as is always the case in domestic disputes when evil women know how to manipulate the system. The man always loses if he doesn't call the police first.

Later, she had a change of heart about what she did and admitted her lie to the D.A. She asked that the charges dropped. Ooops. Too late! He was in the hands of the D.A. now who wouldn't drop charges. Apparently the D.A. doesn't offer 'refunds' in his business to customers who change their mind. Rex's celly was in jail for ninety days before he could even get a meaningful hearing. That alone is enough to ruin most people's lives. What would it mean to you and your life if you were in jail for no reason for 90 days? What would happen to your job Your bills? Your pets & family?

Rex went to work trying to help some of these poor guys who didn't know what to do. During his previous visits to WashCo jail he had put in at least twenty kites (written requests) to get into the law library. The jailers only let him go in there maybe two or three times over a period of several weeks which is an unreasonable denial of rights. Once there, the tiny room had very little in the way of helpful law books and was a complete joke.

This time around it was a different story altogether. The library was moved to a newly expanded room and there were, instead of just a few old books, there were sections upon sections of shelves stuffed with nearly everything he could ask for. He asked about this turnabout and quickly learned that an inmate sued the county in Federal Court for violating inmates' rights with a woefully inadequate law library. WashCo finally buckled under and was forced by Federal Court order to spend the money necessary for new books and furnishings. They also worked out a new procedure for inmates to get more frequent access.

Now, for each kite he put in he was getting prompt access to a vastly improved law library. He was thrilled! This is unfortunately a classic example of government not obeying its own laws until challenged and forced to comply by someone who in this case was another sharp inmate.

Why does it take a Federal lawsuit to gain government's compliance with the law? What is wrong with this picture?

One poor man in Rex's pod who was almost illiterate was being severely taken advantage of by not only the court and D.A. but even his own attorney! Rex helped him fire his attorney and set the record in court for reversible error on his case so he could get it overturned on appeal if he needed to. Rex couldn't fight his case for him, but he helped him do that much anyway.

He helped another man determine that his charges and pending sentence were illegal. He now had the ammo to get everything overturned, walk free and have grounds for damages and a Federal suit against his oppressors for acting under *color of state law*, outside their delegated scope of authority to violate his Federally protected constitutional rights.

Too bad a guy couldn't just set up an office in there and work full time! He'd never run short of work to do so long as the prosecutors seek only convictions as opposed to justice. They just run the numbers through the mill.

Rex's sentencing hearing was fast approaching. He was reserved to reality yet hopeful based upon two things going in his favor:

1) The probation department's pre-sentence interview report recommended probation without prison time. Although they did also make the comment that due to Rex's strong Christian upbringing and firm beliefs, he "...probably wouldn't successfully complete the probation period". We have to wonder how they determined that? Rex's odds for completing probation successfully are diminished because of his faith?

2) One of the court rules for sentencing only leaves the judge one 'out' to overrule the recommended probation. That 'out' is only if he deems him to be a 'threat to public safety'. Since in Rex's case there was no intended victim, let alone an 'actual victim' to Rex's 'crime' of impersonating himself, he had no prior record, no violence... no drugs, etc. He felt that he at least had some ammunition to present to the judge in getting him to order the recommended probation. This was also in view of all the time he had already spent in jail during pre-trial hearings, etc. and this amounted to many weeks.

Well, the time came upon him and he was soon hauled back into court to get his sentence. There was a long underground tunnel inmates would have to walk through to get from the jail complex to the courthouse. Then you'd go up an elevator under guard and restrained by handcuffs.

During this trip he had visions of the French Revolution and the trip so many thousands of unhappy French citizens would make on their way to the guillotine. In those days, you could lose your head for simply complaining about the price of bread as this was perceived as a complaint against how government was running things which made you an 'instigator'. It was not so dissimilar from the modern day. Fortunately for him, WashCo didn't own a guillotine, at least to Rex's knowledge.

Judge Perriman, who was now an adverse party debtor to private security interests he owned, went through his administrative duties, setting the record and so on and then asked if Rex wished to make a statement to the court. He did of course. Are you surprised?

He calmly and respectfully reminded Chief Justice Perriman of all of the mitigating factors involved in the case. He also brought to his attention that nothing on the record would give any indication that there was any 'threat to the public' either real or perceived and that it would be entirely appropriate to follow the recommendations of the probation department.

Perriman promptly and without any basis or foundation forthrightly declared, on the record, that he determined that Rex was a "threat to the public". Having done so, he then proceeded to give him the maximum allowable sentence of 18 months in the department of corrections on each of two counts AND that each count was to run consecutively making it a 36 month prison term as the 'just' penalty for a first time "offender" of the heinous victimless crime of using his own given name.

This sentence was a message being sent to all the other rotten, despicable, social misfits like Rex who might also be tempted to use their own names in an attempt to impersonate themselves! Caveat actor! Well done Judge Perriman! You got your man and saved the public once again. Hail to the Chief!

Obviously, the sentence had little to do with the crime, but had everything to do with 'who he was' and the threat he was posing to the Masonic empire which the bar association had built for themselves in Colorado (and all other states). The net effect was that they have effectively stolen the government from the people in a bloodless 'coup d' etat'.

Within a few days Rex was put in a van with about seven other guys and delivered over to the Denver Reception & Diagnostic Center (D.R.D.C.) This is the intake processing unit for all department of corrections inmates heading to prison.

D.R.D.C. would do a complete medical and dental evaluation which he needed anyway. They also submitted him to a week's worth of testing on aptitudes, attitudes, educational levels, psychological profiles and tendencies, etc. He was poked, prodded and psychoanalyzed.

This data would later be reviewed by a case manager along with other data pertaining to prior criminal history, drug history, rating the current charges and escape history in order to determine a) the classes and programs one needed to take, and b) the level of security that was needed which would determine which facility he would be sent to.

The interview with Rex's case manager was interesting. He asked Rex to explain his crime and why he thought he was here. The truthful response was to the effect that he was a political prisoner being held on a charge of criminally impersonating himself for using his own name. He further explained what went on in the courtroom in the second trial to enable them to obtain the verdict and the fact that due to Rex's involvement in exposing fraud and corruption in WashCo along with teaching people the truth about the fraud our government is involved in, evidently this was sufficient cause for WashCo to come after him with whatever they could find. So here he was! Hello Mr. Case Manager !

Apparently this opened the door for the case manager as he told Rex that he knew who he was from listening to Rex's radio show. After quickly reviewing Rex's file and asking some prerequisite questions, he made the comment, "You know Rex, in my eleven years in this job, I have never seen a more ridiculous case than yours. There is no reason for you to be here", he said. Rex shrugged his shoulders and agreed with a wry smile.

They talked some more and Rex sensed that his case manager wanted to come right out and express his support and encouragement, but he worked hard at maintaining his neutral objectivity as a good government employee. He had his job to do which he respected. Nevertheless, he knew they were brothers in spirit.

Interestingly enough, during Rex's wait to get shipped out, he noticed Joe Mentlick in the chow hall. Joe was one of the insiders involved in promoting the farm claims' program that we discussed earlier. He was convicted of fraud just like Gary was and evidently was put in D.R.D.C. just prior to Rex's arrival unbeknownst to him. It was more than a pleasant surprise to see him!

He was in a separate 'pod' in D.R.D.C. than Rex was. Each pod would eat in its own designated area and they weren't allowed to visit inmates outside of our own pods. So he waited for him to get up from his table to go and get a drink from the soda fountain which was a common area.

Rex went up and said hello and Joe knew who he was. They chatted only briefly as they had to keep moving, but agreed to meet at chapel service which was a combined service for both pods.

Several days' later Chapel service was announced. They finally got together and Joe brought him up to speed on a couple items of interest.

First... He told him, James Black (remember 'Buck James'?) had been released out in Oklahoma. After he got back on his feet health wise here in WashCo they shipped him out after they brought so much attention to his plight on Rex's radio show. WashCo couldn't take the heat. This was great news and it was very satisfying since Rex had a hand in bringing his situation to the world's attention.

Next, Joe told him that James, of course, was under intense surveillance and monitoring upon his release, which was anticipated. He went on to tell him that it had been confirmed that James had slipped out from under his 'big brothers' watchful eyes. He was now making select rendezvous collecting his stored away artifacts and evidence that would go a long way in exposing the truth about some of our public servants over the last twenty five years.

Joe and he talked about what was going on with the claims and other projects involving the restoration of our republic. Joe told him he'd happily do 10 years or more in prison if he could just see these things come to fruition. Well, it certainly seemed like the ball was rolling in the right direction. The cat was out of the bag and it would be hard to put back in.

To Rex's surprise Joe was later moved into Rex's pod. He enjoyed talking with Joe and they spent the next week together comparing notes and looking to the future. Joe got released on an appeal bond and went home to Kansas. He later told Rex that the guards knew all about his efforts in the claims and treated him like a V.I.P. as they processed him out. One guard even made the comment to another guard, "you'd better open the door for Mentlick, he could be our next president!"

During this time Rex's stepfather died from leukemia. Rex's mom called D.R.D.C. on a Thursday to try to make arrangements for him to be at the funeral on Saturday. Unfortunately, nobody at D.R.D.C. bothered to notify him until the following Tuesday. To Rex's chagrin this would typify the level of competence he would have to deal with on a regular basis in D.O.C. (department of corrections)

Rex's point total on the scoring sheet with his case manager was about as low as it could possibly be which was good. This meant he was stable and a low security risk with no needs for special classes or programs.

He was assigned straightaway to a minimum security camp in the Colorado countryside on the western slope in a small town called Rifle.

Rex's case manager in D.R.D.C. told him that it would probably be another week or so before he got shipped out of D.R.D.C. and to be patient. He gave him a couple of tips for getting along in D.O.C. and wished him good luck.

Interestingly enough, one of the 'labels' put on him by the government and the minions in the media was 'Colorado ringleader for the Montana militia'. With this in mind he found it ironic that they would send him to a place called 'Rifle'. It seems to have some poetic justice.

This type of facility was usually the last stop for guys who had worked their way through the system and were ready to get out. It was a very open facility with freedom of movement, fresh air and really not too bad of a place to be.

Rex soon shed his orange D.R.D.C. jumpsuit for a brand new custom tailored (one pocket was accidentally sewn shut) D.O.C. 'Greens' outfit. He was then loaded onto the 'Bluebird' prison bus and sent on his way to camp Rifle. Oh boy!

He took the long way to Rifle having made a couple of scheduled overnighters at other prison facilities along the way. The trip was made a couple of days longer when an avalanche closed one of the mountain passes they were needing to cross. It was the dead of winter and cold in the mountains.

When he finally got to the Rifle facility he was pleasantly surprised to see that it was nestled in a beautiful mountain valley out of town and adjacent to a reservoir lake and wildlife refuge. There were no fences or security doors. It was a small compound with several buildings serving various functions much like a small community college campus. The inmate population was only about one hundred fifty.

He was processed in quickly and got to know some of the guys. He made quite a few friends in short order by hanging out in the law library and chapel for Bible studies and various services.

It wasn't long before a number of Rex's inmate buddies were intrigued with Rex's knowledge of the government fraud and how to deal with it. Perhaps that's not a surprise in a place like this. It wasn't long before 'THE AMERICAN LAW CLUB' had a new chapter and informally began holding discussion groups so that they all could expand their knowledge and capabilities in protecting and preserving our rights!

At the second meeting, they had a pretty good group and the law library was filled to capacity and then some. Upon seeing this, one female guard stuck her nose in and listened for a while, which was fine. She just wanted to see what was going on. It was a bit unusual for the guards to pay much attention.

After the meeting she called Rex into her office to advise him of posted operational rule number 19 which prohibits unsupervised gatherings of four or more as they are characteristic of 'gang' related activity and disruptive of facility purposes. She continued with a comment to the effect that, in reviewing your 'jacket' (file) with your known associations with, or involvement in *white supremacist militia's* you'd better be very careful about your behavior here! You will be in serious trouble if you are found recruiting for your white supremacist militia in here, she said.

She was advising him in a friendly, 'advance warning' manner but he was still taken back a bit by her comment about Rex's 'associations'. So as soon as our meeting ended he went and got a couple of his better friends who helped him organize the new prison law club. It was a moonless, dark night.

With Rex's two key organizers at his side, the three of them went over to the control center where he got her attention again. They were outside under a roofed area which was poorly lit and they were a bit in the shadows. He politely informed her that, "in the event that you ever need to communicate with my group and I'm not around, I'd like to introduce you to my Lieutenant Commander and the Colonel of my 'white supremacist militia' group, Anthony and Jay."

Anthony and Jay are as black as the night. Rex's two black buddies were grinning ear to ear and waved at her through the window. In the shadows of the night you could see little more than the whites of their eyes and their big grins! While the three of us were nearly splitting a gut the sergeant looked very confused and concerned and didn't know how to react. The poor girl, she took the whole thing so very seriously. Hey, who says you can't have a little fun in prison?

Everyone (well the inmates anyway) was very excited about the law club meetings and wanted to continue. Since they were warned about P.O.R. 19, they couldn't risk disciplinary action meeting again unless they did it properly. They didn't want to submit to formal requirements for scheduled activity as this would be asking for the warden to allocate personnel to supervise and create a whole bureaucratic mess. They would need to have arrangements for a classroom and because of all this trouble the answer more than likely be a resounding NO!

As an alternative Rex drafted a 'Constructive Notice' to Captain Pierce who had oversight on these matters at this facility. The 'Notice" was a good faith advisement to Captain Pierce of the activities. They outlined the fact that they were using the law library for its intended purpose, that the gatherings there of four or more was no different than gatherings in the day room for T.V. viewing or chow hall for meals or chapel for service. The activities served a productive and educational purpose and were being conducted in a peaceful and orderly manner for the educational benefit of the inmates. Due to these facts relating to the intent they therefore felt that P.O.R. 19 did not apply.

They informed him that they would continue the meetings unless or until they were advised differently from his office. Eight inmates signed it and it was presented the next day. The 'Notice' was constructed keeping in mind that the easiest thing for someone to do is nothing! They wanted him to say 'yes' by doing nothing and then they'd be in the clear. It was the shortest route to a 'yes' he could think of. Rex learned this from doing the commercial liens. If you disagree, you must object and support your position. It's much easier to do nothing (and agree)!

The strategy worked. Captain Pierce did exactly that! 'Nothing'. So they continued the meetings without any concern for P.O.R. 19. Silence is acquiescence and they had their tacit 'approval'.

Several weeks after this little showdown, the inmate working as law clerk in the library was shipped out for medical treatment. He had recently won a lawsuit against D.O.C. for an injury he incurred while he was incarcerated and the court awarded him $170,000 plus proper medical care. Needless to say he and Rex got along great.

He put in a good word for Rex to replace him as law clerk while he was gone and Rex got his job. This was great because he was already spending his free time there anyway doing all of his legal research. Now he had his own private office with typewriters, office supplies and everything at his disposal full time. This was a gift from heaven! It was all that Rex would need to complete his work. He now had unlimited access to the law library; his own private office where he tended as 'clerk' for the inmates!

With Rex's creative perspective and 'incisive' applications on the 'law... word traveled quickly in this small camp and the inmate access logs always seemed full as he had these guys learning some amazing things. This apparently didn't go unnoticed by the camp administration. After about a month of freewheeling and aggressive educating, Rex's case manager called him into her office. She advised him that they were going to put someone else in that position. She said, "Mr. Freeman, based upon your history and background, we don't feel it would be a good idea for you to be influencing too many inmates." He could only laugh to himself. Of course she was right, he was very bad for 'business', from their perspective.

Rex replied... "My opinions don't change the law. What are people afraid of, the law or truth?" In any event, it didn't matter. That was that! They obviously don't want inmates knowing very much for obvious reasons.

Rex was never in Rifle for more than two to three weeks at a time because he was continuously being shipped back to Denver for court on two other cases that were now pending. One was the new bond jumping case in WashCo for supposedly not showing up for his sentencing there even though the case was removed by a bonded action by our one supreme Court and he did make an appearance by affidavit.

The other was a case in Denver based upon charges of writing a bad check involving the C.M.O. used for the Mercedes. This case started prior to Rex's self-imposed exile. We'll get into these shortly.

But what he found interesting was the fact that his mode of transportation back to Denver was not the same as the other inmates going to court. Rather than travelling with the other inmates who would normally go by van or bus in a herd, dressed in their normal greens, Rex was given exception which he always appreciated.

Rex had his own private car with two special E.R.U. (emergency response units) or S.W.A.T. personnel to accompany him. They always gave him a very special 'red' jump suit, the private car and two escort cars to take him to court in comfort, speed and style. Evidently word had spread that judge Perriman declared him a threat to public safety and he required extra security for fear of 'ambush' by all of Rex's 'white supremacist militia' buddies, even though he was at a minimum security camp with no fences and no armed guards. Figure that one out!

It was comical really, the hysterical paranoia that he created in officialdom by doing nothing more than teaching people the law and broadcasting his faith and belief in good government.

Anyway, the four hour drive through the beautiful Colorado Rockies was always a nice break. It gave him a chance to make new friends and plant seeds of thought with his public servant chauffeurs, which is exactly what he did. During Rex's escorted trips back to court in Denver he usually had enjoyable and very interesting conversations with the personnel assigned to him and they had plenty of time to discuss the ins and outs of each other's worlds. He learned a lot and no doubt they did too!

Having the chance now to adjust to the relaxing pace of Rex's paid vacation, he channeled his energies into writing and research. This, he figured, would be one way to continue to contribute to others' enlightenment and perspectives on truth, law and good government and further develop some of his own ideas. There wasn't a minute to waste!

He wrote several articles on various issues of law, scripture and prophecy, his national heritage and related topics. In view of the many inquiries he began to receive from friends and radio followers on the outside, he decided to write an article about his story and how he got to camp Rifle. Being a fairly complicated story, the article was eight pages and was entitled:

"And Justice for All: The Making of a Prisoner - American Style."

Rex sent the article to several publications. It was finally published in THE AMERICAN FREEDOM magazine published by the radio station KHNC which broadcast Rex's radio show. This way, most of Rex's listeners would get the story and he could make a few copies and mail them off when needed without the dreary task of getting writer's cramp telling the same story again and again. KHNC sent him about a half dozen complimentary issues of the magazine with the article.

Rex's mail censors at camp Rifle wouldn't allow him more than one copy for fear he'd be disseminating information to cause unrest. (There's that paranoia again). Captain Nagle was responsible for screening incoming mail. He read the article and was intrigued by it. Thereafter, for quite some time he would corner Rex when nobody was around and he'd ask Rex questions about his view and research on issues like: the I.R.S., government fraud & abuse, personal rights, etc.

He agreed with many of Rex's positions and they hit it off pretty good. Of course who isn't interested in preserving their own personal rights against encroachments by excessive and unlawful power? That's the bottom line. We're all in the same boat. Nagle did allow him to send the extra copies to friends on the outside rather than just throw them in the trash, which Rex appreciated. However... the warden saw a copy while it was on Capt. Nagle's desk and he wanted to read it also. The story was a big splash on the magazine cover so it was hard to miss.

The article contained Rex's new Rifle address and he started receiving mail from around the country in response. This high exposure was another perceived 'security threat' and it 'spooked' Rex's captors. It wasn't long before he was transferred down to another minimum security camp called 'Skyline' located in the Cañon City prison complex in southern Colorado.

CHAPTER 20

THE DENVER TWO STEP

FROM REX'S NEW 'BASE' IN Rifle Correctional Center, several, trips were made back to district court in Denver for the case which they threw at him which was centered around the private credit he issued. Remember the 'invasion' and kidnapping in Cañon City? Yep, that one.

Again, a private negotiable instrument was tendered to Mercedes Benz Credit Corp pursuant to a private agreement he reached with a Mr. Farthing from Kansas who wanted to get out from under his lease obligation with M.B.C.C.

According to the agreement it was only 'after' M.B.C.C. had confirmed acceptance of the instrument and released the title was Farthing then to deliver the car to Rex. There was no risk or obligation for Farthing whatsoever. Nor was there for Rex as he was acting legally in good faith with full disclosure. Everything was based on M.B.C.C. accepting the tender of payment in full for the car.

M.B.C.C. was given explicit written instructions in a cover letter on the exact nature of the instrument and how to redeem it with the private party against whom it was drawn. They were told explicitly that this was not a public debt instrument and they could not deposit it at their local bank.

M.B.C.C. accepted the instrument, released the lien, cancelled the lease contract and delivered the certificate of title to Farthing in Kansas as per normal procedure. Farthing informed Rex of the good news and promptly drove to Denver to deliver the beautiful red 190SL to him with the key, the certificate of title, a smile and much thanks!

It wasn't until six months after the initial transaction that any indication of problem arose. At this point Rex wasn't able to determine if M.B.C.C. either wasn't able to redeem the instrument for more credit, or if they just couldn't follow instructions properly.

It turns out that they failed to follow the instructions they were given and they tried to deposit the instrument in a Federal Reserve member bank which they were told in good faith was 'not' the proper procedure for redemption. Of course their local bank rejected the instrument.

To make a long story short, Rex tried for a year and a half through correspondence to try and get them to simply follow simple instructions; for prompt redemption which was to mail the endorsed instrument to private party bank in Texas whereupon they would be issued a certified cashier's check for 'private credit' in the form of 'Money of Account' of the United states (which has never been legally defined or determined, but in practice is only 'credit' i.e. promises to pay which never get paid).

So what did Mercedes Benz Credit Corp do? Two things:

A) They hired a local Denver firm to try and repossess the car. Rex caught on to this early and out maneuvered them. They never got it. Some time later, a guy who was a skinhead, full of tattoos showed up at one of the Law Club meetings and stood out like a sore thumb. The skinhead approached Rex afterwards and complimented him on what was going on in the meetings. He was impressed. Later he asked Rex, "Are you the one who has the red Mercedes?" Rex replied in the affirmative. He went on to explain how he was the one who was instructed to repo the car. Normally in this process they confirm who is the real owner. In this case he found out that Rex had the full unencumbered certificate of title to the car as per Rex's agreement and there was acceptance by all involved in the transaction. He explained how he had asked his superior, 'If this guy has the title they can't do a repo on it can they?" He said he was told to do it anyway!

B) Rather than following simple instructions or pursuing a civil action for a commercial dispute where they would have to spend money on lawyers, M.B.C.C. got the Denver D.A. to press charges against Rex for theft and writing a bad check. This was a class three felony which carried a four to twelve year prison term if found guilty.

Rex's initial reaction was twofold:

1. He was quite interested as to how they would try to prove that it was a bad check when they never made an attempt to process it according to the instructions they were given. This is bad faith on their part. On the contrary, he had continued to communicate with M.B.C.C. and had done nothing other than exhibit good faith and continued support to help them in the process.
2. He was quite excited by the prospect of being able to bring the 'money issue' into court and make all of this a matter for public record. He was highly confident in his position and this could turn the entire system on its ear! The dummies in the Denver D.A.'s office had no idea what they were getting into!

Rex read the charging documents against him and they were so fraught with obvious errors of fact, law and procedure that he put together a 'Notice of Violation of Ethics' document. This document was extensively detailed as to each and every element that violated the Bar Association code of ethics and was fully supported with exhibits and documentation. He notified the office of the American Bar Association of the ethical standards it would be violating if it proceeded to prosecute the case based on erroneous information. This 'Notice' was given to all parties and filed simply as a matter of record to establish reversible error should it be needed in the future.

Of course this didn't faze them one bit. Continuing on this track, he went to the Colorado Supreme Court to file a petition for a 'Writ of

Prohibition'. This writ is based on the Court's own previous decisions wherein they have ruled that a prosecution cannot proceed upon knowingly false and erroneous information.

Rex filed the petition to the Supreme Court with 'Emergency' status. The court heard the petition right away. This in itself was a small victory. However they ignored their own precedents and case law, sided with the bankers and the 'system' and denied the petition. He thought this was quite curious when the Supreme Court doesn't even recognize and act on its own previous decisions!

The next step was to go to the Ethics Committee and review board for the bar association. They would most certainly recognize obvious violations of their very specific tenets of conduct and want to maintain their ethical standards by putting some pressure on the D.A.s office, right? Wrong again. The fox was not about to let anyone else into this hen house!

He further reviewed the paperwork and found his 'good friend' Gary Clayman of the Attorney General's office on the witness list. Here he was again! Rex was keeping this boy busy wasn't he? Was it any coincidence that he was the key lynch pin to do an undercover investigation and set up Gary Woodland to take a fall? Then he appeared as a witness again in Rex's 'self-impersonation' case. Now he shows up again on Rex's Denver credit case. The bell finally rang for him. the Attorney General's office and the same minions of the M.J.T.F. were behind all of these persecutions!

It was quite obvious that these were not just ordinary prosecutions. There was clearly a deliberate and willful attempt to use the full weight of the government machine to destroy him and all others like him who were showing people how to use the law to protect themselves and hold public officials accountable. This is nothing less than a 'war' against the people.

This 'freedom movement' is more of a threat to the power structure and 'status quo' than any form of military or terrorist threat. From their perspective, he had to be dealt with and dealt with harshly to set an example, with whatever means possible. This was clear from the experience in WashCo.

When they couldn't convict him in the first trial, despite their best efforts, they pulled out all the stops. Rules, law and procedure were notwithstanding. In the second trial in WashCo they didn't even try to maintain any appearances of proper procedure and a level playing field. They did *the necessary* to get their conviction on a trumped up charge which was baseless in the first place and ended up being a joke.

Now the same was happening in Denver County. The charging documents were full of gaping holes and errors to begin with yet they wanted to proceed despite having been put on notice. Neither the court nor the Bar Association ethics committee would honor their published standards and the Supreme Court refused to honor its own standing decisions and act accordingly. The writing was on the wall and he didn't need an interpreter!

Rex was on a horse with two ropes: one binding his hands and the other around his neck. This was a precarious position. He was facing 'four to twelve'!

Rex felt strong about his case. The facts, law and common sense were on his side. To get a criminal conviction the prosecution would have to show 'intent' to commit a crime. This was easy for him because he had acted at all times in good faith and his intent was always to get M.B.C.C. to just follow instructions, which they never did. Nobody could ever say the check was bad because nobody ever tried to redeem it properly. And he continued to communicate with them. He didn't run and hide. Based on intent alone this should be a slam dunk case for him.

The only challenge he had was to properly manage the twelve jurors.

He decided to switch up the strategy a little. He would use the court appointed attorney to handle preliminaries and initial case administration in the early stages. This way he could handle early case management so that the record would be well set and he would play their little game with a 'club approved' intermediary. Later, when necessary, he would ultimately have to release the attorney from the case and do the trial himself in order to effectively make the necessary points. Surely the attorney didn't understand the money issue like Rex did and he would certainly butcher the case.

Rex was prepared to proceed and have fun doing it. This could be a landmark case for the nation.

Lo and behold around mid-April after all the initial posturing, the D.A.s office told Rex's attorney Fernando that they were willing to make a deal.

Fernando told Rex that they were willing to offer 'only' five years' probation and all he would need to do was: plead guilty, pay the check, for $25,000 withdraw the commercial liens which he had filed, and agree not to file any more commercial liens or other lawsuits against any public officials.

In other words, all he would have to do is become a complete whore and prostitute everything he believed in, sell himself out, and still live as a convicted felon all for the small benefit of staying out of prison!

The fact that this offer came as it did, told him one thing: They were scared as hell and they didn't want this thing going any further. They tipped their hand and Rex was more emboldened than ever at this point.

After the offer was made and he had his little discussion with the D.A. Fernando came back to the sheriff's holding cell area where Rex was being held in the court house waiting to be called. With a straight face he was trying desperately to understand a few things. Fernando came back and was VERY curious now. He said to Rex "Tell me about this lawsuit and lien you have on judge Perriman!"

Fernando didn't know about Rex's $50 million lien against Perriman previously. So Rex explained in the briefest terms possible. Fernando was intrigued but still didn't quite understand it all, which was fine. Rex wasn't prepared to educate him entirely.

Fernando's initial knee jerk reaction to the offer was "they can't stop you from filing further grievances. That's ridiculous!" Rex agreed and patted him on the back. He was starting to like Fernando.

Fernando then explained some of the finer details of the offer and what it meant and how it would work. If Rex accepted it, or they accepted a counter offer, it would be agreed to and then a hearing would be set in a couple weeks to present it to the judge and resolve the case accordingly.

Rex was thinking about his options. He thought about how they sent the S.W.A.T. team after him, after tracking him down, pulled him out of bed into the snow at 3 AM in the morning, violated every rule in the book to try and nail him and now they had him, but wanted to strike a deal? This is not a position of strength.

An idea came to mind. He would accept their deal (for now). This would give them a false sense of security and they would stop preparing for trial thinking that the matter is resolved. Their request to have him agree 'not to file any more lawsuits or liens' was ridiculous and they couldn't make that stick anyway. So that was a dead issue.

When the hearing came up to enter the plea and the plea deal, Rex would change his mind and inform the judge he wanted to move to trial. This would burn time off of their fuse to prepare, leaving them to chase loose ends before the trial and set them back on their heels with a surprise move. Rex would pay the restitution anyway which would completely eliminate their 'intent' issue and they'd have nowhere to go with the case other than to allow him to enter onto the record the facts about the fraudulent money system and private credit which would pave the way for others to follow him. He liked it.

He told Fernando he'd take the deal but they couldn't preclude him from filing any further grievances and they knew that. He informed them accordingly and then Rex had to wait for his chauffeur before ending the episode and heading back to 'camp'.

Three weeks later back in Rifle, the S.W.A.T. team escort came for him to bring him back to Denver. After a nice trip, he was brought into the courtroom in his special red jumpsuit. He was seated in the jury box and who did he see sitting in the courtroom with an entourage? Gary Clayman and his cronies! The whole M.J.T.F., A.G. and C.I.B. team was there and he could only surmise that apparently they wanted to be present to gloat over Rex's submission to the 'guilty' plea which would be their conquest and final victory!

Rex had everything worked out with Fernando. He already had it clear that he would be breaking the bad news that Rex had changed his mind about accepting the deal, and that he wanted to go to trial. This was going to be fun!

What they wanted was to suspend the sentence in lieu of the 5 years supervision they were offering, understanding that if he failed the terms of the supervision (which they felt was likely due to Rex's character and strong beliefs) he would end up doing the time anyway.

So for him, the offer was B.S. and it was never seriously considered, other than to use the offer as a ploy for more shenanigans and play with them a little.

The judge entered the courtroom and called the case. He asked the D.A. if he had a disposition. She replied and said, 'Well apparently judge there has been a change of course here. We need some more time to sort things out.'

"Fine," Judge Collins said, "you can come back again in thirty minutes." He called another case and started working on that.

The entire team of government persecutors got together in the back of the courtroom. There were about ten of them standing in a huddle and they called Fernando over to discuss with them.

The whole time he was sitting in the jury box observing the Chinese fire drill. Rex made no attempt to hide the fact that he was watching them intently. He occasionally got a return stare. They all looked so serious and concerned. It was clear that this was not what they'd expected today.

They finally came back with another offer: three years supervision, contingent upon restitution with the stipulation that he'd admit in open court that the court here does in fact have jurisdiction over him.

This was obviously the result of the Letter Rogatory and other documents he had filed in WashCo from the peoples' One Supreme Court

which they were clearly aware of. If in fact this court 'did' have jurisdiction over him, and the peoples' court did not have supremacy, why
would they even bother with this request? Because once again, Rex had
them on the run and they were trying everything in the book to 'rectify'
things in any way they could.

When they came at him with this one he couldn't control himself
and had to laugh out loud the sound of which pierced the somber mood
of the courtroom. They were really grasping at straws now! This was
proof positive that they felt very vulnerable and Rex was relishing every
moment. After a good laugh he told Fernando that they should prepare
for trial. Fernando delivered the message. Rex's laugh clearly commu-
nicated the answer to them even though they were across the room.

If they did in fact 'have' jurisdiction, why would they have him admit it openly on the record? The only reason was to force Rex's 'willing
consent' and submission to the court as a part of the deal because they
know they don't have it once it is properly challenged.

Judge Collins called the case again and all parties approached
their respective tables and podiums. The judge asked again: "Have you
reached a disposition?" The D.A. responded, "Well your honor... apparently there's been a change of heart and we do not have a disposition.
we're prepared to go to trial.

This was not what the judge anticipated and he sternly ordered
counsel to approach the bench. He turned his microphone off, leaned
over and tried to talk quietly but forceful. It was easy to see that he was
upset and he didn't want this to go to trial. This was good for Rex.

Despite trying to keep the encounter private, the podium Rex was
at, was right in front of the bench and he could hear every word spoken.

Judge Collins asked, "What's going on here?" The D.A. tried to reply
but was flummoxed and incoherent. That's when Fernando stepped in
and tried to explain Rex's position vis-à-vis the crazy offer including the
request to admit jurisdiction on the record, which he refused.

Looking very stern, judge Collins said, "What's wrong with you people? You want to bring this onto the record in open court? If this issue

were raised and people knew what Rex is raising here, that the court doesn't have jurisdiction over people like him, we wouldn't have hardly any cases and you'd all be out of a job!"

Fernando turned around and looked at Rex and literally started banging his head on the wooden rail in front of the bench to express his complete dismay at the prosecution and this whole situation. It was quite a scene!

They talked some more and fashioned a 'new deal' at the judge's urging. This deal was driven by Fernando who was aware of the other case and sentence Rex had in WashCo. They finally agreed to offer him a sentence to run concurrent with what he already had in WashCo on the impersonation case, which meant there would be *no additional time* and no additional conditions or ridiculous requests. They would reduce the charges to a simple fraudulent/bad check if he would make a guilty plea and pay court costs and just go away.

Rex had to think really hard. This was not an easy decision. On one hand, he had a solid defense against a case they were bringing which was full of holes big enough to drive a truck through. He could make history by getting this issue and District Court case on the record and setting precedent in a court of record on the 'money issue' and blow the whole 'Fed Fraud' wide open. Plus, upon victory, he could chase every malevolent state actor from here to kingdom come, lien up their assets and create enough credit to set entire state free from the bondage of the money powers.

On the other hand, he also knew that they had the police, the detectives, the M.J.T.F. the C.B.I., the operatives, the banks, the courts and the entire system behind them. Right or wrong, the old saying goes, 'It's dangerous to be right, when your government is wrong!' The stakes went beyond this little local fiefdom. It had national and international implications.

He saw what they did to him in WashCo. They did what they had to do no matter what it took. Was he going to be naïve enough to think that they would play fair in the courtroom and allow him to single handedly expose their entire financial fraud system using their flawed legal system?

Rex's sense of reality took hold of his thinking and dashed the dreams he had to try the case. The stakes were high enough that in the event he was prevailing in the courtroom on the case, which would be likely, it would also be likely that they would find a way to put him six feet under before the end of the trial. They would not allow him to succeed to single handedly destroy the Fed financial system.

He decided to take the deal and live to fight another day on a different battlefield. He felt he had already won on the spiritual level and he beat them up pretty badly. He knew it. They knew it. Sadly it wasn't on the public record as he would have hoped.

They settled accordingly and the case was closed with the record showing he was involved in issuing a fraudulent check. They got their brownie points and Rex went back to his cozy little mountain camp in Rifle, Colorado.

This is how most convictions are obtained these days. They pile on so many onerous charges with ridiculous prison sentences base on charges which make almost no sense at all. Then, from the fear and intimidation, they get the poor sucker defendant to cop a plea when in many cases they are not guilty of anything, or when they are it is a small infraction compared to the case they build up. They get the conviction and a new customer for the system and they don't even have to try the case. The wonders of modern legal practice. It's not about justice anymore. It's all about 'business' and 'control'.

CHAPTER 21

WashCo Comes Again

WASHCO INITIATED NEW CHARGES; VIOLATION of Bail Bond Conditions as a result of the removal of Rex's District Court case to the peoples' One Supreme Court, whereupon Rex did not volunteer back into the District Court jurisdiction. Upon learning of this, Rex's attorney in Denver made the comment, "That's chicken shit" in reference to the prosecutorial behavior. Of course, Rex couldn't disagree.

As if WashCo hadn't witnessed against themselves enough by their behavior in the previous case, they continued to try to plow him under even deeper. In this case, the 'Violation of Bail Bond Conditions' charge amounted to another class 6 felony which carried another possible 18 months which was mandatory to run consecutive to any other sentences.

As expected, the District court ignored the lawful orders from its principals and masters. They refused to subject themselves to lawful process and thus allow the people to set an historic precedent to challenge their police powers and control.

Having now had firsthand experience with the fraudulent nature of this corrupt statutory jurisdiction, Rex realized that he would need to take a different approach to his predicament.

Truth and law obviously didn't have any place in Perriman's courtroom and thus Rex would never get the opportunity to advise the jurors of the 'facts' AND 'the law' which was the entire foundation of his defense.

When 'intent' is required to prove a criminal charge, and your 'intent' is based wholly upon your frame of mind which consists of your understanding of the law, as it is written, and the court doesn't allow you to discuss or even bring up 'the law', then it's pretty safe to say that your fate is sealed.

Contrary to the supreme law of the land and the judge's oath to support that contract with the people, judge Perriman made a point to specifically instruct the jury in the previous case that "HE" was the only one to determine 'the law' in this case and that the jurors were to follow His instructions only as it relates to 'the facts' presented.

Rex didn't expect that anything which he could do would have any positive effect on the outcome of his case, the way this court was conducted. The best he could hope for would be to maximize his effectiveness in forcing the persecutors to expose their fraud and corruption.

He started with the source of the charges, the bail bond contract. In reviewing the Bail Bond agreement he noticed some interesting facts;

(1) They had Rex's name in all capital letters as if he were a fictional entity such as a corporation or acronym. He had learned through his studies in law that this is a deliberate tactic used to create a fiction to bring into the court which was not operating 'in law' but rather was operating under the fictional public policy modus operandi of a 'bankrupt' not 'sovereign' entity.

This misnomer 'person' was not him, as Rex's Christian name is spelled in both upper and lower case letters. The case was a misnomer. The 'Person' they named was not him and 'misnomer' is a lawful defect which gives rise to a demurrer.

(2) They had written down an address which he knew for a fact was erroneous and non-existent. This being the case, it certainly did not apply to him. Wrong 'person' and 'misnomer' again.

(3) The Bond agreement curiously made a demand for payment in, of all things, 'lawful money of the United States'.

Of course, lawful money (by definition) does not exist since H.J.R. 192 in 1933. The law cannot require the impossible. If we accept Federal Reserve Notes as 'lawful money' then they have to accept 'private credit' and we now know what we can do with that.

(4) Rex had signed the bond agreement 'without prejudice' above his name which is a reservation of all rights and a waiver of none. Pursuant to the contract, in the event that should future events dictate, Rex's signature should not be construed as a waiver of any rights, which can often be the case when the court takes 'silent judicial notice' of certain facts to then proceed upon assumptions and presumptions which are secret to the court. This would preserve Rex's right to raise issues on any defects or lawful deficiencies in the agreement and would not compromise his position in relation to the agreement.

Based upon the above mentioned facts, he swore out an *Affidavit of Refusal for Cause' pursuant to U.C.C. 3-501 whereby he refused the implied or express liability of the agreement for the lawful reasons (cause) which he cited as...

1... MISNOMER. To get a grasp of this issue and its lawful foundation search the subject of 'non-statutory abatement'

2... MISTAKE. The incorrect and nonexistent address listed under Rex's name in the agreement obviously was not his.

3... UNCONSCIONABLE CONTRACT. Under this doctrine, as outlined in U.C.C. 2-302, the courts may deny enforcement of a contract because of unfair or oppressive terms or procedural or substantive abuses. In this case, demand for payment of the amount stipulated in the Bond Agreement in 'lawful money of the U.S.' was too vague and impossible to perform and thus could not require specific legal performance.

Here's why; if 'lawful money' of the U.S. (gold and silver coin) is not available as a currently circulating medium of exchange, and if the state statutes define 'Legal Tender' as the same gold or silver minted coin which is not available, and The U.S. Code (Federal Statutes) tell us at 31 U.S.C. 5101 that 'money of account of the United States has never been determined by any court or government agency', then it's clear they can't tell him what exactly it is.

So then, how can a contract require you to pay in something that is either unavailable or undefined? Again, the law does not, nor can it, require impossibilities.

3... LACK OF INFORMED CONSENT. Rex was not aware of these defects when he put his signature on the agreement and therefore did not knowingly, willingly and intentionally accept the liability of the agreement under these conditions.

4... DURESS. Since they were going to keep him in their stinking jail if he did not sign as they told him to, he had no choice but to sign under duress and again Rex's signature was not voluntary or binding.

5... NO BONA FIDE SIGNATURE. Since he had made an explicit reservation of his rights upon the original signature (U.C.C. 1-201) and was now exercising these rights to establish more than one affirmative defense to the intended compelled performance of the agreement, he therefore wished to withdraw, cancel, annul and vacate his signature off of the agreement *ab inicio* which leaves no bona fide signature to demand compliance and or liability pursuant to the agreement.

He further demanded that all parties either:

a) show cause within ten days as to what lawful grounds they have to proceed on this matter, or
b) cease and desist.

Failure to do so would be willful and a knowing violation of Rex's rights and property to which could attach criminal liability to each violator and co-conspirator.

The establishment of Rex's 'prima facie' case would be a matter of record and could not be ignored without establishing either dismissal or criminal intent by the prosecution and/or the court if not both.

This was Rex's initial thrust in exposing more corruption in WashCo. This however was just the first step.

Rex's next little endeavor would be a *non-statutory abatement* procedure. You can find info on this procedure on the internet.

Part One of the non-statutory abatement consists of paperwork which sets the stage. The stage that they are setting is such that 'while he have received the charging documents alleging this crime, we do not accept them and thus refuse to enter into any implied consent agreements with the accusers for the reason that my accusers' paperwork is fraught with fraud, inconsistencies, irregularities and they lack the lawful authority vis-à-vis the true supreme law of the land including due process.

Rex outlined fifteen marks of fraud in their charging documents in Part One.

Part Two related to jurisdictional issues which were known to be valid since they've been confirmed by Judge Collins in the Denver. courtroom escapade.

Part Three related to factual errors which was the base of the case. It gave them grace to correct the defects and remedy the situation promptly or in the alternative, cease and desist.

Part Four was the final notice giving them Notice of Fraud which, if left uncorrected without remedy, made it very clear that there was nothing but criminal intent on the part of the prosecution to proceed illegally with malicious ill will which is, of course, the basis for further action.

And now you understand the 'non-judicial' commercial lien process and how that can be used, was used and would be used again to 'correct' errant officials and gain remedy without having to use the corrupt courts.

In the end, this final attack WashCo launched against him amounted to nothing and was taken apart as mentioned above, to die a slow death. They had their way with him and had gotten all they were going to get.

Rex appealed his 'impersonation' conviction with more than enough reversible error to achieve success. But it went nowhere and the appeals court would have none of it. Rex was too much of a political hot potato and apparently had not earned a position as a 'favorite son' to be granted the benefit of establishing legal precedent, especially when it would only serve to dismantle the machine of the cabal.

Rex's battles in court were over. At least for now.

So finally, after only spending a portion of his 36 month sentence, he got released early for good behavior. He did a short stint in a halfway house and was back on the street menacing the world once again with threats of 'impersonating himself' at any given moment!

He then began pondering the next phase in the 'War' and in his life.

Having fought and survived in the belly of the beast, he was now fearless of 'man' and committed to God.

This only emboldened him and the next phase of life would be quite different. It would get even more interesting!

CHAPTER 22

CONCLUSION

SOME PEOPLE WHO DON'T UNDERSTAND, feel that the prison sentence is a black mark on Rex's record and an embarrassment in his life.

To the contrary, the fact is, that this was Rex's 'badge of honor'. He had every opportunity to make a plea bargain in the impersonation case and avoid jail time from the very beginning. All he had to do was to repudiate everything he believed in and submit to evil.

He refused this course. Rex stood by his principles and took the government persecutors to the wall giving them fits every step of the way. In the process he exposed them for who they really are, and for all to see. There is no longer any doubt about it, as this book now confirms.

The year he spent in prison (camp) was one of the best years of Rex's life. It was relaxing and educational. He didn't have to worry about paying bills or fixing the car or fighting city traffic to get somewhere. He was working in the kitchen and he ate very well. He played handball, volleyball and softball and had plenty of recreation. He didn't even have to do his own laundry!

Rex's greatest joy and intellectual endeavor was that he had plenty of time to study and compare God's law, with what he had learned about 'Man's Law'.

This was a special project he took on. He dissected the new testament and categorized scripture in a way that made it clear as a bell that everything he was learning and doing to separate himself from the corporate state police powers jurisdiction to live as a 'free man', was scripturally correct and corroborated in every way.

He knew this to be the case beforehand but now, having the time to go through a laborious exercise and have the complete detail from his own handiwork, gave it special meaning, impact and importance.

One of the greatest benefits to this entire experience was that he now 'knew' the beast and how he operates. He has exposed his weaknesses and strengths. The result of all of this is that there is no more fear.

People fear the unknown. Once you've been in the belly of the beast, it is no longer unknown and the fear dissipates. The people in government who want to oppress us are just people. Most are not that well educated in terms of real knowledge. Degrees and certificates mean nothing in this regard. They believe as they are told and taught. They are striving in their careers so they do as they are told and notch benchmarks (convictions) whenever they can. We should pity them really. They don't know freedom like we know it.

Very few, if any, really understand law, history or the age old proven maxims that are derived from a spiritual level before they were ever implemented into a code of law for man. We refer you here back to our diagram in the Introduction showing the 'hierarchy of order'.

Nevertheless, as the USA and the world are being pushed down the slippery slope into a socialist, totalitarian, one world, secular system, the enlightenment of those empowered 'Patriots' who dare to risk life, limb and honor to preserve the God given constitutional republic, have enabled truth to rise to the surface. This gives us hope. With God, there is always hope. Our adversaries don't have that comfort. Without God, there is NO hope!

The country is in dire straits. We are on the verge of losing it. You can see from Rex's experiences nearly 20 years ago how the legal system has been hijacked. This was all back in the 90's. It's much, much worse now.

The USA will only survive if the people turn back to God, pray for guidance, courage and his almighty protection and do the following:

* Turn off the TV and get your kids out of public school.
* Don't waste your time or money on party politics. The federal government is not your friend no matter what color shirt the president is wearing. None of it addresses the core issues.
* Re-create your local government and courts.
* Read and study history, law and the bible
* Get off your duff, get involved and get others involved in restoring our heritage and lawful processes.
* Take control of your local government working directly with your local sheriff.
* Understand who you are under God and separate yourself from the corporate democracy known as the UNITED STATES. Breathe new life into the *'de jure'*, organic republic of the united States of America!

The commercial processes Rex had learned and used in the nineties have evolved substantially and people are using them with significant success. Look up the search term 'Accepted for Value' or 'A4V' on YouTube and follow the trail.

This book contains numerous other references which you can pick up on and do further research to expand your knowledge and understanding. We hope you do. We have enough notes, sidebars and follow up on the previously mentioned stories to fill another book but it will have to wait for now.

Remember, once ignorance is removed, you cannot get it back! Now it's up to you to do something about it!

As for Rex, he had served his people and his country by being as vocal and public as he could to sound the alarm and educate. Several years of weekly public meetings, private tutoring, and courtroom assistance without financial compensation was a sacrifice and a serious commitment.

Doing this service, hosting the radio show 'The Citizens Rights Forum' involved driving to Johnstown Colorado every Saturday from Denver, about 40 minutes each way, plus the airtime, plus the time preparing each show in advance. This was an unpaid volunteer job which reaped huge rewards in other ways.

Taking risks to stand on correct principles and 'just say no' is something more Americans need to accept as their own responsibility if we want to preserve the values and life which made America great. Rex did it at a time when most people were asleep and most patriots were 'in the closet'. Today, the sleeping giant is awakening. When the multitudes stand up and 'just say no', the system is only equipped to deal with the few, not the multitudes. We all need to recognize our strength and stand on righteousness!

In hindsight, It was a fantastic experience for Rex which has shaped his character in a way that nothing else could have.

Upon release from prison, his war would continue on a different level and take on a new twist. Rex's days fighting in court were over but he was not done educating, informing and providing an escape route on a higher level. Realizing that many of the laws were just great, if only they could be enforced properly, (they aren't) brought him to a point of knowing that we are living in a lawless society.

The tyrants will use the law against you when it is good for their business. When it is not good for their business, you cannot use the law to your benefit against the powers that be, at least if you are not on the 'politically correct' club list. Rex obviously wasn't.

With this in mind, he found true freedom after all. The ultimate victory is his. He has no 'income', no assets, no government benefits or ties and yet he lives like a king in a natural paradise where he lives like a retiree yet works from any hammock with wireless internet.

Curious? Find W.G. Hill's book 'PT - The Perpetual Traveler'.

Please discover who you really are, who created you and to whom you should serve. You cannot serve two masters. Many people don't know who they are. They serve the wrong master and thus will always be handled on the 'corporate farm' as chattel unless they find a way to get back to the 'original status' which is.... Freeman!

APPENDIX

COME OUT AND SEPARATE

Warning: To Escape Babylon's Judgment…

"Then he heard another voice from heaven say:
Come out of her my people, so that you will not share in her sins,
so that you will not receive any of her plagues…"
-Revelation 18:4

NEVER BEFORE IN HISTORY HAS this warning been so relevant.

As a result of Rex's time in prison, his study of God's law confirmed to him what he already knew by instinct. These tables are the result of his work which was made possible by the hospitality of 'the state' to whom he offers great thanks for making all of this possible! Read these select passages, look them up, and be thinking in the context of both: the spiritual meaning and in the context of life in modern day 'systems' as you recall Rex's story. You may make some new discoveries yourself! Both contexts fit together. Remember the words: "…Let your will be done on earth as it is in heaven", and live the glory here and now!

The Book of John	
10:5	A stranger they will not follow, but the will flee from him, for they do not know the voice of strangers.
10:14-16	I am the good shepard; I know my own and my own know me, as the Father knows me and I know the Father; and I lay down my life for the sheep, and I have other sheep that are not of this fold; I must bring them also and they will heed my voice. So there will be one flock, one Shepard.

John 11:47-48	So the chief priests and the Pharisees gathered the council and said, "What are we to do? For this man performs many signs. If we let him go on thus, everyone will believe in him, and the Romans will come and destroy both our Holy place and our nation."
13:16	"…a servant is not greater than his master, nor is he who is sent, greater than he who sent him. If you know these things blessed are you who do them."
18:36	Jesus answered, "My kingship is not of this world; if my kingship were of this world, my servants would fight, that I might not be handed over to the Jews."

The Book of Matthew	
10:23	When they persecute you in one town, flee to the next.
15:14	Let them alone, they are blind guides. And if a blind man leads a blind man, both will fall into a pit.
17:25	Jesus spoke, "What to you think Simon? From whom do the kings of the earth take toll or tribute? From their sons or from others? Simon said, "From others." Jesus said to him, "Then the sons are free."
23:4	They bind heavy burdens, hard to bear, and they lay them on men's shoulders: but they themselves will not move them with their finger.
23:13	But woe, you scribes and pharisees, you hypocrites! Because you shut the kingdom of heaven against man; for you neither enter yourselves, nor allow those who would enter, to go in.
23:23	Woe to you hypocrites! For you tithe mint and cumin and have neglected the weightier matters of the law, justice, mercy and faith: these you ought to have done, without neglecting the others. You blind guides, straining out a gnat and swallowing a camel.
13:11	To you it has been given to know the secrets of heaven, but to them it has not been given.

	The Book of Luke
6:22	Blessed are you when men hate you and when they exclude you and revile you and cast out your name as evil on account of the son of man! Rejoice in that day and leap for joy, for behold your reward is great in heaven...
9:61	Another said, "I will follow you Lord: but let me first say farewell to those at my home." Jesus said to him, "No one who puts his hand to the plow and looks back if fit for the kingdom of God."
11:17	..every kingdom divided against itself is laid waste and a divided house falls.
11:23	He who is not with me is against me, and he who does not gather with me, scatters.
12:9	But he who denies me before men will be denied before the angels of God.
12:37	Blessed are those servants who the master finds awake when he comes.
12:47	And that servant who knew his masters will, but did not make ready or act according to his will, shall receive a severe beating. 48: Everyone to whom much is given, of him much will be required. And of him to whom men commit much, they will demand the more.
12:51	Do you think that I have come to give peace on earth? No I tell you, but rather division...
12:56	You hypocrites! You know how to interpret the appearances of the earth and sky but why do you not know how to interpre the present time?
12:57	And why do you not judge for yourselves what is right?
16:13	No servant can serve two masters...You cannot serve God and mammon.
21:15	...for I will give you a mouth and wisdom, which none of your adversaries will be able to withstand or contradict. You will be delivered up. By your endurance, you will gain your lives.

| Luke 21:34 | But take heed to yourselves lest your hearts be weighed down with dissipation and drunkenness and cares for this life, and that day come upon you suddenly like a snare. |
| 22:36 | and let him who has no sword sell his mantel and buy one. |

II Thessalonians

| 3:14 | If anyone refuses to obey what we say in this letter, note this man and have nothing to do with him, that he may be ashamed. |

II Timothy

| 2:2 | And what you have heard from me, before many witnesses, entrust to faithful men who will be able to teach others also. Share in suffering as a good soldier of Jesus Christ. No soldier of service gets entangled in civilian pursuits, since his aim is to satisfy the one who enlisted him. |
| 3:1 | But understand this, that in the last days there will come a time of stress. For men will become lovers of self, lovers of money, proud, arrogant, abusive, haters of good, lovers of pleasure rather than lovers of God, holding the form of religion but denying the power of it. Avoid such people. |

Acts

2:40	Save yourselves from this crooked generation
5:38	So in the present case I tell you, keep away from these men and let them alone; for if this plan or this undertaking is of men, it will fail...
7:3	God said to Abraham, "Depart from your land and from your kindred and go into the land which I will show you."

| Acts 7:6 | And God spoke to this effect, that his posterity would be aliens in a land belonging to others, who would enslave them and ill treat them…"But I will judge the nation which they serve," said God. |

Philippians	
3:2	Look out for the dogs, Look out for the evil workers, look out for those who mutilate the flesh.
3:20	But our citizenship is in heaven and from it we await a Savior.

Galatians	
1:10	Am I now seeking the favor of men, or of God? Or am I trying to please men?. If I were still pleasing men, I should not be a servant to Jesus.
2:4	But because of false brethren secretly brought in, who slipped in to spy out our freedom which we have in Christ Jesus, that they might bring us into bondage-to them we did not yield submission even for a moment, that the truth fo the gospel might be preserved for you.
2:20	I have been crucified with Christ: it is no longer I who live, but Christ who lives in me; and the life I now live in the flesh I live by faith in the Son of God who loved me and gave himself for me.
3:29	And if you are Christ's then you are Abraham's offspring, heirs according to the promise.
4:8	Formerly, when you did not know God, but you were in bondage to beings that by nature are no gods; but now that you have come to know God, how can you turn your back again to the weak and beggarly elemental spirits whose slaves you want to be once more?

Galatians 4:30	But what does the scripture say? "Cast out the slave and her son; for the son of the slave shall not inherit with the son of the free woman."
5:1	For freedom Christ has set us free; stand fast therefore, and do not submit again to a yoke of slavery.
5:13	For you were called to freedom brethren; only do not use your freedom as an opportunity for the flesh, but through love be servants of one another.

I John
2:15	Do not love the world for the things in the world. If any one loves the world, love for the Father is not in him.
2:18-19	Children, it is the last hour, and as you have heard that antichrist is coming, so now many antichrists have come; therefore we know it is the last hour. They went out from us, but there were not of us. But you have been anointed by the Holy One and you all know.
3:1	See what love the Father has given us, that we should be called children of God; and so we are. The reason why the world does not know us is that it did not know HIM.
3:13	Do not wonder brethren that the world hates you. We know that we have passed out of death into life because we love the brethren. He who does not love abides in death.
4:4	Little children, you are of God, and have overcome them; for he who is in you is greater than he who is in the world. They are of the world, therefore what they say is of the world, and the world listens to them. We are of God, Whoever knows God listens to us, and he who is not o fGod, does not listen to us. By this we know the spirit of truth and the spirit of error.

II John
1:10	If anyone comes to you and does not bring this doctrine, do not receive him into the house or give him any greeting; for he who greets him shares his wicked work.

Jude	
1:4	For admission has been secretly gained by some who long ago were designated for this condemnation, ungodly persons who pervert the grace of our God into licentiousness and deny our only master and Lord, Jesus Christ.

1 Peter	
2:9	But you are a chosen race, a royal priesthood, a holy nation, God's own people, that you may declare the wonderful deeds of his, who called you out of darkness into his marvellous light.
3:12	For the eyes of the Lord are upon the righteous, and his ears are open to their prayer. But the face of the Lord is against those who do evil.
3:13	Now who is to harm you if you are zealous for what is right?
4:4	They are surprised that you do not now join them in the same wild profligacy.

II Peter	
1:16	For we did not follow cleverly devised myths when we made known to you the power and coming of our Lord Jesus Christ.
2:2	And many will follow their licentiousness, and because of them te way of the truth will be reviled. And in their greed they will exploit you with false words from of old their condemnation has not been idle and their destruction has not been asleep.
2:12	But these, like irrational animals, creatures of instinct, born to be caught and killed, reviling in the matters of which they are ignorant, will be destroyed in the same destruction with them, suffering wrong for their wrongdoing.

II Peter 2:18-20	For uttering loud boasts of folly, they entice with licentious passions of the flesh men who have barely escaped from those who live in error. they promise them freedom, but they themselves are slaves of corruption; for whatever overcomes a man so that he is enslaved for if after they have escaped the defilements of the world through the knowledge of our Lord and Saviour Jesus Christ, they are again entangled in them and overpowered. The last state has become worse for them than the first.

Romans

1:18	For the wrath of God is revealed from heaven against all ungodliness and wickedness of men who by their wickedness suppress the truth.
6:16	Do you not know that if you yield yourselves to anyone as obedient slaves, you are slaves of the one whom you obey, either of sin, which leads to death, or of obedience which leads to righteousness?
11:15	For if their rejection means the reconciliation of the world, what will their acceptance mean but life from the dead?
12:2	Do not be conformed to this world but be transformed by the renewal of your mind, that you may prove what is the will of God.
13:11	Besides this, you know what hour it is, how it is full time now for you to wake from sleep.
14:4	Who are you to pass judgement on the servant of another? It is before his own master that he stands or falls. And he will be upheld, for the master is able to make him stand.
16:17	I appeal to you brethren, to take note of those who create dissensions and difficulties, in opposition to the doctrine which you have been taught; avoid them, for such persons don't serve our Lord Christ, but their own appetites, and by fair and flattering words they deceive the simple minded.

Ephesians	
2:19	So then you are no longer strangers and sojourners, but you are fellow citizens with the saints and members of the household of God.
5:6	Let no one deceive you with empty words, for it is because of these things that the wrath of God comes upon the sons of disobedience. Therefore, do not associate with them, for once you were in darkness, but now you are light in the Lord, walk as children of the light, take no part in the unfruitful works of darkness but instead expose them…
6:12	For we are not contending against flesh and blood, but against the principalities, against the powers, against the world rulers of this present darkness against the spiritual hosts of wickedness in heavenly places. Therefore, take the whole armour of God.
14:9-11	Another angel, a third followed, saying with a loud voice: "If any one worships the beast and its image, and receives the mark on his forehead or on his hand, he shall also drink the wine of God's wrath, poured unmixed into the cup of his anger, and he shall be tormented with fire and sulphur in the presence of the holy angels and in the presence of the Lamb. And the smoke of their torment goes up forever and ever; and they have no rest, day or night, these worshipers of the beast and its image, and whoever received the mark of its name."
16:15	"Lo I am coming like a thief! Blessed is he who is awake, keeping his garments that he may not go naked and be seen exposed!"
18:4-6	Come out of her my people, lest you take part in her sins, lest you share in her plagues; for her sins are heaped high as heaven and God has remembers her iniquities. Render to her as she herself has rendered, and repay her double for her deeds; mix a double draught for her in the cup she has mixed.
21:7	He who conquers shall have this heritage, and I will be his God and he my son, but as for the cowardly, the faithless, the polluted, as for murderers, fornicators, sorcerers, idolators, and all liars, their lot shall be in the lake that burns with fire and sulphur, which is the second death.
22:7	And behold I am coming soon. Blessed is he who keeps the prophecy of this book.
22:17	The Spirit and the bride say 'come'. And let him who hears say "Come" and let he who is thirsty come, let him who desires take the water of life without price.

James	
4:4	Unfaithful creatures! Do you not know that friendship with the world is enmity with God? Therefore, whoever wishes to be a friend of the world makes himself an enemy of God.

Revelations	
2:20-22	But I have this against you, that you tolerate the woman Jezebel, who calls herself a prophetess and is teaching and beguiling my servant to practice immorality and to eat food sacrificed to idols. I gave her time to repent, but she refuses to repent of her immorality. Behold I will throw her on a sickbed and those who commit adultery with her I will throw into the great tribulation unless they repent of their wrongdoings.
13:10	If anyone is to be taken captive, to captivity he goes; if anyone is doomed to death by sword, with the sword must he be slain. Here is a call for the endurance and faith of the saints.

Revelations 14:9-11	Another angel, a third followed, saying with a loud voice: "If any one worships the beast and its image, and receives the mark on his forehead or on his hand, he shall also drink the wine of God's wrath, poured unmixed into the cup of his anger, and he shall be tormented with fire and sulphur in the presence of the holy angels and in the presence of the Lamb. And the smoke of their torment goes up forever and ever; and they have no rest, day or night, these worshipers of the beast and its image, and whoever received the mark of its name."
16:15	"Lo I am coming like a thief! Blessed is he who is awake, keeping his garments that he may not go naked and be seen exposed!"
18:4-6	Come out of her my people, lest you take part in her sins, lest you share in her plagues; for her sins are heaped high as heaven and God has remembers her iniquities. Render to her as she herself has rendered, and repay her double for her deeds; mix a double draught for her in the cup she has mixed.
21:7	He who conquers shall have this heritage, and I will be his God and he my son, but as for the cowardly, the faithless, the polluted, as for murderers, fornicators, sorcerers, idolators, and all liars, their lot shall be in the lake that burns with fire and sulphur, which is the second death.
22:7	And behold I am coming soon. Blessed is he who keeps the prophecy of this book.
22:17	The Spirit and the bride say 'come'. And let him who hears say "Come" and let he who is thirsty come, let him who desires take the water of life without price.

I Corinthians	
4:13	We have become, and are now, the refuse of the world, the off scouring of all things.
4:20	For the kingdom of God does not consist of talk but of power

I Corinthians 6:1	When one of you has a grievance against a brother, does he dare go to law before the unrighteous instead of the saints? And if the world is to be tried by you, are you incompetent to try trivial cases? If then you have such cases, why do you lay those before those who are least esteemed by the church?
6:15	Do you not know that your bodies are members of Christ? Shall I therefore take the members of Christ and make them members of a prostitute?
7:21	Were you a slave when called? But if you can gain your freedom, avail yourself of the opportunity. For he who was called in the Lord as a slave is a freedman of the Lord. Likewise he who was free when called is a slave of Christ. You were bought with a price; do not become the slaves of men.
9:19	For though I am free from all men, I have made myself a slave to all.
15:33	Do not be deceived! Bad company ruins good morals!

II Corinthians	
2:11	...to keep satan from gaining an advantage over us; for we are not ignorant of his designs.
6:14	Do not be mismated with unbelievers
6:17	Therefore, come out from them and be separate from them, says the Lord, and touch nothing unclean; then I will welcome you, and I will be a Father to you.
10:3	For though we live in the world, we are not carrying on a worldly war, for the weapons of our warfare are not worldly but have divine power to destroy strongholds. We destroy arguments and every proud obstacle to the knowledge of God, and take every thought captive to obey Christ, being ready to punish every disobedience when your obedience is complete.

Hebrews	
9:28	So Christ having been offered once to bear the sins of many, will appear a second time, not to deal with sin, but to save those who are eagerly waiting for him.
11:13	These all died in faith, not having received what was promised, but having seen it and greeted it from afar, not having acknowledged that they were strangers and exiles on the earth.
11:16	But as it is, they desire a better country, that is a heavenly one. Therefore, God is not ashamed to be called their God, for he has prepared for them a city.
11:24	By faith Moses, when he was growing up, refused to be called the son of the Pharaoh's daughter, choosing rather to share ill-treatment with the people of God than to enjoy the fleeting pleasures of sin. He considered the abuse suffered for Christ was greater than the wealth of Egypt for he looked to his reward in heaven.
12:16	...that no one be immoral or irreligious like Esau, who sold his birthright for a single meal. for you know that afterward, when he desired to inherit the blessing, he was rejected, for he found no chance to repent though he sought it with tears.

**All Glory and Honor to my Lord Jesus Christ
for making my life, this book and the thought of
redemption possible!**

*"My people are destroyed for lack of knowledge: because thou hast rejected
knowledge, I will also reject thee"
- Hosea 4:6*

Printed in Great Britain
by Amazon

84834770R10222